Generators, Bots, and Tutors:

Creative Approaches to Human-AI Synergy in Classroom Instruction

Bosede Iyiade Edwards
Universiti Sains Malaysia, Malaysia

Hassan Abuhassna
Sunway University, Malaysia

Damola Olugbade
First Technical University, Nigeria

Olayinka Anthony Ojo
University of Bolton, UK

Wan Ahmad Jaafar Wan Yahaya
Universiti Sains Malaysia, Malaysia

IGI Global
Scientific Publishing
Publishing Tomorrow's Research Today

Vice President of Editorial Melissa Wagner
Director of Acquisitions Mikaela Felty
Director of Book Development Jocelynn Hessler
Production Manager Mike Brehm
Cover Design Jose Rosado

Published in the United States of America by
IGI Global Scientific Publishing
701 East Chocolate Avenue
Hershey, PA, 17033, USA
Tel: 717-533-8845
Fax: 717-533-7115
Website: https://www.igi-global.com E-mail: cust@igi-global.com

Library of Congress Cataloging-in-Publication Data
Names: Edwards, Bosede, 1971- editor. | Abuhassna, Hassan, 1986- editor. | Olugbade, Damola, 1989- editor. | Ojo, Olayinka, 1975- editor. | Yahaya, Wan Ahmad Jaafar Wan, 1968- editor.
Title: Generators, bots, and tutors : creative approaches to human-AI synergy in classroom instruction / edited by Bosede Edwards, Hassan Abuhassna, Damola Olugbade, Olayinka Ojo, Wan Ahmad Jaafar Wan Yahaya.
Description: Hershey, PA : IGI Global Scientific Publishing, [2026] |
Includes bibliographical references and index. | Summary: "This book explores the transformative impact of emerging technologies on teaching, learning, and educational outcomes across diverse educational contexts. Artificial Intelligence (AI) is rapidly reshaping the landscape of education. This edited volume explores the innovative ways in which AI-powered tools like generators, bots, and tutors are transforming classroom instruction"-- Provided by publisher.
Identifiers: LCCN 2024061690 (print) | LCCN 2024061691 (ebook) | ISBN 9798337308470 (hardcover) | ISBN 9798337308487 (paperback) | ISBN 9798337308494 (ebook)
Subjects: LCSH: Artificial intelligence--Educational applications.
Classification: LCC LB1028.43 G478 2025 (print) | LCC LB1028.43 (ebook) | DDC 370.285/63--dc23/eng/20250221
LC record available at https://lccn.loc.gov/2024061690
LC ebook record available at https://lccn.loc.gov/2024061691

British Cataloguing in Publication Data
A Cataloguing in Publication record for this book is available from the British Library.

To all educators, researchers, and learners who envision a future where Artificial Intelligence empowers equitable, ethical, and transformative learning experiences.

Table of Contents

Detailed Table of Contents

This study presents a bibliometric analysis and SLR of research trends in AI-driven (PLP), exploring the evolving landscape of how artificial intelligence transforms education through adaptive, learner-centric models. By systematically analyzing academic publications from the past five years using data extracted from the Scopus database and tools like VOSviewer, the study maps the growth, key contributors, and emerging trends in the field. It identifies influential authors, leading institutions, and prevalent sources, while also examining the distribution of publications across countries and over time. The analysis of this study highlights predominant methodologies, AI-powered learning models, and sample types frequently employed in empirical studies, providing a comprehensive understanding of how AI technologies are utilized to enhance personalized learning experiences. Moreover, key findings reveal the challenges in implementing AI-driven solutions and underscore the importance of interdisciplinary collaboration among education, computer science, and psychology to drive innovation.

Generative AI has numerous applications in education. This chapter investigates the use of AI tools among students in the context of learning mathematics. Guided by the Technology Acceptance Model, the study evaluates AI tools in terms of perceived ease of use, credibility, and usefulness. Data were collected from 67 education students major in mathematics at a public university in the Southern Philippines. Results show that a significant majority are already using AI tools to support their learning in mathematics. The popularity of these tools is attributed to features such as offline functionality, image-based input, and the ability to generate step-by-step solutions. The chapter offers insights into current practices of AI tool usage in mathematics learning and highlights its pedagogical implications. It concludes with practical recommendations for teachers and policymakers, supporting the need to shift current classroom practices in response to the growing AI integration in education.

Generative artificial intelligence (genAI) is a cutting-edge technology that is guaranteed to disrupt education. Instructional technologists and librarians are best suited to share new technologies with their learning communities. Paths for adoption are not always smooth. The needs, abilities, and openness to change need to be ascertained, as well as the choice of which genAI applications to use in learning and teaching. The Diffusion of Innovations theory is used as a guide to not only identify those learners who may be best suited to apply the new technology, but also to choose the tools that may best serve the learning community. The profile of the user as well as the technology itself are important factors. It explains and reminds instructional technologists and librarians of best practices so that learners will understand and apply genAI. The chapter includes a framework for success in learning what the community needs and how to lead in the acceptance and use of

While AI tools are widely used by students as sources of scholastic information, their emotional and psychosocial impacts remain less explored. This chapter examines how interactions with AI algorithms foster emotional bonds with students, offering insights into future human-AI interactions. It focuses on students' experiences and emotional attachments to AI tools. Using a phenomenological research design, data were collected from 20 college students who met defined inclusion criteria. Findings reveal that students use AI not only for academic purposes but also for emotional support. Some participants reported feeling uplifted, satisfied, and secure when interacting with AI rather than with humans. The chapter concludes that AI tools can be integrated into the teaching-learning process as holistic resources, providing academic assistance while also serving as sources of motivation, entertainment, and emotional well-being. The chapter recommends the development of appropriate school policies and guidance on the responsible use of AI tools in education.

This systematic literature review examines the current state of AI-based tutoring systems in education, focusing on their roles in personalized learning, intelligent agent integration, and learning analytics within classroom instruction. A thorough analysis of 30 relevant studies reveals that AI-based tutoring systems significantly enhance educational outcomes by adapting learning experiences to individual needs through tailored feedback and customized learning trajectories, leading to improved student engagement and performance. Intelligent agents are central to these systems, providing social-emotional support, interactive feedback, and fostering motivation and deeper understanding. Learning analytics further support educators by enabling real-time monitoring of student progress, facilitating data-driven instructional

Preface

In the past decade, artificial intelligence (AI) has transcended the realm of speculative fiction and research laboratories to become a practical and increasingly central force in education. Classrooms today are rapidly evolving ecosystems where traditional pedagogical strategies intersect with intelligent systems capable of adapting, personalizing, and extending human capabilities. As we venture deeper into this digital age, it becomes imperative to examine not only how AI is reshaping instruction, but also how educators, learners, and institutions can creatively harness this synergy to enrich learning experiences.

Generators, Bots, and Tutors: Creative Approaches to Human-AI Synergy in Classroom Instruction emerges at the confluence of technological innovation and educational transformation. This volume offers a timely and diverse collection of scholarly perspectives, empirical investigations, and practical insights on the integration of AI into teaching and learning. By bringing together contributions from a global community of researchers and practitioners, the book captures the pulse of contemporary educational practice while offering visions for its near and distant future.

THE RELEVANCE OF AI IN THE WORLD TODAY

The emergence of large language models, machine learning algorithms, adaptive tutoring systems, and emotionally aware AI agents has radically altered what it means to teach and learn. AI technologies are now embedded in assessment platforms, virtual learning environments, administrative systems, and even in classroom discourse through tools like ChatGPT. While these technologies hold immense promise for enhancing personalization, engagement, and efficiency, they also bring forth complex questions about ethics, equity, privacy, and the evolving role of human educators.

This book is particularly relevant in today's world because it confronts these opportunities and challenges head-on. It offers not only critiques but also creative, constructive frameworks for understanding and applying AI in educational settings. From exploring sentiment analysis in remote learning to mapping personalized learning trajectories, the chapters in this volume reflect the multifaceted nature of human-AI collaboration.

TARGET AUDIENCE

This book is intended for a broad yet specific audience. It speaks to:

1. Educators and instructional designers seeking practical insights into integrating AI tools into their teaching strategies.
2. Educational researchers exploring the pedagogical, psychological, and socio-technical dimensions of AI in learning.
3. Policy makers and institutional leaders interested in shaping the future of education through informed decision-making around AI adoption.
4. Graduate students and early-career scholars looking for cutting-edge studies and frameworks in the rapidly expanding field of AI in education.
5. EdTech developers and AI specialists who want to better understand the classroom implications and educational expectations for their technologies.

CHAPTER DESCRIPTIONS

Mapping Research Trends in AI-Driven Personalized Learning Pathways: A Scoping Review: A comprehensive review of the literature reveals trends, gaps, and opportunities in the personalization of learning through AI, offering a valuable roadmap for future research.

Students' Learning Math with the Aid of AI and the Need of Shifting Classroom Instructions: This contribution addresses the AI-enhanced learning of mathematics, emphasizing the need to reconfigure traditional instruction to accommodate AI-driven feedback and problem-solving processes.

Start Small, Think Big!: Exploring GenAI in Learning and Teaching: This opening chapter sets the stage by encouraging educators to take incremental yet visionary steps in adopting generative AI tools. Through classroom anecdotes and practical frameworks, it shows how small interventions can lead to transformative teaching outcomes.

Integrating ChatGPT into Teaching: Educators' Insights Using the SAMR Model and Bloom's Taxonomy: This chapter bridges theory and practice by aligning ChatGPT's classroom use with Bloom's cognitive levels and the SAMR model, offering a structured path for AI integration.

Revolutionizing Higher Education with Generative AI: Prospects, Challenges, and Future Directions: A sweeping look at how generative AI is poised to disrupt higher education, this chapter forecasts trends and offers strategies to navigate the change.

Students Building Emotional Connections with AI: Insights into the Future AI-Infused Classroom: This chapter explores the psychological dimensions of AI companionship in classrooms, questioning what it means to "connect" emotionally with non-human agents.

AI-Based Tutoring Systems in Education: A Systematic Literature Review: Focusing on intelligent tutoring systems, this chapter examines how AI tutors are reshaping the classroom, drawing on findings from learning analytics and adaptive learning research.

From NPCs to AI Assistants: A Scoping Review of AI in Immersive STEM Learning: With a focus on gamification and immersive learning, this chapter examines how AI agents are being used to scaffold, support, and enhance STEM learning environments.

Classifying Student Sentiments in Learning on Video-Conference Platforms: Through a sophisticated blend of machine learning and the Self-Determination Theory, this chapter uncovers the emotional dimensions of online learning, showing how AI can help detect and respond to learner sentiments in real time.

CONCLUDING REFLECTIONS

This book is more than a collection of case studies and reviews—it is a declaration that the future of education is not about choosing between humans and machines, but about designing intelligent systems that elevate human agency, compassion, and creativity. Through its varied and rigorous contributions, Generators, Bots, and Tutors moves the conversation beyond hype and fear, toward grounded, hopeful, and critically informed applications of AI in education.

As editors, contributors, and readers, we are all participants in shaping this evolving narrative. We hope this volume serves as both a guide and an inspiration for those committed to realizing the full potential of human-AI synergy in teaching and learning.

Acknowledgment

This book is the culmination of shared vision, scholarly collaboration, and unwavering dedication from contributors across the globe. We extend our deepest gratitude to all authors for their expertise, to our peer reviewers for their critical insights, and to our respective institutions for supporting this endeavor. Special thanks to our families and mentors whose encouragement made this journey possible.

Chapter 1
Mapping Research Trends in AI-Driven Personalized Learning Pathways: A Scoping Review

Mohammed Adi Al Battashi
https://orcid.org/0009-0007-2866-1862
University of Malaya, Malaysia

Mohamad A. M. Adnan
https://orcid.org/0000-0002-3578-3581
Academy of Islamic Studies, Malaysia

Asyraf Isyraqi Bin Jamil
Academy of Islamic Studies, Malaysia

Majid Adi Al-Battashi
Ministry of Education, Oman

ABSTRACT

This study presents a bibliometric analysis and SLR of research trends in AI-driven (PLP), exploring the evolving landscape of how artificial intelligence transforms education through adaptive, learner-centric models. By systematically analyzing academic publications from the past five years using data extracted from the Scopus database and tools like VOSviewer, the study maps the growth, key contributors, and emerging trends in the field. It identifies influential authors, leading institutions, and prevalent sources, while also examining the distribution of publications across countries and over time. The analysis of this study highlights predominant methodologies, AI-powered learning models, and sample types frequently employed in

DOI: 10.4018/979-8-3373-0847-0.ch001

empirical studies, providing a comprehensive understanding of how AI technologies are utilized to enhance personalized learning experiences. Moreover, key findings reveal the challenges in implementing AI-driven solutions and underscore the importance of interdisciplinary collaboration among education, computer science, and psychology to drive innovation.

I. INTRODUCTION

Over the past decade, Artificial Intelligence (AI) has transformed multiple sectors, with education emerging as a key domain for its applications. AI has enabled a shift from traditional teaching methods toward data-driven, student-centered learning models that emphasize personalized learning experiences. Unlike conventional systems, which often deliver static content to all students, AI-powered technologies analyze individual learner data to design customized learning pathways, thus optimizing the educational process (Zawacki-Richter et al., 2019). This personalized approach aligns with the growing demand for lifelong learning, adaptability, and tailored educational experiences in the digital age (Holmes et al., 2021).

One of the most significant contributions of AI to education is the development of personalized learning pathways. These pathways leverage AI algorithms to recommend content, predict learner performance, and adapt instructional strategies in real-time based on students' unique needs and progress (Chen et al., 2020). Personalized learning pathways promote more engaging and efficient learning experiences by fostering autonomy, encouraging self-regulated learning, and improving overall learner outcomes (Khosravi et al., 2022). Technologies such as natural language processing (NLP), predictive analytics, and machine learning have further advanced the design and scalability of personalized learning systems. As a result, educational institutions are increasingly adopting AI-based tools to ensure that learning is not only more accessible but also more effective and personalized.

Globally, research on AI in education has expanded significantly, particularly in exploring its role in enhancing learning outcomes and supporting personalized instruction (Spector et al., 2021). Studies from the United States, Europe, and East Asia have contributed to a growing body of literature on AI-based adaptive learning environments, focusing on both technological and pedagogical perspectives (Luckin et al., 2018). The most prominent areas of research include intelligent tutoring systems, recommendation algorithms for educational content, and predictive models for learner success. Despite these advancements, challenges such as data privacy concerns, algorithmic biases, and the digital divide remain significant barriers to widespread adoption (Williamson & Eynon, 2020). Addressing these challenges is crucial for ensuring equitable and ethical use of AI in personalized learning.

The present study contributes to the growing research on AI in education by providing a comprehensive bibliometric analysis of research trends in AI-based personalized learning pathways. Bibliometric analysis is a powerful tool for identifying key themes, influential publications, and emerging research areas within a specific field. By mapping the research landscape, this study aims to highlight patterns in publication growth, collaboration networks, and thematic clusters related to personalized learning pathways. The findings will offer a clear understanding of how the field has evolved, guide future research, and inform policymakers and educators about current developments.

The primary goal of this paper is to provide a detailed and critical examination of the impact of AI-driven personalized learning pathways. By analyzing a wide range of scholarly articles, research papers, and academic contributions, this study aims to map out current trends, challenges, and future directions in the field of AI-based personalized learning. The use of artificial intelligence technologies to create diverse personal learning paths has revolutionized the world of education and sparked significant innovation, revolutionizing how educational experiences are customized to meet individual learners' needs. Through this scoping review, we aim to offer educators, researchers, and policymakers a clear understanding of key advancements and insights in AI and personalized learning pathways (PLP), laying the groundwork for shaping the future of personalized education and improving adaptive learning strategies.

What sets this study apart is its unique approach, combining bibliometric analysis with a systematic literature review using the PRISMA methodology. This research followed author researchers work for instance (Abuhassna et al., 2022a; Van et al., 2021; Samsul et al., 2023). This dual approach allows for a comprehensive exploration of how AI is integrated into personalized learning pathways, identifying major contributors, emerging trends, and potential future directions. By thoroughly collecting and analyzing relevant articles, this paper provides valuable insights into the influence of AI-driven personalized learning pathways. It also addresses future opportunities and ethical considerations, making it a significant contribution to the field of educational technology research.

To achieve the objectives of this study, the review is structured into two main sections: a bibliometric analysis and a systematic literature review. The bibliometric analysis addresses key questions in the preliminary phase, while the systematic review delves deeper into the findings. Together, these sections aim to provide a holistic understanding of AI's role in personalized learning and its implications for the future of education. These questions apply to the review's preliminary phase (the bibliometric analysis). The following questions are stated to address the objectives of this review:

What is the main contribution in AI and Personalized Learning Pathways research field in accordance with years distribution, top countries, top educational institutions, authors, sources and trends and co-occurrences in the last 5 years?
Which methodologies have been most employed in AI and Personalized Learning Pathways research over the past five years?
Which AI-powered PLPs are most frequently implemented in educational research?
What types of samples are most often used in studies on AI-driven PLPs?
What are the most frequently proposed future agendas and recommendations in recent literature?

II. BACKGROUND

Over the past decade, artificial intelligence (AI) has emerged as a transformative force in education, clearly reshaping traditional learning models and programs, transforming them into dynamic, learner-centered environments that are driven by learners' needs and abilities. With the growing global interest in and development of education systems, particularly those powered by AI, personalized learning paths have become a critical focus. These paths leverage AI to adapt content and learning methods based on individual student needs, enhancing engagement and improving outcomes. Despite AI's advanced potential in education, challenges emerge when implementing these programs. These challenges include ethical concerns, data privacy, algorithmic bias, and unequal access to technology, which continue to raise fundamental questions about the fairness and sustainability of these innovations. Research in this field is increasingly interdisciplinary, integrating perspectives from computer science, pedagogy, psychology, and data science. While numerous studies have explored the technical applications of AI, there is still a need for structured reviews that contextualize these efforts within broader educational goals, highlight methodological trends, and identify existing gaps. This study aims to address this gap by examining the development, scope, and focus of AI-based PLP research published over the past five years.

2.1 Theoretical Background

The integration of AI technologies and programs into educational contexts has evolved significantly over the past decade, gaining transformative power that has made it an influential element in reshaping traditional learning models. Personalized Learning Paths (PLPs) have emerged from this evolution as adaptive educational approaches that tailor instruction to individual learners. Early concepts of PLPs focused on learner autonomy and differentiated instruction, but with the emergence of AI, the focus has shifted toward real-time dynamic personalization. This has contributed to the increasing use of AI models, such as adaptive learning systems, recommendation engines, intelligent tutoring systems, and generative AI tools, to facilitate individualized learning experiences. These developments align with broader shifts toward data-driven education and highlight the potential for improved engagement, retention, and performance outcomes, while raising numerous concerns, particularly those related to ethical aspects of monitoring, data privacy, and algorithmic bias.

2.2 Literature Review

Several studies have explored various dimensions of AI-based personalized learning paths and their various technologies. Regarding AI models, Chen, Huang, and Liu (2020) highlighted adaptive content delivery as a key function, emphasizing AI's role in dynamically adjusting learning materials based on learner performance in real time. Khosravi and Cooper (2022) expanded this field by using machine learning algorithms to design predictive models that improve learner engagement. Regarding the concept of personalized learning, Lukin et al. (2018) proposed a framework focused on "intelligence amplification," suggesting that AI should support, not replace, human decision-making processes in education. Spector et al. (2021) mapped prevalent AI applications, identifying intelligent tutoring systems and recommendation platforms as prevalent technologies, but criticized the field's narrow focus on short-term academic outcomes. In examining the impact of personalized learning programs, Liu et al. (2024) proposed algorithmic frameworks that aim to promote sustainable learning by identifying learning paths in the real world, emphasizing the need to strike a balance between automated systems and human-centered approaches. Zawacki-Richter et al. (2019) emphasized the importance of involving teachers in the design of AI systems to ensure meaningful interpretation and application of data in learning analytics and data-driven personalization. Finally, Williamson and Eynon (2020) critically addressed ethical and privacy concerns, highlighting risks such as surveillance, loss of learner autonomy, and systematic biases in AI personalization frameworks. Together, these studies demonstrate the multifaceted landscape of AI-based personalized learning programs, emphasizing their transformative potential and the urgent need for ethical, inclusive, and pedagogically informed design principles.

III. PROBLEM STATEMENT

Despite the growing volume of research on AI in education, there is a noticeable absence of comprehensive mapping studies that focus exclusively on personalized learning pathways. Many existing reviews either lack methodological rigor or are too narrow in focus, overlooking critical dimensions such as ethical implications, practical applications across diverse contexts, and the long-term effectiveness of AI-driven systems. Furthermore, a disproportionate reliance on a small number of studies and repeated citations of the same authors in literature reveals a narrow scope of inquiry. This study seeks to fill this void by presenting a well-structured scoping review, identifying the most prevalent research methodologies, sample types, and emerging themes in the field.

IV. MATERIALS AND METHODS

A. Research Design

This search took place on 4th January 2025, using Scopus database because it is one of the largest bibliographic databases, providing indexing and citation tracking for scholarly research across various academic disciplines. Moreover, it is widely utilized by researchers as it grants access to peer-reviewed studies and offers precise citation analytics, facilitating the evaluation of research quality and impact on a global scale. The initial search was utilized based on the main keywords used "ai AND personalized AND learning" using the query as follow, TITLE-ABS-KEY (ai AND personalized AND learning). The search included the recent five years starting from 2020 – 2024, as documented in the query "AND PUBYEAR > 2019 AND PUBYEAR < 2025". Three main subject areas were included, computer science and arts and humanities and social sciences as the query "AND (LIMIT-TO (SUBJAREA, "COMP") OR LIMIT-TO (SUBJAREA, "SOCI") OR LIMIT-TO (SUBJAREA, "ARTS"))". Only article were included "AND (LIMIT-TO (DOCTYPE, "ar"))" any other sources were excluded for instance, conference's, book chapters, press articles. Only articles written in English language were included, any other languages were excluded "AND (LIMIT-TO (LANGUAGE, "English")). In addition to the above, the researcher relied on open access articles only as one of the criteria to obtain results from research papers.

Following the application of the predefined selection criteria established by the researcher to align with the scope of this study, a total of 343 research papers relevant to the field were identified. Furthermore, to ensure the accuracy and relevance of the findings within the study's scope, 210 educational design publications indexed in the

Scopus database were retrieved. Additionally, to enhance the precision of the search process, specific filtering options were implemented, the options LIMIT-TO (EXACTKEYWORD, "Artificial Intelligence") OR LIMIT-TO (EXACTKEYWORD, "Artificial Intelligence (AI)") OR LIMIT-TO (EXACTKEYWORD, "AI") OR LIMIT-TO (EXACTKEYWORD, "Generative AI") OR LIMIT-TO (EXACTKEYWORD, "Generative Artificial Intelligence") OR LIMIT-TO (EXACTKEYWORD, "Artificial Intelligence Technologies") OR LIMIT-TO (EXACTKEYWORD, "Knowledge Management")) were selected from the additional capabilities offered by the Scopus database's new look search. Following a Scopus search, 36 articles were included in this study's first draught. In the Final round of the quality assessment the total of 14 articles were included in this study.

Table 1. The inclusion and exclusion criteria

Inclusion	Exclusion
All research papers regarding Artificial Intelligence, leadership, workplace engagement	Any other articles were excluded
Only articles published 2020-2024	Any articles before 2020 were excluded, 2025 articles were not included because it's not over yet.
Only articles	Conferences, book chapters and any other publications were excluded
Only articles written in English	Any other languages were excluded

B. Years distribution

The attached graph illustrates the distribution of research contributions in the field of artificial intelligence (AI) and personalized learning pathways (PLP) over the past five years, from 2020 to 2024. The data shows a significant and steady increase in the number of publications, reflecting the growing interest and advancements in this field. In 2020, there were 15 publications, which increased to 25 in 2021 and 35 in 2022. The most notable growth occurred in 2023, with 94 publications, and this trend continued sharply into 2024, reaching 174 publications. This exponential rise indicates a heightened focus on AI-driven PLP, likely driven by the increasing recognition of AI's potential to transform education through personalized and adaptive learning solutions.

Previous studies in this area have primarily focused on the development and implementation of AI technologies to create tailored educational experiences. Researchers have explored various methodologies, including machine learning algorithms, natural language processing, and reinforcement learning, to enhance the personalization of learning pathways. These studies have highlighted the importance of data-driven approaches in understanding learner behaviors and preferences, enabling the creation of more effective and engaging educational environments.

The analysis of these studies reveals a consistent emphasis on the need for interdisciplinary collaboration, combining insights from education, computer science, and psychology to drive innovation. Additionally, there is a growing awareness of the ethical considerations and challenges associated with AI integration in education, such as data privacy and algorithmic bias. Overall, the increasing volume of research underscores the transformative potential of AI in personalizing education and improving learning outcomes.

Figure 1. The distribution of research contributions over the past five years

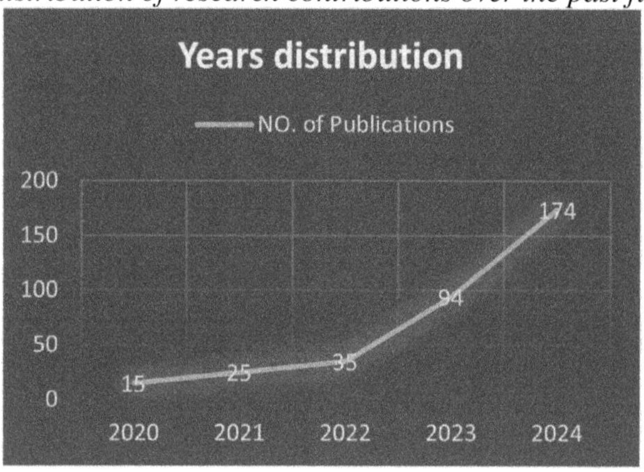

C. Top 10 countries

The data provided highlights the contributions of the top 10 countries in the field of artificial intelligence (AI) research and personalized learning pathways (PLP). It is noted that countries with high populations and an increasing interest in technological development activities have topped the list of countries in this field. The United States leads with 68 contributions, reflecting its strong technological infrastructure and significant investment in AI research. China follows with 47 contributions, showcasing its focus on large-scale AI implementations and advancements in educational technology. India ranks third with 37 contributions, indicating its growing role in AI-driven educational innovations.

The United Kingdom (32 contributions) and Germany (17 contributions) emphasize ethical considerations and inclusive AI applications, while Saudi Arabia (25 contributions) demonstrates its increasing investment in AI for education. Countries like Italy (19 contributions), Australia (18 contributions), South Korea (15 contributions), and Spain (12 contributions) also show notable involvement, reflecting a global interest in leveraging AI to enhance personalized learning.

Previous studies in this field have highlighted the importance of international collaboration and knowledge sharing. Research from leading countries often focuses on developing advanced AI algorithms, integrating AI into educational platforms, and addressing challenges such as data privacy and algorithmic bias. These contributions underscore the transformative potential of AI in creating personalized, effective, and engaging learning experiences, while also emphasizing the need for equitable and inclusive AI applications in education.

Figure 2. The top 10 countries leading the charge in publications showcase the artificial intelligence (AI) research and personalized learning pathways (PLP)

D. Top 10 educational institutions

The data provided highlights the contributions of the top educational institutions in the field of artificial intelligence (AI) research and personalized learning pathways (PLP). Hamad Bin Khalifa University leads with 5 contributions, reflecting its strong focus on innovative educational technologies. Institutions like Harvard

Medical School, King Abdulaziz University, Anadolu Üniversitesi, King Faisal University, CQ University Australia, Tallinna Ülikool, and University of South Africa each have 4 contributions, showcasing their active involvement in advancing AI-driven personalized learning.

Other notable institutions, including Stanford University, Prince Sultan University, Consiglio Nazionale delle Ricerche, University College London, Università degli Studi di Foggia, Beijing Normal University, University of North Texas, University of Michigan, Ann Arbor, University of Cambridge, and Princess Sumaya University, each have 3 contributions. These institutions are recognized for their research in developing AI algorithms, integrating AI into educational platforms, and exploring the ethical and practical implications of AI in education.

Previous studies from these institutions have emphasized the importance of interdisciplinary collaboration, combining insights from education, computer science, and psychology to drive innovation. They also highlight the need for addressing challenges such as data privacy, algorithmic bias, and equitable access to AI-driven educational tools. The contributions from these top institutions underscore the transformative potential of AI in creating personalized, effective, and engaging learning experiences, while also emphasizing the importance of ethical and inclusive AI applications in education.

Table 2. Publications distributions by universities

AFFILIATION	TP*	AFFILIATION	TP*
Hamad Bin Khalifa University	5	Stanford University	3
Harvard Medical School	4	Prince Sultan University	3
King Abdulaziz University	4	Consiglio Nazionale delle Ricerche	3
Anadolu Üniversitesi	4	University College London	3
King Faisal University	4	Università degli Studi di Foggia	3
CQUniversity Australia	4	Beijing Normal University	3
Tallinna Ülikool	4	University of North Texas	3
University of South Africa	3	University of Michigan, Ann Arbor	3
UCL Institute of Education	3	University of Cambridge	3
Vellore Institute of Technology	3	Princess Sumaya University	3

TP*= Total Publications

E. Authors

The table provides a detailed overview of the top authors contributing to the field of artificial intelligence (AI) research and personalized learning pathways (PLP). Hooshyar, Danial leads with 71 publications (TP), 1,532 citations (TC), and an H-index of 21, reflecting his significant impact on adaptive learning systems and AI-driven educational technologies. Al-Fuqaha, Ala Isam follows with 241 publications, 15,874 citations, and an H-index of 38, highlighting his extensive contributions to AI research, particularly in interdisciplinary applications. Chamola, Vinay also stands out with 220 publications, 9,105 citations, and an H-index of 50, emphasizing his influential work in AI and its integration into educational systems.

Other notable authors include Bozkurt, Aras (88 publications, 2,913 citations, H-index 26), who focuses on open and distance learning, and Dinov, Ivo D. (198 publications, 8,100 citations, H-index 49), known for his work in data science and AI applications in education. Yang, Yeongwook (43 publications, 603 citations, H-index 13) and Laverde, Andrés Chiappe (48 publications, 315 citations, H-index 8) contribute to the field with research on AI-driven learning models and educational technologies.

These authors represent a diverse range of countries, including Estonia, Qatar, India, the United States, Turkey, and Colombia, reflecting the global nature of AI research in education. Their work underscores the importance of interdisciplinary collaboration, combining insights from computer science, education, and data science to drive innovation in personalized learning. The high citation counts, and H-indices of these authors highlight their influential roles in advancing AI-driven PLP, addressing challenges such as scalability, ethical considerations, and equitable access to educational technologies.

Table 3. The top authors in the field of AI/PLP

#	Author	TP*	TC*	H-index	Scopus ID	Affiliation	Country
1	Hooshyar, Danial	71	1532	21	56572940600	Tallinna ÜlikoolThe institution	Estonia
2	Yang, Yeongwook	43	603	13	42662613900	Gangneung-Wonju National University	South Korea
3	Al-Fuqaha, Ala Isam	241	15874	38	57220421072	Hamad Bin Khalifa University, College of Science and Engineering	Qatar
4	Alkurd, Rawan	16	133	6	56028744100	Larus Technologies Corporation	Canada
5	Bozkurt, Aras	88	2913	26	56566181600	Anadolu Üniversitesi	Turkey
6	Castro, Gina Paola Barrera	2	5	1	59073443200	Universidad de La Sabana	Colombia
7	Chamola, Vinay	220	9105	50	55427784900	Birla Institute of Technology and Science	India

continued on following page

Table 3. Continued

#	Author	TP*	TC*	H-index	Scopus ID	Affiliation	Country
8	Laverde, Andrés Chiappe	48	315	8	22833507400	Universidad de La Sabana	Colombia
9	Dhananjaya, G. M.	13	13	2	58142308700	Visvesvaraya Technological University	India
10	Dinov, Ivo D.	198	8100	49	6603200380	University of Michigan, Ann Arbor	United States

F. Top sources

The data provided highlights the top sources for publications in the field of artificial intelligence (AI) research and personalized learning pathways (PLP). IEEE Access is a leading source, reflecting its broad coverage of cutting-edge research in technology and engineering, including AI applications in education. Sustainability Switzerland and Applied Sciences Switzerland are also prominent, with 23% and 7% contributions respectively, indicating a focus on sustainable and applied aspects of AI in education. International Journal of Advanced Computer Science and Applications and Applied Mathematics and Nonlinear Sciences are significant sources, contributing 6% each. These journals emphasize advanced computational techniques and mathematical models that underpin AI-driven personalized learning. Computers and Education Artificial Intelligence is another key source, highlighting the intersection of computer science and educational technology. Previous studies published in these sources have explored various methodologies, including machine learning algorithms, natural language processing, and adaptive learning systems, to enhance personalized learning experiences. They also address challenges such as data privacy, algorithmic bias, and the integration of AI into traditional educational frameworks. The diversity of these sources reflects the interdisciplinary nature of AI research in education, combining insights from computer science, mathematics, and educational theory. The contributions from these top sources underscore the transformative potential of AI in creating personalized, effective, and engaging learning experiences, while also emphasizing the importance of ethical and inclusive AI applications in education.

Figure 3. The top sources for publications in the field of AI/PLP

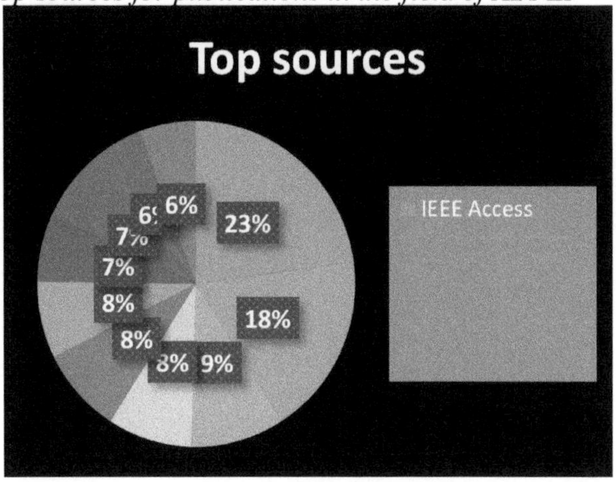

G. Trends, keywords

Figure (4) shows the keyword analysis shows Artificial Intelligence (AI) at the center, with the highest frequency (68) and total link strength (111), highlighting its wide-reaching impact across different fields. Machine Learning and Deep Learning follow closely, playing key roles in education, predictive modeling, and neural networks. NLP and Predictive Models have solid connections, focusing on language processing and data analysis. Meanwhile, emerging technologies like ChatGPT and Generative AI are gaining momentum, with strong links to personalized learning and educational innovation. Overall, these connections show how AI is weaving its way into multiple sectors like education, healthcare, and technology, driving change and new possibilities.

Figure 4. The most used keywords used in publication in the field of AI/PLP

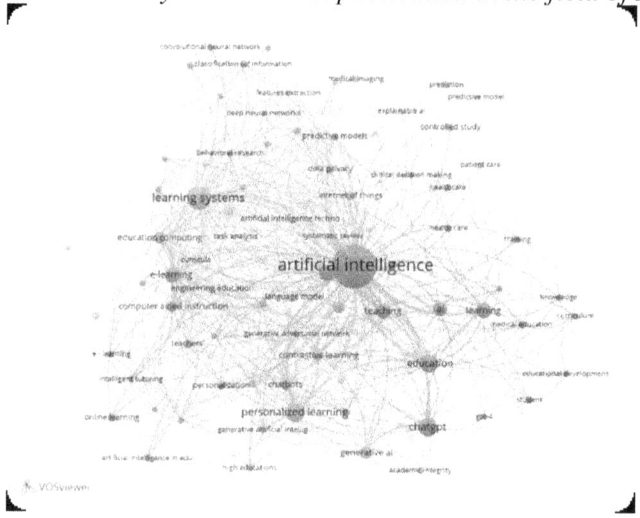

V. SLR (SYSTEMATIC LITERATURE REVIEW)

This bibliometric analysis explores the evolving research landscape on AI-driven personalized learning pathways. The study systematically examines academic publications to identify trends, influential works, key authors, and leading institutions contributing to the field. By leveraging bibliometric tools like VOSviewer and Scopus data, the analysis provides insights into the integration of artificial intelligence in tailoring educational experiences to individual learner needs. Key findings include an overview of how AI technologies are being utilized to enhance learning personalization, the challenges in implementation, and the future research directions for optimizing AI-driven solutions in education. The study also highlights the importance of interdisciplinary collaboration, encompassing education, computer science, and psychology, to drive innovation in personalized learning. This analysis contributes to academic discourse by offering a comprehensive understanding of the growth and impact of AI in transforming traditional learning pathways into adaptive, learner-centric models. As figure (5) shows the PRISMA framework, the researcher got total of (5230) records at the beginning. However, the total of (343) research is only downloaded from the Scopus database. Total research were excluded later and (174) papers were not retrieved. Out of (36) papers, a total of (22) were excluded because they are SLR papers. The final remaining papers were (14) papers only.

Figure 5. PRISMA framework

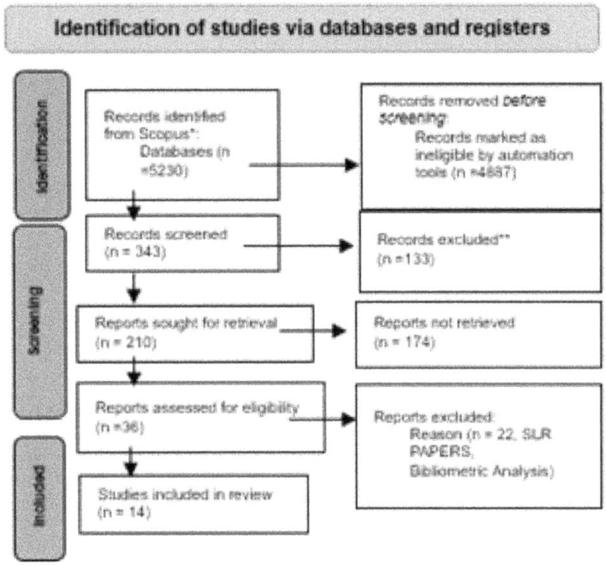

VI. THE RESULTS

A. Methodology

As shown in table (4), the analysis of methodologies in the field of AI-driven personalized learning pathways shows a clear preference for quantitative approaches with 10 out of 14 studies (71%) using data-driven techniques like machine learning, reinforcement learning, and natural language processing. These methods focus on analyzing large datasets, predicting student performance, and creating adaptive learning systems. For example, studies like (Sayed et al., 2023) and (Bagunaid et al., 2024) use advanced AI models to optimize learning pathways, while others, such as (Dhananjaya et al., 2024), employ chatbots powered by AI to provide personalized support. This trend reflects the field's emphasis on precision, scalability, and measurable outcomes. On the other hand, qualitative studies (4 out of 14, 29%) explore the practical and human side of AI in education. These studies, such as (Albdrani & Al-Shargabi, 2023) and (Chadha, 2024), use methods like case studies to examine how AI tools are implemented in real-world educational settings and how users interact with them. While these studies provide valuable insights into the challenges and experiences of using AI, they are fewer in number and often limited in scope. A notable gap in the research is the lack of mixed-methods studies, which could combine the strengths of both quantitative and qualitative approaches. Additionally, there is limited discussion on ethical concerns, such as data privacy, bias in algorithms, and the potential over-reliance on technology. Future research should address these gaps by focusing on ethical AI design, long-term impacts, and user-centered perspectives to ensure that AI-driven personalized learning is not only effective but also fair and inclusive. By balancing technical innovation with human and ethical considerations, the field can create more holistic and sustainable solutions for education.

Table 4. The methodologies used in the researches of AI/PLP

Author	**methodology**
(Sayed et al., 2023)	**quantitative** (Deep Q-Network Reinforcement Learning (DQN-RL) and rule-based decision-making)
(Sajja et al., 2024)	**Quantitative** (AI-enabled intelligent assistant (AIIA) using NLP, Large Language Models (LLMs), and GPT-based frameworks)
(Hooshyar et al., 2024)	**Quantitative** (Neural-Symbolic AI (NSAI) integrating deep neural networks with symbolic knowledge representation)
(Chen et al., 2020)	**Quantitative** (Hybridized Deep Neural Network (HDNN) for predicting student performance in Education 4.0)
(Hao, Wang, & Peng, 2024)	**Quantitative** (Empirical research using AI-supported precision teaching model)
(Dhananjaya et al., 2024)	**Quantitative** (AI-driven chatbot (ChatGPT) for education, employing machine learning and NLP for interactive learning)
(Pesovski et al., 2024)	**Qualitative** (Generative AI using Large Language Models (LLMs) integrated into LMS)
(Albdrani & Al-Shargabi, 2023)	**Qualitative** (Case study approach with the 5Es model and ChatGPT-based personalized learning)
(Liu et al.,2024)	**Qualitative** (Collaborative Structure Search Framework (CSSF) using AI-driven causal inference and evolutionary algorithms)
Duan, 2024)	**Qualitative** (AI-supported digital training model using multi-factor reasoning and integrated clustering)
(Deng et al., 2024)	**Qualitative** (Dynamic model using Non-Homogeneous Hidden Markov Model (NHMM) and incremental learning)
(Eltahir & Babiker, 2024)	**Quantitative** (Quasi-experimental design with pre-test and post-test comparison)
(Chadha, 2024)	**Qualitative** (Case study methodology examining AI-driven pedagogical innovations in higher education)
(Bagunaid et al., 2024)	**Quantitative** (Deep Reinforcement Learning (DRL) using ID2QN and Federated Learning for secure AI-driven education)

B. Personalized Learning Pathways

The analysis of AI-driven personalized learning pathways (PLPs) over the last five years reveals a strong focus on adaptive learning systems, AI-powered virtual assistants, and personalized resource recommendations. Studies like (Sayed et al., 2023) and (Hooshyar et al., 2024) use adaptive models to tailor content based on student performance and preferences, while (Sajja et al., 2024) and (Dhananjaya et al., 2024) employ AI-driven virtual assistants and chatbots to provide real-time support and engagement. Additionally, research by (Chen et al., 2020) and (Duan, 2024) leverages learning analytics and knowledge graphs to recommend personalized resources and interventions. Innovative approaches, such as (Pesovski et al., 2024), use generative AI to create customizable learning materials, making education more engaging and contextually relevant. Despite these advancements, there is a lack of standardized frameworks, limited exploration of long-term outcomes, and insufficient attention to ethical challenges like data privacy and algorithmic bias. Future research should address these gaps to ensure that AI-driven PLPs are not only effective but also equitable, scalable, and sustainable, paving the way for more inclusive and holistic educational solutions.

Table 5. The types of PLP used in researches over the last five years

Author	Personalized Learning Pathways
(Sayed et al., 2023)	Adaptive personalized learning using VARK model and gamification techniques
(Sajja et al., 2024)	AI-driven virtual teaching assistant (VTA) integrated with LMS for adaptive and personalized learning
(Hooshyar et al., 2024)	AI-driven adaptive learning system for computational thinking in an educational game
(Chen et al., 2020)	AI-driven student performance analysis and personalized intervention based on learning analytics
(Hao, Wang, & Peng, 2024)	AI-driven precision teaching model integrating educational diagnostics, feedback, and intervention for high school science subjects
(Dhananjaya et al., 2024)	AI-powered personalized learning assistant for student engagement and teacher support
(Pesovski et al., 2024)	AI-generated customizable learning materials tailored to different personas (e.g., traditional teacher, Batman, Wednesday Addams)
(Albdrani & Al-Shargabi, 2023)	AI-driven personalized learning using ChatGPT for deep learning education
(Liu et al.,2024)	AI-driven learning path recognition using real-world data and optimization techniques
(Duan, 2024)	AI-driven personalized training based on learner profiling and knowledge graph-based recommendations

continued on following page

Table 5. Continued

Author	Personalized Learning Pathways
(Deng et al., 2024)	AI-driven adaptive PLP resource recommendation system
(Eltahir & Babiker, 2024)	AI-driven personalized learning using ChatGPT, Moodle LMS, and AI-powered educational tools for pre-service teachers
(Chadha, 2024)	AI-driven personalized learning using Stanford's AI platform, University of Murcia's chatbot, Knewton's adaptive learning, and an intelligent tutoring system
(Bagunaid et al., 2024)	AI-assisted adaptive e-learning system (E-FedCloud) with automated recommendations and engagement tracking

C. Samples

The analysis of samples used in AI-driven personalized learning pathways (PLPs) research over the last five years reveals a diverse range of participants, with K-12 students representing approximately 21% of studies (e.g., Sayed et al., 2023; Hao, Wang, & Peng, 2024), higher education learners accounting for 36% (e.g., Sajja et al., 2024; Pesovski et al., 2024), and large-scale educational datasets making up 21% (e.g., Liu et al., 2024; Bagunaid et al., 2024). Additionally, 14% of studies include teachers or pre-service teachers (e.g., Eltahir & Babiker, 2024), highlighting their role in implementing AI tools. While these samples demonstrate the versatility of AI-driven PLPs across educational levels, there is limited focus on lifelong learning (0%) and inclusive sampling (e.g., underrepresented groups, learners with disabilities), as well as insufficient attention to ethical considerations in data collection. Future research should address these gaps, ensuring that AI-driven PLPs are equitable, scalable, and applicable across diverse educational contexts, fostering more inclusive and effective learning solutions.

Table 6. The types of samples used in researches of AI/PLP

Author	samples
(Sayed et al., 2023)	26 Grade 3 students (ages 9-10)
(Sajja et al., 2024)	Higher education students using an AI-enabled VTA system
(Hooshyar et al., 2024)	427 players of the Auto Thinking game
(Chen et al., 2020)	Data from students in an Education 4.0 environment
(Hao, Wang, & Peng, 2024)	540 high school students (Grade 2) in China (6 intervention classes, 3 control classes) + 19 teachers surveyed

continued on following page

Table 6. Continued

Author	samples
(Dhananjaya et al., 2024)	No specific sample; discuss implementation cases in various schools and institutions
(Pesovski et al., 2024)	20 undergraduate students in a software engineering course at a European university
(Albdrani & Al-Shargabi, 2023)	20 students (10 in experimental group using ChatGPT, 10 in control group using traditional methods)
(Liu et al.,2024)	Real-world datasets from Eedi and Diagnostic Questions platforms, covering 6400 students and 65,000 test sessions
(Duan, 2024)	Higher vocational college students in China (Data collected from 2021 cohort)
(Deng et al., 2024)	Online education platform and LMS datasets, including MOOC platforms, K-12 education, and university systems
(Eltahir & Babiker, 2024)	110 pre-service teachers (55 experimental, 55 control) enrolled in the Educational Technology course at Ajman University
(Chadha, 2024)	Various case studies, including university implementations of AI-driven learning
(Bagunaid et al., 2024)	Open University Learning Analytics Dataset (OULAD) - 32,593 students, 22 courses, 10,655,280 interaction records

VII. THE FUTURE AGENDA

The analysis of future agendas and recommendations in AI-driven personalized learning pathways (PLPs) research over the last five years reveals several recurring themes, reflecting the field's priorities and challenges. Approximately 64% of studies emphasize the need to enhance AI techniques for better personalization, such as improving adaptive algorithms (e.g., Sajja et al., 2024; Hooshyar et al., 2024) and integrating advanced AI models like reinforcement learning (e.g., Sayed et al., 2023). These recommendations highlight the ongoing effort to make AI systems more accurate, dynamic, and responsive to individual learner needs. Around 57% of studies call for expanding AI applications to broader educational contexts, including different age groups, subjects, and institutions (e.g., Chen et al., 2020; Duan, 2024). This reflects a recognition of the potential for AI-driven PLPs to benefit diverse learners, from K-12 students to higher education and vocational training. A significant portion of studies (50%) stress the importance of addressing ethical concerns, such as AI bias, data privacy, and academic integrity (e.g., Pesovski et al., 2024; Chadha, 2024). These recommendations underscore the need for responsible AI development, ensuring that personalized learning tools are fair, transparent, and secure. Additionally, 36% of studies highlight the need for teacher training in digital literacy and AI integration (e.g., Hao, Wang, & Peng, 2024), recognizing that educators play a critical role in implementing and optimizing AI-driven solutions. Improving AI interpretability is another key recommendation, mentioned in 29% of studies (e.g., Hooshyar et al., 2024), as it is essential for building trust and understanding among educators and learners. Furthermore, 21% of studies advocate long-term research to assess the sustained impact of AI-driven PLPs on learning outcomes and educational equity (e.g., Deng et al., 2024; Chadha, 2024). This highlights the need for longitudinal studies to move beyond short-term evaluations and understand how AI tools influence learning over time. Other recommendations include enhancing AI-generated content (e.g., Pesovski et al., 2024), improving computational efficiency (e.g., Deng et al., 2024), and developing hybrid AI-human teaching models (e.g., Albdrani & Al-Shargabi, 2023) to balance automation with human expertise. In overall, the future agendas in AI-driven PLPs research focus on three main areas: advancing AI capabilities for better personalization, ensuring scalability across diverse educational contexts, and addressing ethical and practical challenges. By prioritizing these areas, the field can develop more effective, equitable, and sustainable personalized learning solutions that meet the needs of learners, educators, and institutions alike.

Table 7. The future agenda related to AI/PLP

Author	**future agenda**
(Sayed et al., 2023)	- Enhance adaptive personalized learning with more AI techniques. - Extend to other age groups and subjects. - Integrate multi-agent RL for collaborative learning.
(Sajja et al., 2024)	- Enhance AI-enabled VTAs with real-time video interaction - Improve personalization through adaptive learning algorithms - Expand integration with multiple LMS platforms - Address ethical considerations and academic integrity
(Hooshyar et al., 2024)	- Improve NSAI framework by incorporating additional educational constraints - Enhance AI interpretability for broader educational applications - Expand dataset diversity to improve generalizability - Integrate NSAI into real-world digital learning platforms
(Chen et al., 2020)	- Enhance HDNN by integrating more AI-driven personalization techniques - Improve predictive modeling for early intervention - Expand to different educational contexts and institutions - Address potential biases in AI-driven assessments
(Hao, Wang, & Peng, 2024)	- Improve AI precision teaching models for broader subject applicability - Address teacher training challenges in digital literacy - Expand empirical research on AI-driven teaching at different educational levels - Enhance AI-driven assessment tools for better personalized learning interventions

continued on following page

Table 7. Continued

Author	future agenda
(Dhananjaya et al., 2024)	- Improve AI-powered chatbots for better contextual understanding and adaptive learning - Address ethical concerns, data privacy, and misinformation risks - Enhance AI integration in traditional and online education platforms - Expand research on AI's long-term impact on education
(Pesovski et al., 2024)	- Expand AI-driven content personalization for diverse learning preferences - Integrate generative AI tools with more LMS platforms - Address ethical concerns like AI bias and misinformation - Improve AI-generated quizzes and feedback mechanisms
(Albdrani & Al-Shargabi, 2023)	- Improve AI-based tutoring models for broader application in various subjects - Address ethical concerns and AI biases in educational settings - Expand research on AI-driven personalized learning in STEM education - Develop hybrid AI-human teaching models for enhanced student engagement
(Liu et al.,2024)	- Improve AI-based learning path recognition models for different age groups - Address ethical concerns related to AI-driven education - Enhance AI personalization through adaptive learning techniques - Integrate CSSF into large-scale learning management systems
(Duan, 2024)	- Enhance AI-based learner profiling for more accurate personalization - Expand research on AI-driven digital training models across multiple disciplines - Address challenges of AI integration in vocational education - Improve adaptive learning through AI-powered analytics
(Deng et al., 2024)	- Improve AI-driven dynamic PLP models for real-time adaptability - Address computational efficiency challenges in incremental learning - Expand research on long-term impact of AI-driven PLPs - Investigate ethical considerations and fairness in AI-based education
(Eltahir & Babiker, 2024)	- Expand AI integration in pre-service teacher training programs - Enhance AI-powered tutoring systems for real-time personalized feedback - Investigate ethical implications and student attitudes towards AI in education - Develop AI-driven frameworks for improving instructional design models
(Chadha, 2024)	- Expand AI-based pedagogical innovations for higher education - Address AI ethics and fairness in personalized learning models - Improve AI chatbots for adaptive learning and student engagement - Conduct long-term studies on AI's impact on educational equity
(Bagunaid et al., 2024)	- Improve AI-driven early warning systems for student performance prediction - Enhance federated learning-based authentication for e-learning security - Expand AI-generated personalized learning recommendations - Address ethical concerns in AI-driven education, including bias and data privacy

VIII. LIMITATIONS

Despite the efforts made to ensure the comprehensiveness and accuracy of the analysis in this study, there are some limitations that need to be acknowledged, as they may affect the generalizability of the findings and the ability to provide a broader perspective on the field of artificial intelligence and personalized learning pathways. First, the study relied solely on research published within the last five years, which may have excluded some earlier studies that could contribute to a deeper understanding of long-term developments in this field. While this temporal limitation was necessary to focus on recent trends, it may have overlooked some early contributions that remain relevant and significant. Second, the study primarily focused on research published in Scopus only, which may have led to the omission of valuable studies published in other databases or local journals or conferences not indexed in Scopus. This limitation may affect the comprehensiveness of the analysis and restrict the representation of certain regional or cultural educational contexts, warranting caution when generalizing the findings. Third, the reviewed studies encompassed diverse research methodologies (quantitative and qualitative), making it challenging to integrate the findings into a comprehensive and comparative analysis. While this diversity reflects the multidimensional nature of AI research in education, it also poses a challenge in deriving unified and generalizable conclusions. Fourth, although the study provided important theoretical insights into trends and methodologies, there is a need for more applied research to explore how these solutions can be implemented in real-world educational settings. The gap between theoretical research and practical application remains a key challenge that needs to be addressed in future studies to ensure the effectiveness of these solutions in practice. Fifth, the analysis did not sufficiently address the implications of algorithmic bias or the challenges associated with protecting learner data. These issues require further research and scrutiny to ensure that AI applications in education remain fair and adhere to strict ethical standards for user privacy. Considering these limitations, future studies can contribute to addressing these gaps by expanding the temporal scope of analysis, incorporating additional data sources, and focusing on practical applications to improve the design of personalized learning pathways. Additionally, future research should pay greater attention to ethical and technical challenges, such as algorithmic bias and data protection, to ensure that AI solutions in education are inclusive, effective, and equitable for all users.

IX. DISCUSSION

This section aims to critically analyze the study's findings within the broader context of advancements in artificial intelligence (AI) and personalized learning, while identifying key trends, challenges, and future opportunities. By situating the results within existing literature, this discussion seeks to provide a nuanced understanding of the implications of AI-driven educational technologies and their applications in institutional settings.

1. Key Research Contributions and the Evolving Research Landscape

The bibliometric analysis revealed a marked increase in research productivity related to AI applications in education, particularly in the domain of personalized learning pathways. This surge aligns with the global technological advancements of the past decade, as educational institutions increasingly adopt AI-driven solutions to enhance teaching and learning processes. The United States, China, and India emerged as the leading contributors to this field, a trend attributable to robust government funding, advanced research infrastructure, and a strong emphasis on innovation. In contrast, Arab nations, including the Sultanate of Oman, lag behind despite incremental efforts to modernize digital infrastructure and integrate technology into educational frameworks. This disparity underscores the need for greater investment in research and development within these regions.

Existing literature, such as Chen et al. (2021), corroborates the potential of AI to revolutionize education while highlighting ethical concerns, particularly regarding data privacy and algorithmic transparency. These findings resonate with the current study, emphasizing the dual nature of AI as both an opportunity and a challenge in educational contexts.

2. Research Methodologies: Balancing Quantitative and Qualitative Approaches

The analysis identified a predominance of quantitative methodologies, accounting for 71% of the studies reviewed. This preference reflects researchers' reliance on statistical tools and predictive models, such as neural networks and deep learning techniques, to analyze large datasets and forecast learner behaviors. These methods are particularly valued for their ability to handle complex data and generate actionable insights.

Conversely, qualitative methodologies, though less prevalent, play a critical role in uncovering contextual challenges associated with AI implementation. For instance, qualitative studies have shed light on practical barriers, including resistance to change among educators, insufficient training, and inadequate digital infrastructure. These insights align with the recommendations of Hooshyar et al. (2023), who advocate for a mixed-methods approach to achieve a holistic evaluation of AI applications in education.

3. AI-Driven Personalized Learning Models

A significant finding of this study is the growing reliance on adaptive learning models, which leverage real-time data analytics to deliver personalized educational content. These systems, including Intelligent Tutoring Systems (ITS) and Personalized Learning Platforms, have demonstrated efficacy in enhancing academic performance and fostering learner engagement, as evidenced by Olga & Zhiyenbayeva (2022). However, challenges persist, particularly in ensuring the accuracy of AI-generated recommendations and mitigating algorithmic bias. Addressing these issues is critical to maximizing the potential of adaptive learning technologies.

4. Sample Analysis and Identification of Research Gaps

The study revealed a disproportionate focus on higher education (36% of studies), followed by basic education (21%). This emphasis reflects the growing demand for flexible and adaptive educational systems tailored to diverse learner needs. However, significant gaps remain in the exploration of AI applications in lifelong learning and technical or vocational education. These underserved areas warrant further investigation to ensure that AI-driven solutions are inclusive and equitable, particularly for marginalized and underrepresented populations.

5. Future Directions and Recommendations

The findings underscore the need for continued innovation in adaptive algorithms and user interface design to optimize the learning experience. Key recommendations emerging from the literature include:

- Collaborative Innovation: Strengthening partnerships between academia and industry to develop AI-driven educational tools.

- Teacher Training: Investing in professional development programs to equip educators with the skills needed to effectively utilize AI technologies.
- Ethical Frameworks: Establishing robust regulatory guidelines to address data privacy concerns and safeguard learner rights.

X. CHALLENGES AND OPPORTUNITIES

The integration of AI in education is not without challenges. Key issues include:

1. Data Privacy and Security: The collection and analysis of vast amounts of learner data raise significant privacy concerns.
2. Algorithmic Bias: Poorly designed algorithms risk perpetuating biases, potentially undermining the fairness and accuracy of AI-driven recommendations.
3. Digital Divide: Disparities in technological infrastructure exacerbate inequalities between well-resourced and under-resourced institutions.

Despite these challenges, opportunities abound for future research, such as developing transparent and interpretable algorithms, ensuring equitable access to AI technologies, and exploring their applications in underserved educational sectors.

XI. CONCLUSION

This study contributes to providing an in-depth understanding of the role of AI in developing personalized learning paths, with a careful analysis of the prevailing trends and methodologies followed over the past five years. By combining bibliometric analysis and a systematic literature review, we were able to explore the different aspects of this rapidly evolving field, highlighting the leading research contributions, the most widely used methodologies, and the most prominent AI-powered learning models.

The results indicate a significant increase in the use of AI technologies in education, with an increasing focus on adaptive models that enhance individual learning experiences. However, this development is not without multiple challenges related to privacy, algorithmic neutrality, and digital gaps between different educational institutions. These challenges, although complex, provide new research opportunities to develop innovative and sustainable solutions that ensure equity and inclusiveness in education.

In terms of methodologies used, it was found that quantitative methodologies dominate the research landscape, reflecting the increasing reliance on statistical analyses and predictive models to improve learning strategies. Despite the importance of these methodologies, combining quantitative and qualitative approaches will remain essential to provide a comprehensive vision that combines digital accuracy with an understanding of educational contexts.

The study emphasizes the importance of developing educational policies that support the integration of AI technologies at all levels of education. This effort requires collaboration between researchers, educational institutions, and policy-makers to ensure that regulatory frameworks are in place to protect personal data and enhance transparency in the design of algorithms.

On a practical level, the study recommends the need to provide ongoing training programs for teachers on how to use AI tools effectively. It also calls for enhancing research in the fields of lifelong education and technical education, to ensure that AI applications are comprehensive and sustainable.

In conclusion, this study represents a call for researchers to continue exploring this vital field, with a focus on developing innovative educational models that benefit from the capabilities of AI and providing realistic solutions to current challenges. These efforts will pave the way for a more inclusive and efficient educational future, where AI plays a pivotal role in improving educational outcomes and enhancing academic performance.

REFERENCES

Abuhassna, H., & Alnawajha, S. (2023a). Instructional design made easy! Instructional design models, categories, frameworks, educational context, and recommendations for future work. *European Journal of Investigation in Health, Psychology and Education, 13*(4), 715–735. DOI: 10.3390/ejihpe13040054 PMID: 37185907

Abuhassna, H., & Alnawajha, S. (2023b). The transactional distance theory and distance learning contexts: Theory integration, research gaps, and future agenda. *Education Sciences, 13*(2), 112. DOI: 10.3390/educsci13020112

Abuhassna, H., Awae, F., Bayoumi, K., Alzitawi, D. U., Alsharif, A. H., & Yahaya, N. (2022b). Understanding online learning readiness among university students: A bibliometric analysis. [iJIM]. *International Journal of Interactive Mobile Technologies, 16*(13), 81–94. DOI: 10.3991/ijim.v16i13.30605

Abuhassna, H., Van, N. T., Yahaya, N., Zakaria, M. A. Z. M., Awae, F., Al Zitawi, D. U. D., & Bayoumi, K. (2022a). Strategies for successful blended learning—A bibliometric analysis and reviews. [iJIM]. *International Journal of Interactive Mobile Technologies, 16*(13), 66–80. DOI: 10.3991/ijim.v16i13.30739

Albdrani, R. N., & Al-Shargabi, A. A. (2023). Investigating the Effectiveness of ChatGPT for Providing Personalized Learning Experience: A Case Study. [IJACSA]. *International Journal of Advanced Computer Science and Applications, 14*(11). Advance online publication. DOI: 10.14569/IJACSA.2023.01411122

Bagunaid, W., Chilamkurti, N., Shahraki, A. S., & Bamashmos, S. (2024). Visual Data and Pattern Analysis for Smart Education: A Robust DRL-Based Early Warning System for Student Performance Prediction. *Future Internet, 16*(206), 206. Advance online publication. DOI: 10.3390/fi16060206

Chadha, A. (2024). Transforming Higher Education for the Digital Age: Examining Emerging Technologies and Pedagogical Innovations. *Journal of Interdisciplinary Studies in Education, 13*(S1), 53–70. https://ojed.org/jise. DOI: 10.32674/em2qsn46

Chen, X., Huang, Y., & Liu, S. (2020). Artificial intelligence for personalized learning pathways: Current status and future directions. *Computers & Education, 156*, 103940.

Chen, X., Zou, D., Cheng, G., & Xie, H. (2021). Artificial intelligence-assisted personalized language learning: A systematic review and bibliometric analysis. *Computer Assisted Language Learning, 34*(7), 934–957. DOI: 10.1080/09588221.2019.1901492

Chen, Z., Zhang, J., Jiang, X., Hu, Z., Han, X., Xu, M., Savitha, V., & Vivekananda, G. N. (2020). Education 4.0 using artificial intelligence for students performance analysis. *Inteligencia Artificial*, *23*(66), 124–137. DOI: 10.4114/intartif.vol23iss66pp124-137

Deng, W., Wang, L., & Deng, X. (2024). Strategies for Optimizing Personalized Learning Pathways with Artificial Intelligence Assistance. *International Journal of Advanced Computer Science and Applications*, *15*(6), 605–616. DOI: 10.14569/IJACSA.2024.0150662

Dhananjaya, G. M., Goudar, R. H., Govindaraja, K., Kaliwal, R. B., Rathod, V. K., Deshpande, S. L., & Kulkarni, A. (2024). Enhancing Education with ChatGPT: Revolutionizing Personalized Learning and Teacher Support. *EAI Endorsed Transactions on Internet of Things*, *10*. Advance online publication. DOI: 10.4108/eetiot.6998

Duan, H. (2024). Research and Practice of Digital Training Model Based on Artificial Intelligence Technology. *Applied Mathematics and Nonlinear Sciences*, *9*(1), 1–17. DOI: 10.2478/amns.2023.2.01507

Eltahir, M. E., & Babiker, F. M. E. (2024). The Influence of Artificial Intelligence Tools on Student Performance in e-Learning Environments: Case Study. *Electronic Journal of e-Learning*, *22*(9), 91–110. DOI: 10.34190/ejel.22.9.3639

Hao, M., Wang, Y., & Peng, J. (2024). Empirical Research on AI Technology-Supported Precision Teaching in High School Science Subjects. *Applied Sciences (Basel, Switzerland)*, *14*(7544), 7544. Advance online publication. DOI: 10.3390/app14177544

Holmes, W., Bialik, M., & Fadel, C. (2019). Artificial intelligence in education: Promises and implications for teaching and learning. Center for Curriculum Redesign. Retrieved from https://curriculumredesign.org/wp-content/uploads/AI-in-Education-CCR-2019.pdf

Hooshyar, D., Ahmad, R. B., Yousefi, M., Yusop, F. D., & Horng, S. J. (2015). A flowchart-based intelligent tutoring system for improving problem-solving skills of novice programmers. *Journal of Computer Assisted Learning*, *31*(4), 345–361. DOI: 10.1111/jcal.12099

Hooshyar, D., Azevedo, R., & Yang, Y. (2024). Augmenting Deep Neural Networks with Symbolic Educational Knowledge: Towards Trustworthy and Interpretable AI for Education. *Machine Learning & Knowledge Extraction*, *6*(1), 593–618. DOI: 10.3390/make6010028

Ilie, M. D., & Frăsineanu, E. S. (2019). Artificial intelligence applications in education: A review. Proceedings of the International Conference on Virtual Learning, 11, 105–110. Retrieved from https://www.icvl.eu/2019/abstracts/ICVL2019_Section_III_Paper01.pdf

Khosravi, H., & Cooper, A. (2022). Personalized learning pathways using machine learning: Enhancing learner engagement and outcomes. *International Journal of Educational Technology in Higher Education*, *19*(1), 8–20.

Liu, T.-Y., Jiang, Y.-H., Wei, Y., Wang, X., Huang, S., & Dai, L. (2024). Educational Practices and Algorithmic Framework for Promoting Sustainable Development in Education by Identifying Real-World Learning Paths. *Sustainability (Basel)*, *16*(6871), 6871. Advance online publication. DOI: 10.3390/su16166871

Luckin, R., Holmes, W., Griffiths, M., & Forcier, L. B. (2018). *Intelligence Unleashed: An Argument for AI in Education*. Pearson Education.

Pesovski, I., Santos, R., Henriques, R., & Trajkovik, V. (2024). Generative AI for Customizable Learning Experiences. *Sustainability (Basel)*, *16*(3034), 3034. Advance online publication. DOI: 10.3390/su16073034

Sajja, R., Sermet, Y., Cikmaz, M., Cwiertny, D., & Demir, I. (2024). Artificial Intelligence-Enabled Intelligent Assistant for Personalized and Adaptive Learning in Higher Education. *Information (Basel)*, *15*(596), 596. Advance online publication. DOI: 10.3390/info15100596

Sayed, G., Hassan, M. M., & Rizk, H. (2023). Quantitative methods in personalized learning: A meta-analysis of AI-driven educational tools. *Journal of Artificial Intelligence in Education*, *33*(4), 223–245. DOI: 10.1007/s40593-023-00211-8

Sayed, W. S., Noeman, A. M., Abdellatif, A., Abdelrazek, M., Badawy, M. G., Hamed, A., & El-Tantawy, S. (2022). AI-based adaptive personalized content presentation and exercises navigation for an effective and engaging E-learning platform. *Multimedia Tools and Applications*, *82*(3), 3303–3333. DOI: 10.1007/s11042-022-13076-8 PMID: 35789938

Spector, J. M., Ifenthaler, D., Sampson, D. G., & Isaias, P. (2021). Trends and research on artificial intelligence in education: A comprehensive review. *Computers in Human Behavior Reports*, *4*, 100125.

Williamson, B., & Eynon, R. (2020). Algorithmic systems in education: Surveillance, autonomy, and equity in AI-driven learning platforms. *Learning, Media and Technology*, *45*(3), 254–267.

Zawacki-Richter, O., Marín, V. I., Bond, M., & Gouverneur, F. (2019). Systematic review of research on artificial intelligence applications in higher education – where are the educators? *International Journal of Educational Technology in Higher Education*, *16*(1), 1–27. DOI: 10.1186/s41239-019-0171-0

Chapter 2
Students' Learning Math With the Aid of AI and the Need of Shifting Classroom Instructions

Potchong M. Jackaria
https://orcid.org/0009-0006-1678-4841
Mindanao State University-Tawi-Tawi College of Technology and Oceanography, Philippines

Al-adzran G. Sali
https://orcid.org/0009-0009-3542-5643
Mindanao State University-Tawi-Tawi College of Technology and Oceanography, Philippines

Hana An L. Alvarado
https://orcid.org/0009-0006-6550-616X
Mindanao State University-Tawi-Tawi College of Technology and Oceanography, Philippines

Rashidin H. Moh. Jiripa
https://orcid.org/0009-0003-7253-452X
Mindanao State University-Tawi-Tawi College of Technology and Oceanography, Philippines

Al-sabrie Y. Sahijuan
Pagasinan National High School, Philippines

DOI: 10.4018/979-8-3373-0847-0.ch002

ABSTRACT

Generative AI has numerous applications in education. This chapter investigates the use of AI tools among students in the context of learning mathematics. Guided by the Technology Acceptance Model, the study evaluates AI tools in terms of perceived ease of use, credibility, and usefulness. Data were collected from 67 education students major in mathematics at a public university in the Southern Philippines. Results show that a significant majority are already using AI tools to support their learning in mathematics. The popularity of these tools is attributed to features such as offline functionality, image-based input, and the ability to generate step-by-step solutions. The chapter offers insights into current practices of AI tool usage in mathematics learning and highlights its pedagogical implications. It concludes with practical recommendations for teachers and policymakers, supporting the need to shift current classroom practices in response to the growing AI integration in education.

INTRODUCTION

The integration of artificial intelligence (AI) into education has brought about a transformative era in teaching and learning. In particular, the rise of generative AI has significantly impacted teaching and learning processes by offering personalized experiences tailored to individual students' needs (Hwang, G., 2021; Ka et al., 2023; Yu & Guo, 2022). With AI's ability to swiftly provide answers and customize learning experiences, AI-powered tools can become a powerful vehicle for AI-driven education, as they are accessible (Nikolopoulou et al., 2020; Ouédraogo, 2024). This ever-present combination of mobile devices and the speed of AI responses can enhance the accessibility of AI as an effective learning tool.

In addition, AI-powered learning applications have huge potential to address current educational inequalities by providing high-quality learning resources to students regardless of location or socioeconomic background (Khandor et al., 2023; Patil et al., 2024). For instance, AI applications on mobile phones could significantly impact students who lack access to private tutorials. One of the primary advantages of these applications is the ability to provide instant feedback for both teachers (Jackaria et al.,2024) and students (Eden et al., 2024). Artificial intelligence tools have primarily been tested in language teaching and learning. It is commonly used to construct and automate ratings of written works (Jackaria et al., 2024).

While mathematics is often considered a challenging subject, consistent practice is key for students to retain math concepts (Ayu et al., 2020). With the available AI tools, these can be utilized by students to effectively learn mathematics, such as in providing timely correction of problem-solving strategies. AI-based application tools can offer a convenient and supportive platform for students to engage with math problems. These AI tools offer personalized and interactive learning experiences that may help students develop a more profound understanding of mathematical concepts while at the same time improving motivation and engagement (Francis & Davis, 2018; Wu, 2021).

However, along with the advantages, concerns have been raised regarding students' use of AI tools in schools and mathematics in particular. Some worry that instead of serving as aid, students may become over-reliant and may reduce their ability to critically think and problem-solve (Fuchs, 2021; Jackaria et al., 2024). With answers readily available, the students may become less willing to engage in the processes that facilitate deep learning (Zhai et al., 2021). Additionally, there are concerns about the accuracy of AI-generated responses, particularly in a subject as precise as mathematics (Drori et al., 2022; Frieder et al., 2024).

With the many potentials of AI-driven tools as an aid in learning mathematics and the concerns surrounding their possible misuse, the chapter explores the current usage and acceptance of AI-driven tools in learning mathematics. The chapter explains the AI usage and acceptance based on the established Technology Acceptance Model (TAM), particularly in terms of the AI tools' usefulness, ease of use, and credibility appropriate for emerging AI technologies in the context of learning mathematics.

This chapter assessed the current usage of AI application tools among mathematics pre-service teachers while learning mathematics content. The pre-service teachers provide the vantage point as they are the users of these AI tools and are training to be future teachers. The chapter provides valuable insights into the technical and pedagogical implications of AI use, providing insights that aid in improving policies and instruction on integrating AI in mathematics instruction.

RELATED LITERATURE

This section presents current studies and literature that helped conceptualize this chapter. The chapter comprehensively presents and analyzes the impact of Artificial Intelligence, the challenges it poses, and its application in mathematics teaching and learning.

Artificial Intelligence's Impact on Education

In the fast-evolving landscape of education, Artificial Intelligence is one of the key factors that affect today's education. Artificial Intelligence is gradually reshaping and transforming the world of teaching and the learning landscape. AI's integration into education can pave the way for new possibilities in making learning more relevant and meaningful for students (Roll & Wylie, 2016).

Yim and Su (2024) posited that AI can aid teachers in improving student performance by transforming the students' learning experiences and providing effective pedagogy methods. Hwang et al. (2020) and Yufeia et al. (2020) underscore that teachers can use AI to enhance feedback, automatic grading systems, distance learning, and personalized learning. Additionally, Akgun and Greenhow (2022) emphasize that valuable applications of AI in education include personalized learning systems, which are also referred to as adaptive learning platforms, designed to support both learners and instructors. AI assists teachers in precipitating the integration of personalized learning in the classroom. It helps by adapting content and teaching methods based on student needs, performance, and engagement (Holmes et al., 2019). On a similar note, Ayeni et al. (2024) pointed out that AI can also help teachers tailor instruction for each student based on the difficulty levels and the student's ability. Sruthi and Mukherjee (2020) and Wakelam et al. (2020) highlighted that AI helps educators analyze student data to better tailor learning activities and experiences based on students' needs.

Similarly, AI grants students numerous learning materials to explore, learn, and understand the concepts based on their needs and interests. Luckin et al. (2016) point out that AI can align and tailor to the student's experiences and drastically change the traditional way of teaching and learning. It is underscored by Peng et al. (2019) and Cho et al. (2019) that AI can help students improve their performance by providing learning materials that are more tailored and relevant. With AI rapidly spreading in education, students interact and collaborate with this AI by offering them personalized instruction, thus building a connection and relationships.

The AI-driven adaptive learning systems have the potential to effectively improve the engagement of the students by aligning content delivery with students' learning preferences and paces. This approach provides students with material to explore, be motivated, and be interested in learning. It is noted by Owoc et al. (2019) that one of the most promising benefits of AI in education is adaptive learning, which is different from the traditional way of teaching one-size-fits-all. Adaptive learning can potentially improve the student's performance and maximize learning efficiency by aligning the content delivery with students' learning pace. In addition, it is affirmed by Raja et al. (2024) that adaptive learning systems are frequently used in different subjects; students who use them tend to perform much better academically than those who do not.

Several studies investigate the impact of integrating Artificial Intelligence (AI) on students' learning outcomes and reveal promising results. Suntharalingam (2024) and Xu (2024) noted that integrating AI technologies, such as virtual reality and even intelligent tutoring systems, significantly enhances students' academic performance, motivation, and engagement. It is also corroborated by Sugiarso et al. (2024), who found that at the high school level, AI is known for assisting teachers in improving students' overall learning. Furthermore, Nguyen et al. (2024) underscore that AI's interactive and engaging nature could be a transformative tool to make learning more dynamic and relevant to the student's needs. Nemorin et al. (2023) found that AI empowers and motivates students by providing dynamic, engaging, and interesting classes.

Concerns about the use of artificial intelligence

While AI provides ample benefits for education, it is vital to acknowledge the concerns and potential disadvantages it may bring. Many have expressed apprehension about the negative impact of using AI in education. These concerns encompass a broad scope of issues, including over-reliance, ethical concerns, the decreasing of human interaction, and the potential bias reinforcement; all of these raise critical questions about how AI can enhance the learning experiences of the students and its long-term impact on students, instructors, and education.

One of the primary concerns many educators raised is the students' over-reliance on AI tools, which could be detrimental and hinder their ability to think independently and critically. It is highlighted by Mhlanga (2023) that most of the teachers are pretty concerned that students are relying too much on AI. Educators emphasize that rather than AI helping students learn more, it hinders students' ability to learn independently and think creatively and critically. This perspective is further supported by Zanetti et al. (2019), underscoring that AI tools could hamper the development of vital skills of students and, worst, even decrease human interaction. The ease of accessing and using AI to provide answers in assignments and activities may encourage students to use and rely on it, thus diminishing their intellectual growth. Students may become too reliant on AI tools, which could hamper the development of students' creativity and innovation (Duhaylungsod & Chavez, 2023). It is further explored by Koos and Wachsmann (2023), who found that the over-reliance on AI has detrimental effects on the students' development of essential skills such as analyzing, critiquing, and evaluating information and constructing rational arguments, which are both salient for their academic and professional success.

While AI can assist students in understanding their subjects, Crowe et al. (2017) cautioned that AI may promote dishonesty in education, hindering academic integrity and meaningful learning for the students. This situation poses a significant risk and may lead to research misconduct, including plagiarism, falsification, and fabrication. It is noted by Chaka (2023) and Kleebayoon and Wiwanitkit (2023) that even though AI tools can be a potential tool that helps students understand complex concepts or assists them in gathering data or generating ideas, the ease of using it can encourage the student to plagiarize. This is further supported by Mohammadkarimi (2023), who states that students usually submit AI-generated work and claim it as their own, undermining the educational objectives of fostering original thinking and academic integrity. Most students are tempted to submit AI-generated work to their teachers as it becomes easy to access, encouraging academic dishonesty.

Another significant challenge in AI integration in education is the ethical impact, especially concerning the privacy and data security of the users. AI systems in educational contexts often require extensive data collection and even personal student information. This raises an issue since there is an inherent risk of data breaches or misuse of sensitive and personal information. This issue is also raised by Yang et al. (2023) and Baskara (2023), noting that if data is not adequately secure, all of the students' sensitive information could be exposed and cause harm to the students. Also, using AI systems raises a question on consent, which is emphasized by Gupta and Jain (2023), who state that students and educators must understand how these AI manage their data, giving importance to informed consent. It is vital that users of AI, most notably students and educators, fully understand what data is being collected from them, how it will be used, and how they can be vigilant with their data to avoid exposing personal information. Without informed consent, using AI in education could violate fundamental privacy rights.

In addition to privacy concerns, there are concerns about AI systems' biases and misinformation. The AI tools are trained on large datasets collected from the internet, which may contain inherent biases. Kooli (2023) and Talanquer (2023) argue that using AI presents a significant risk to the students through bias reinforcement and misinformation. This is dangerous and problematic as it impairs the overall goal of education. It can also promote stereotypes and misinformation to students and teachers (Eubanks, 2018). Educators must not underestimate the risk of exposing students to biases, as it could significantly impact the decision-making and understanding of the students, thus contributing to an inequitable educational environment.

The ease of using AI poses an issue with the rapid spreading of misinformation, particularly with Chatbots. AI tools like Chatbots rely heavily on extensive data from the internet to generate user responses (Adetayo, 2023). The internet is replete with plenty of misinformation that could leak into the AI's responses, raising another significant concern about AI's outputs' accuracy and reliability. Akgun and Greenhow (2021) also stress that teachers and students must know when and how to use AI and how to assess the reliability and validity of AI outputs. Xie et al. (2021) emphasize that students who use unverified AI output can lead to misinformation.

While AI revolutionizes the teaching and learning landscape, there is still a need for careful consideration of its adoption while mitigating the potential risk to students. The research stressed the need to carefully look at how AI affects education and the importance of proper rules and assessments to make sure that using AI improves students' learning instead of distracting them from the main goals of education. However, the advantages of the integration of AI in education undoubtedly outweigh the disadvantages of it, as evidenced by several studies.

The Use of AI Tools in Mathematics Teaching and Learning

In mathematics education, Artificial Intelligence (AI) is a potential tool to transform mathematics teaching and learning, making mathematics more intriguing and engaging for every student. The development of AI technology has raised interest in its potential to improve learning outcomes. Popenici and Kerr (2017) note that integrating AI into mathematics education can enhance student learning and teaching practices. Furthermore, Hwang et al. (2020) highlighted that AI has roles in education. It serves as a teacher, friend, learning tool, partner, and policy-making advisor. Teachers could use AI technologies by helping them provide personalized guidance, feedback, or support to students during the learning process.

AI tools can help students access more lesson information quickly and efficiently, allowing them to study at their pace and explore mathematical concepts outside the classroom. Mohammed (2023) suggests that AI helps students find answers faster and easier. Students can easily access all information about the lesson using this innovative intelligence software.

Subsequently, AI has a unique ability to make learning more interactive for students, which is the key factor in its success. Francis and Davis (2018) argue that an AI-driven approach to teaching mathematics can foster an engaging and dynamic learning environment. AI applications encourage the development of students' problem-solving and critical thinking skills, both salient in understanding mathematics. Voskoglou and Salem (2020) noted that using AI-enhanced mathematical software, especially animated mathematical figures and representations, can provide students with a foundation to improve their imagination and problem-solving abilities.

Other studies have revealed that AI systems can increase student engagement by offering immediate feedback, personalized learning experiences, and opportunities for exploration. For instance, Wu's (2021) research concludes that it is highly effective to use AI in assisting teachers in teaching introductory mathematics concepts. The result of Wu's study is that through learning AI, students' mathematics scores are higher than with traditional teaching methods, and a sense of cooperation between students is reached. This finding is also consistent with Min et al. (2021), who suggest that AI's influence on student accomplishment extends beyond academic performance to include learning attitude (Liao & Gu, 2022), creative skills, and computing thinking (Kim et al., 2023), contributing to the overall development of creative problem-solving skills and positive learning attitudes.

AI can personalize the learning experience and significantly impact students ' cognitive and affective skills. Mathematics learning software uses AI to adjust the difficulty level of questions according to students' abilities, thereby increasing learning motivation. Using AI makes it easier for educators to identify specific individuals who require extra help and guidance through the process or are motivated and encouraged to do more within a classroom setting (Crompton et al., 2024). Furthermore, these AI-driven platforms encourage the development of essential skills such as critical thinking, problem-solving, reasoning, and collaboration, which are vital for mathematics and other disciplines (Huang & Qiao, 2024; Nagaraj et al., 2023).

AI also supports mathematics teachers' instructional practices by providing real-time data on student performance. Forsström and Afdal (2020) suggest that educators must explore AI more in order to apply technology during classes. Mathematics teachers should consider upskilling their programming skills to improve their mathematics teaching methods. Teachers must know the strategies and skills needed to use AI during the teaching and learning process to meet the needs of individual students. It is suggested by Moore et al. (2023) that AI's integration can transform mathematics education by using intelligent tutoring systems, computer grading, adaptive learning systems, and data analysis. These AI applications in mathematics education promote learner-centered educational systems and help educators monitor and guide their students effectively. AI can support education to effectively create differentiated instruction for each student's unique learning needs (García-Martínez et al., 2023).

Furthermore, AI also fosters creativity and problem-solving skills among students by providing opportunities for active learning. Darmayanti (2024) stressed that AI tools such as Mathway, Photomath, and Aleph allow students to work independently on different and complex mathematical problems. It offers guidance to the students even when working at home and encountering difficulties. Grájeda et al. (2024) highlight that by using AI, students can visualize complex functions, explore geometry, and manipulate equations through AI-based graphing calculators and algebra systems. Students can understand more abstract concepts through a hands-on approach and by making them tangible.

In conclusion, using AI in mathematics education offers much potential for both teachers and students. It has the potential to transform teaching and learning by providing an engaging and enjoyable learning environment. AI can provide adaptive learning experiences, enhancing critical thinking and problem-solving skills and fostering student engagement. However, teachers must equip themselves with knowledge and skills about AI, taking into account its limitations, to successfully integrate and implement it into the classroom. Understanding the current usage of artificial intelligence in learning mathematics among students provides insights into the current adoption needed to inform teaching and policies pertaining to AI use.

METHODOLOGY

The chapter follows the scientific format of a research study in terms of both process and presentation. This section explains the methodology, including data collection, participants, analysis, and results presentation.

Research design. This chapter employed a descriptive research design that incorporated both quantitative and qualitative data sources. It aimed to describe the utility of the different AI-powered application tools in learning mathematics among math pre-service teachers. We used the Technology Acceptance Model (TAM) as a framework to describe the utility of AI-powered mobile application tools. Particularly, the study described these AI-powered mobile application tools' perceived ease of use (PEU), perceived usefulness (PU), and credibility from the perspective of pre-service teachers. TAM's core variables, perceived ease of use and perceived usefulness, have been proven to be antecedent factors affecting acceptance of learning with technology (Granic & Marangunic, 2019). While the authors' focus on the credibility variable of the TAM model, particularly on the Artificial Intelligence (AI) acceptance, is due to the many issues surrounding the accuracy and reliability of the AI tools. Credibility is an important factor for AI acceptance among students (Stevens & Stetson, 2023). Finally, in-depth one-on-one interviews with selected students were conducted to triangulate the quantitative responses that provide insights into AI use in learning mathematics.

Research respondents. The respondents of this study are mathematics pre-service teachers at the Mindanao State University-Tawi-Tawi College of Technology and Oceanography, a public university in Southern Philippines. The researchers used a total enumeration of 84 pre-service teachers enrolled in the Bachelor of Secondary Education major in Mathematics (BSEd-Math) during the academic year 2024-2025. Seventeen of them were included for reliability testing, while the remaining 67 were considered the final respondents. The choice of mathematics pre-service teachers as respondents of this study is crucial, as the respondents are currently taking core mathematics subjects, many of them are using AI-powered mobile application tools, and their background in education makes them the ideal candidates to give insights into the uses of AI-powered application tools in learning mathematics.

Research instrument. The instrument used in this study is a researcher-made survey questionnaire. We drafted the questionnaire based on the Technology Acceptance Model (TAM), a powerful model that describes the aspects of technology adoption. It is a model that explains behavioral intention and the use of technology (Scherer, 2019). We modified Yilmaz et al.'s (2024) TAM-based questionnaire for this study. The questionnaire used in this study consists of items about the participants' usage of AI-powered mobile application tools. In this part, the respondents can choose from none to multiple options depending on their usage of AI tools. The next part of the questionnaire consists of items about the utility of AI tools in terms of ease of use, usefulness, and credibility from the original six components of Yilmaz et al. (2024). We asked the respondents to rate on a scale ranging from 1-very low to 5-very high. The final form of the questionnaire underwent validation and reliability testing using Cronbach's alpha and was found to be reliable at $\alpha = 0.782$. For the follow-up one-on-one interview, a semi-structured interview questionnaire was used, focusing on participants' experiences in the utilization of AI-powered mobile applications in learning mathematics. We used the results from the follow-up interview to guide our discussion of the study.

Data-gathering procedure. The data gathering started with a preliminary survey of students regarding their use of AI application tools. The initial results provided a list of the AI tools that students frequently used for learning mathematics. This was used in the finalization of the research questionnaire combined with the questionnaire on the Technology Acceptance Model. The researchers then personally administered the questionnaire to the respondents during their most comfortable time. Before administration, permission was sought and the respondents were made aware of the ethical considerations, such as the privacy of the collected data. To gain in-depth insights into AI used among students, follow-up one-on-one interviews with eight selected participants were conducted using a semi-structured interview questionnaire. The interview sessions were tape-recorded. Finally, the results were then tallied and analyzed using appropriate statistical tools, while qualitative data obtained were transcribed, translated into English, and thematically organized.

Statistical data analysis. Descriptive statistics such as frequency count, percent, and mean were computed using Microsoft Excel 2010 was used in the computation and data visualization. For the qualitative data obtained from the students' responses during the follow-up interview, they were transcribed, translated into English and analyzed using thematic analysis to obtain recurring codes and themes.

RESULTS AND DISCUSSION

The following section presents the result of the data obtained from the survey with 67 pre-service teachers. The result is presented in three subsections: The presentation of common AI tools used by students in learning mathematics, quantitative evidence on reasons for continuous use, and the students' qualitative responses.

What Are the Common AI Tools Students Use in Learning Mathematics?

The result showed that a huge majority of the students are using AI-powered mobile applications in learning mathematics, with 62 out of the 67 participants. This high prevalence of usage of AI among the participants supports the need for teachers to recognize and integrate AI in mathematics classrooms. Among the six most popular AI-driven application tools, three of which are exclusively made for mathematics learning (e.g., Photomath, Gauthmath, and Mathway), while the other three are for general-use generative artificial intelligence (e.g., Cici, ChatGPT, and Gemini).

Among the most popular AI-driven tools, Cici (n=47,70.15%), Photomath (n=40, 59.70%) and ChatGPT (n=28, 41.79%) top the list. The popularity of CiCi AI and ChatGPT among the participants is due to their ability to provide explanations for solutions and respond to follow-up questions in an almost human-like manner. As for Photomath, its offline features make it very helpful in solving math problems.

Other AI tools used by mathematics pre-service teachers are Mathway (n=13, 19.0%), Gemini (n=7, 10.45%), and Gauthmath (n=5, 7.46%). While Google's Gemini has the same features as ChatGPT and CiCi AI, its relatively new release may have contributed to its low popularity among the respondents. Finally, only a few of the participants use other AI-driven mobile application tools, including Perplexity and Question.AI.

Figure 1. Common AI Application Tools Used in Learning Mathematics

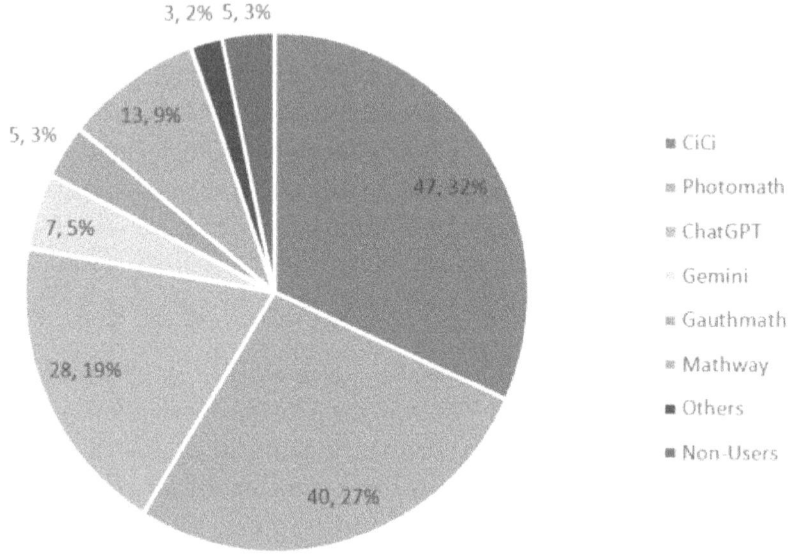

The findings showed that the majority of the pre-service teachers are already using AI application tools as an aid in learning mathematics. This result implies the need for teachers to discuss proper usage of AI tools, particularly with pre-service teachers.

Reasons for Continuous AI Tools Utilization in Learning Mathematics

The students' reasons for the utilization of AI application tools were evaluated based on the Technology Acceptance Model (TAM). We specifically focus on the three components. These are ease of use, credibility, and usefulness.

Ease of Use of AI Application Tools in Learning Mathematics

One of the most important features of any application is its user-friendliness. This study investigated the ease of use of six AI-driven mobile application tools based on the ratings of pre-service teachers who have personally used the tools in learning mathematics.

As can be seen in Figure 2, all of the six AI applications were rated high in terms of their ease of use. However, ChatGPT was rated the highest (M = 3.36) followed by Photomath (M = 4.00) and CiCi AI (M =3.81). It can also be noted that these three AI applications are the most used application tools by the pre-service teachers. This implies that the utilization of AI application tools among pre-service teachers is somehow related to their user-friendliness.

Consistent with the above observation, other AI application tools least used by the preservice teachers, such as Mathway (M = 3.69), Gauthmath (M = 3.60), and Gemini (M = 3.42), were rated the lowest in the aspect of ease of use by preservice teachers in the context of learning mathematics.

Figure 2. Ease of Use of AI Application Tools in Learning Mathematics

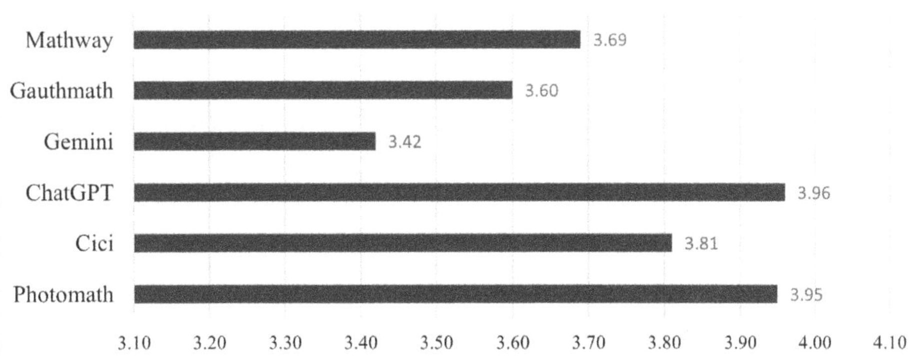

Legend: 1.0-1.79 (Very Low); 1.80-2.59 (Low); 2.60-3.39 (Moderate); 3.40-4.19 (High); 4.20-5.00 (Very High)

The ease of use was the greatest factor in the pre-service teachers' use of AI tools. The three most popular AI tools for learning mathematics (i.e., CiCi AI, Photomath, and ChatGPT) are also among the highest-rated applications in this category. The responses from the participants during the follow-up interview also support this finding. Some selected responses are presented below:

> *"I think that, compared to other AI tools, both Cici and Photomath are easier to use. They provide quick answers to mathematical questions, while other mathematical tools often require more specific input, need a subscription, or follow-up questions to produce an accurate response."*
>
> *Photomath and CiCi AI are easy to use. It is also conversational. While Gemini needs updates, somehow it's more complicated."*

Previous studies have pointed out that some features of Photomath and CiCi AI made them particularly useful for students. In the case of Photomath, the ability to capture and take inputs from the Photos made it popular among students. Another participant also shared that the popularity of some AI application tools over others may be due to the students' familiarity with the application. Such as the case of Photomath and CiCi AI, while other AI tools were only introduced recently.

The Usefulness of AI Application Tools in Learning Mathematics

The mathematics pre-service students were also asked to rate the AI application tools in terms of their usefulness in the learning of mathematics. The result in Figure 3 shows that Gemini (M = 4.00) and Mathway (M = 4.00) are both rated high. This is followed by Photomath (M=3.75) and ChatGPT (M=3.61). Gauthmath was rated the lowest (M = 3.40), while CiCi AI is surprisingly rated second to lowest in terms of usefulness in learning mathematics despite being one of the most used. This may be because CiCi AI is usually used as a companion AI by most of the respondents rather than designed for learning mathematics.

Figure 3. The Usefulness of AI Application Tools in Learning Mathematics

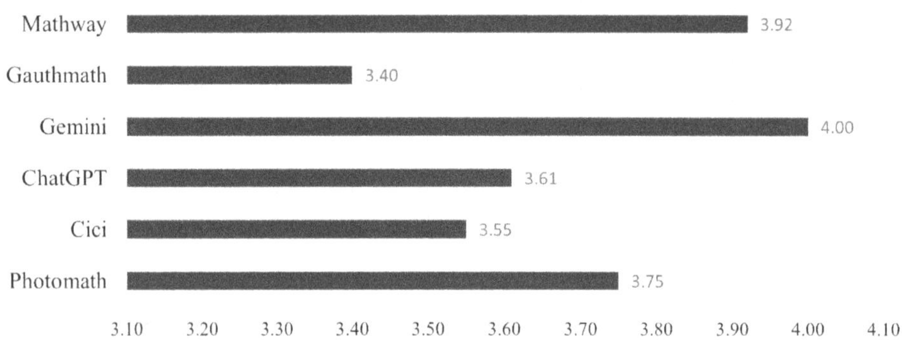

Legend: 1.0-1.79 (Very Low); 1.80-2.59 (Low); 2.60-3.39 (Moderate); 3.40-4.19 (High); 4.20-5.00 (Very High)

During the interview, many preservice teachers believe that AI tools can be useful as they provide solutions to math problems. For the pre-service teachers, the step-by-step mathematics solutions provided by AI have helped them learn math concepts better.

> *"Yes, AI provides step-by-step solutions in explaining the solutions of mathematical problems, which helped me understand more of the process." (P26)*
>
> *"Yes, it's because AI gives me more process and details in solving mathematical problems, especially when the given problem is more difficult to understand and solve." (P9)*

The AI The capability of AI to provide not only solutions but also detailed explanations further helps students understand mathematical problems. the students, the step-by-step solution provided by artificial intelligence tools helped them understand the mathematics concepts better.

"Yes, because in AI it provides a well-explained solution and step-by-step instructions for getting the right answer." (P44)

"Actually, it depends on the problem. I use AI when it is very hard for me to answer; that's why I want to know what the answer is with a complete solution." (P19)

"Yes, but sometimes I use AI when the mathematics teacher did not explain well some concept of mathematics." (P14)

The ability of the AI tools to provide answers to students' math questions is the main reason for students' usage of artificial intelligence when learning mathematics. This ability of artificial intelligence tools to solve and explain mathematics word problems has been shown in previous studies. In the study's findings, Rene (2023) and Poola and Bozid (2023) have demonstrated that generative AI can be utilized as an aid in solving and understanding mathematics problems. Hence, potentially improving students' math achievements.

Credibility of AI Application Tools in Learning Mathematics

The credibility of the AI-powered application tools refers to their ability to provide correct solutions to math problems and respond to students' questions relating to mathematics. This is particularly important because many AI tools have varied capabilities and are still in the process of improvement.

Figure 4 shows many interesting findings showing Gemini (M = 3.86) and Mathway (M = 3.81) were two AI-driven apps that are rated the most credible. Interestingly, the most used AI-driven application tools in learning mathematics previously in Table 1 are not necessarily the most credible in providing solutions (e.g., ChatGPT, Photomath, and CiCi AI).

Overall, two of the AI applications were rated high, while the other four AI tools were rated moderate in terms of their credibility in providing accurate answers. This means that when using these apps, it is important for pre-service teachers to counter-check the solutions given by these AI application tools.

Figure 4. Credibility of AI-powered Mobile Application Tools in Learning Mathematics

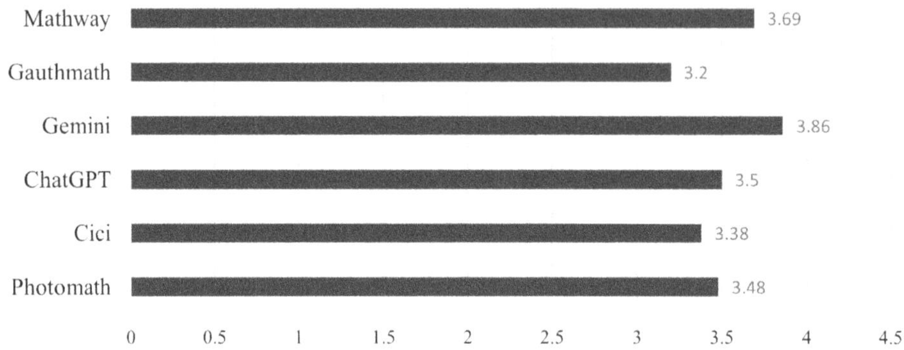

Legend: 1.0-1.79 (Very Low); 1.80-2.59 (Low); 2.60-3.39 (Moderate); 3.40-4.19 (High); 4.20-5.00 (Very High)

The AI-powered application tools were also rated in terms of credibility in providing correct responses to mathematics problems. It turns out that Gemini and Mathway were rated the most credible among the six. Google's Gemini is a very versatile AI, which may have contributed to its credibility among pre-service teachers. This tool can be used to solve a range of mathematical problems. On the other hand, the credibility of Mathway is due to its solving features, especially on math topics like arithmetic, algebra, trigonometry, calculus and statistics. In a similar study conducted by Santos et al. (2022) comparing nine different math application tools, Mathway was also rated the highest in terms of its solving features. The advantages of using Mathway include faster computation. It can provide answers and offer math solutions in detail, helping students answer the easiest to the most complex math. Other AI application tools were rated from moderate to high.

During the follow-up interview sessions, the participants recognized the importance of AI tools as additional guides when learning mathematics.

> *"Yes, I use AI in learning mathematics when I find it difficult to understand mathematics problems and use it as a guiding tool for me to understand the hard mathematics problems." (P26)*
>
> *"AI serves as my guide, and whenever I have questions in my mind I can directly and easily ask AI." (P7)*
>
> *"There are some instances where I use AI, usually when I am doubtful of my answers. I use AI to verify my answer." (P31)*

However, despite the usefulness of these AI tools in learning mathematics, some students have expressed the need for caution when using them in learning:

Sometimes, other answers in these tools are not reliable. (P17)

AI Tools can assist students in learning more quickly and provide them with help at any time. However, the problem is ensuring that they use them appropriately and not merely for copying answers. (P7)

These responses highlight the practical role of AI applications in learning mathematics as a supplemental tool helping the preservice teachers by providing solutions to math problems. However, concerns also arise about the inaccuracy of AI responses and the inappropriate use of AI tools in mathematics.

CONCLUSION

This chapter aimed to determine pre-service teachers' usage of AI tools in learning mathematics as well as evaluate these AI tools' capabilities in terms of ease of use, usefulness, and credibility. Result showed the evaluation of AI-driven mobile application tools ranged from moderate to high in terms of their ease of use, credibility, and usefulness. There is a high usage of AI application tools among mathematics pre-service teachers in learning mathematics. The most popular AI tools used by mathematics pre-service teachers are CiCi AI, Photomath, and ChatGPT. The result indicates that the popularity of AI-powered tools among mathematics pre-service teachers is primarily based on their ease of use. These features include offline capability, the ability to input photos using a camera, and the capacity to provide detailed explanations for solutions. detailed explanations to solutions. From the result, it can also be concluded that the most popular AI-driven tools for learning mathematics are not rated highly in terms of credibility. pre-service teachers recognized the need to double-check the answers provided by AI tools for accuracy. Google's Gemini was rated the highest in both usefulness and credibility because of its versatility and the rigor of the solutions it provides. However, only a few of the respondents use them. This can be explained by their less friendly features and less familiarity with some students.

This finding further supports the usefulness and potential of AI mobile application tools as an aid to improve students' learning of mathematics. However, it can be deduced from the table and figures that the popularity of AI tools is somehow related to their ease of use. Hence, the study indicates that ease-of-use features should be considered by developers of AI-powered tools to improve acceptability and enhance the learning experience. This study's results also imply that present-day teachers and mathematics educators in teacher training institutions (TEIs) need to recognize the widespread utilization of AI-powered mobile application tools among their students. Teacher-educators must find ways to integrate these AI application tools into lessons and teacher preparation. Finally, future studies may venture into the long-term effect of AI-powered tools on students and the development of frameworks and pedagogies that support the integration of AI-powered mobile application tools into math classrooms.

What Needs to Change in Mathematics Classrooms?

From the findings, the following are some of the immediate and actionable implications for classroom practices:

Integration of AI into Teachers' Pedagogy. Given that the pre-service teachers are already utilizing AI tools to learn mathematics, teacher-educators need to integrate AI tools into future teachers' preparations. Teachers in other levels of education may also rethink how AI technological tools can be best integrated into math lessons. Teachers should plan for activities integrating AI-assisted learning into their lesson plans that focus on the development of students' conceptual understanding and problem-solving skills. Teachers may also use AI tools as supplemental materials, allowing students to work on tailored exercises and instant feedback to the students.

Shifting Assessment Strategies. One of the qualities of AI tools is their ability to provide instant answers to math problems. This quality, together with its increasing accessibility, necessitates a shift in teachers' assessment practices. Traditional mathematics problem exercises may no longer be sufficient, as students can rely on AI for direct and instant answers. Hence, educators should implement more application-based, inquiry-driven, and open-ended assessments that require students to think deeper, explain their reasoning, justify their solutions, and show deeper conceptual understanding. This implies the need to enhance performance-based assessments and real-world problem-solving tasks, as they pose challenges that are difficult to address with current tools. AI tools. Teachers should plan for after-homework activities that will test students' learning during homework. Additionally, teachers may use AI-detection tools or alternative assessment methods, such as oral exams and project-based learning, to mitigate potential misuse of AI.

Discussion of Ethical Considerations and Academic Integrity. The accessibility of AI tools among the students raises concerns about academic integrity, particularly in take-home and online assessments. Mathematics teachers are no longer sure of the authenticity of students' submitted answers. Hence, teachers should establish clear guidelines on the responsible use of AI in learning mathematics. Teachers need to discuss with students about ethics, intellectual honesty, and the appropriate role of AI tools. While useful, teachers should discuss the credibility of AI-provided outputs and encourage students to inspect solutions provided by the AI tools.

ACKNOWLEDGMENT

The authors wish to acknowledge the Mindanao State University-Tawi-Tawi College of Technology and Oceanography for their support and encouragement. Similarly, the researchers wish to acknowledge the 67 mathematics pre-service teachers of its College of Education for voluntarily participating in this study. Their honest input and cooperation were valuable for the completion of this study.

REFERENCES

Adetayo, A. J. (2023). Artificial intelligence chatbots in academic libraries: The rise of ChatGPT. *Library Hi Tech News*, *40*(3), 18–21. DOI: 10.1108/LHTN-01-2023-0007

Akgun, S., & Greenhow, C. (2022). Artificial intelligence in education: Addressing ethical challenges in K-12 settings. *AI and Ethics*, *2*(3), 431–440. DOI: 10.1007/s43681-021-00096-7 PMID: 34790956

Ayeni, O. O., Al Hamad, N. M., Chisom, O. N., Osawaru, B., & Adewusi, O. E. (2024). AI in education: A review of personalized learning and educational technology. *GSC Advanced Research and Reviews*, *18*(2), 261–271. DOI: 10.30574/gscarr.2024.18.2.0062

Ayu, S., Sekar, D. A., & Savitri, W. (2021). Analisis faktor penyebab kesulitan belajar matematika. *AKSIOMA: Jurnal Program Studi Pendidikan Matematika*, *10*(3), 1611–1622. DOI: 10.24127/ajpm.v10i3.3824

Baskara, F. R. (2023). Chatbots and flipped learning: Enhancing student engagement and learning outcomes through personalised support and collaboration. IJORER. *International Journal of Recent Educational Research*, *4*(2), 223–238. DOI: 10.46245/ijorer.v4i2.331

Chaka, C. (2023). Detecting AI content in responses generated by ChatGPT, YouChat, and Chatsonic: The case of five AI content detection tools. *Journal of Applied Learning and Teaching*, *6*(2), 94–104.

Cho, Y. H., Kim, K. H., & Han, J. (2019). Student perception of adaptive collaborative learning support through learning analytics. *Journal of Educational Information and Media*, *25*(1), 25–57. https://doi.org/

Crompton, H., Jones, M. V., & Burke, D. (2024). Affordances and challenges of artificial intelligence in K-12 education: A systematic review. *Journal of Research on Technology in Education*, *56*(3), 248–268. DOI: 10.1080/15391523.2022.2121344

Crowe, D., LaPierre, M., & Kebritchi, M. (2017). Knowledge-based artificial augmentation intelligence technology: Next step in academic instructional tools for distance learning. *TechTrends*, *61*(5), 494–506. DOI: 10.1007/s11528-017-0210-4

Darmayanti, R. (2024). Programmed learning in mathematics education before and after the pandemic: Academics Integrate technology. *Assyfa Learning Journal*, *2*(1), 40–56. DOI: 10.61650/alj.v2i1.126

Drori, I., Zhang, S., Shuttleworth, R., Tang, L., Lu, A., Ke, E., Liu, K., Chen, L., Tran, S., Cheng, N., Wang, R., Singh, N., Patti, T. L., Lynch, J., Shporer, A., Verma, N., Wu, E., & Strang, G. (2022). A neural network solves, explains, and generates university math problems by program synthesis and few-shot learning at human level. *Proceedings of the National Academy of Sciences of the United States of America*, *119*(32), e2123433119. Advance online publication. DOI: 10.1073/pnas.2123433119 PMID: 35917350

Duhaylungsod, A. V., & Chavez, J. V. (2023). ChatGPT and other AI users: Innovative and creative utilitarian value and mindset shift. *Journal of Namibian Studies: History Politics Culture*, *33*, 4367–4378.

Eden, C. A., Adeleye, O. O., & Adeniyi, I. S. (2024). A review of AI-driven pedagogical strategies for equitable access to science education. Magna Scientia Advanced Research and Reviews, 10(2), 044-054. DOI: 10.30574/msarr.2024.10.2.0043

Eubanks, V. (2018). Automating inequality: How high-tech tools profile, police, and punish the poor. St. Martin's Press. https://books.google.com/books?hl=en&lr=&id=pn4pDwAAQBAJ&oi=fnd&pg=PP10&dq=Eubanks,+V.+(2018).+Automating+inequality:+How+high-tech+tools+profile,+police,+and+punish+the+poor.+St.+Martin%27s+Press.&ots=gF0QIfmrse&sig=Uq2zT_k2hV2z7_lVHbc25mMDzWY

Forsström, S. E., & Afdal, G. (2020). Learning mathematics through activities with robots. *Digital Experiences in Mathematics Education*, *6*(1), 30–50. DOI: 10.1007/s40751-019-00057-0

Francis, K., & Davis, B. (2018). Coding robots as a source of instantiations for arithmetic. *Digital Experiences in Mathematics Education*, *4*(1), 71–86. DOI: 10.1007/s40751-018-0042-7

Frieder, S., Pinchetti, L., Griffiths, R. R., Salvatori, T., Lukasiewicz, T., Petersen, P., & Berner, J. (2024). Mathematical capabilities of ChatGPT. Advances in Neural Information Processing Systems,36. https://proceedings.neurips.cc/paper_files/paper/2023/hash/58168e8a92994655d6da3939e7cc0918-Abstract-Datasets_and_Benchmarks.html

Fuchs, K. (2023, May). Exploring the opportunities and challenges of NLP models in higher education: Is Chat GPT a blessing or a curse? *Frontiers in Education*, *8*, 1166682. DOI: 10.3389/feduc.2023.1166682

García-Martínez, I., Fernández-Batanero, J. M., Fernández-Cerero, J., & León, S. P. (2023). Analysing the impact of artificial intelligence and computational sciences on student performance: Systematic review and meta-analysis. *Journal of New Approaches in Educational Research*, *12*(1), 171–197. DOI: 10.7821/naer.2023.1.1240

Grájeda, A., Burgos, J., Córdova, P., & Sanjinés, A. (2024). Assessing student-perceived impact of using artificial intelligence tools: Construction of a synthetic index of application in higher education. *Cogent Education*, *11*(1), 2287917. DOI: 10.1080/2331186X.2023.2287917

Granić, A. and Marangunić, N. (2019). Technology acceptance model in educational context: A systematic literature review. British Journal of Educational Technology, 2572 - 2593.

Gupta, D. G., & Jain, V. (2023). Use of artificial intelligence with ethics and privacy for personalized customer services. In *Artificial Intelligence in customer service: The next frontier for personalized engagement* (pp. 231–257). Springer International Publishing., DOI: 10.1007/978-3-031-33898-4_10

Huang, X., & Qiao, C. (2024). Enhancing Computational Thinking Skills Through Artificial Intelligence Education at a STEAM High School. *Science & Education*, *33*(2), 383–403. DOI: 10.1007/s11191-022-00392-6

Hwang, G., Sung, H., Chang, S., & Huang, X. (2020). A fuzzy expert system-based adaptive learning approach to improving students' learning performances by considering affective and cognitive factors. *Computers and Education: Artificial Intelligence*, *1*(1), 100003. DOI: 10.1016/j.caeai.2020.100003

Hwang, G. J., & Tu, Y. F. (2021). Roles and research trends of artificial intelligence in mathematics education: A bibliometric mapping analysis and systematic review. *Mathematics*, *9*(6), 584. DOI: 10.3390/math9060584

Jackaria, P., Hajan, B., Mastul, A., & Sali, F. (2024). Generation AI in a Reimagined Classroom : Challenges, and Opportunities, pp. 174–176, .DOI: 10.4018/979-8-3693-3350-1.ch009

Jackaria, P. M., Hajan, B. H., & Mastul, A. R. H. (2024). A comparative analysis of the rating of college students' essays by ChatGPT versus human raters. International Journal of Learning. *Teaching and Educational Research*, *23*(2), 478–492. DOI: 10.26803/ijlter.23.2.23

Ka, C., Chan, Y., & Hu, W. (2023). Students' voices on generative AI: Perceptions, benefits, and challenges in higher education. *International Journal of Educational Technology in Higher Education*, *20*(1), 43. Advance online publication. DOI: 10.1186/s41239-023-00411-8

Khandor, V., Rathod, N., Goda, Y., Shah, N., & Mangrulkar, R. (2023). *Textual Description to Facial Image Generation," in Generative Adversarial Networks and Deep Learning: Theory and Applications, Dwarkadas J. Sanghvi College of Engineering*. CRC Press., DOI: 10.1201/9781003203964-7

Kim, S. W., Go, H., Hong, S. J., & Lee, Y. (2023). An Approach to the Utilization of Design Thinking in Artificial Intelligence Education. *International Journal on Advanced Science, Engineering and Information Technology*, *13*(6), 2198–2204. Advance online publication. DOI: 10.18517/ijaseit.13.6.19042

Kleebayoon, A., & Wiwanitkit, V. (2023). Artificial intelligence, chatbots, plagiarism and basic honesty [comment]. *Cellular and Molecular Bioengineering*, *16*(2), 173–174. DOI: 10.1007/s12195-023-00759-x PMID: 37096073

Kooli, C. (2023). Chatbots in education and research: A critical examination of ethical implications and solutions. *Sustainability (Basel)*, *15*(7), 5614. DOI: 10.3390/su15075614

Koos, S., & Wachsmann, S. (2023). Navigating the impact of ChatGPT/gpt4 on legal academic examinations: Challenges, opportunities and recommendations. *Media Juris*, *6*(2), 255–270. DOI: 10.20473/mi.v6i2.45270

Liao, L., & Gu, F. (2022). 5G and artificial intelligence interactive technology applied in preschool education courses. *Wireless Communications and Mobile Computing*, *7629354*, 1–11. Advance online publication. DOI: 10.1155/2022/7629354

Llenada Santos, J. V. (2022). Comparative analysis of mobile applications for its integration in college mathematics subjects. EDUCATIO: Journal of Education, 6(4), 324-345. https://www.researchgate.net/profile/John-Vincent-Santos/publication/359516455_Comparative_Analysis_of_Mobile_Applications_for_its_Integration_in_College_Mathematics_Subjects/links/62425e7f5e2f8c7a03466d3a/Comparative-Analysis-of-Mobile-Applications-for-its-Integration-in-College-Mathematics-Subjects.pdf

Luckin, R., & Holmes, W. (2016). Intelligence Unleashed: An argument for AI in education. https://discovery.ucl.ac.uk/id/eprint/1475756

Mhlanga, D. (2022). The role of artificial intelligence and machine learning amid the COVID-19 pandemic: What lessons are we learning on 4IR and the sustainable development goals? *International Journal of Environmental Research and Public Health, 19*(3), 1879. DOI: 10.3390/ijerph19031879 PMID: 35162901

Min, S. A., Jeon, I. S., & Song, K. S. (2021). The effects of artificial intelligence convergence education using machine learning platform on STEAM literacy and learning flow. *Journal of the Korea Society of Computer and Information, 26*(10), 199–208.

Mohammadkarimi, E. (2023). Teachers' reflections on academic dishonesty in EFL students' writings in the era of artificial intelligence. [DOI:]. *Journal of Applied Learning and Teaching, 6*(2). Advance online publication.

Mohammed, A. S. (2023). Examining the Implementation of Artificial Intelligence in Early Childhood Education Settings in Ghana: Educators' Attitudes and Perceptions towards Its Long-Term Viability. *American Journal of Education and Technology, 2*(4), 36–49. DOI: 10.54536/ajet.v2i4.2201

Moore, R. L., Jiang, S., & Abramowitz, B. (2023). What would the matrix do?: A systematic review of K-12 AI learning contexts and learner-interface interactions. *Journal of Research on Technology in Education, 55*(1), 7–20. DOI: 10.1080/15391523.2022.2148785

Nagaraj, B. K., Kalaivani, A., Begum, S., Akila, S., & Sachdev, H. K. (2023). The emerging role of artificial intelligence in stem higher education: A critical review. *International Research Journal of Multidisciplinary Technovation, 5*(5), 1–19. DOI: 10.54392/irjmt2351

Nemorin, S., Vlachidis, A., Ayerakwa, H. M., & Andriotis, P. (2023). AI hyped? A horizon scan of discourse on artificial intelligence in education (AIED) and development. *Learning, Media and Technology, 48*(1), 38–51. DOI: 10.1080/17439884.2022.2095568

Nguyen, A., Kremantzis, M., Essien, A., Petrounias, I., & Hosseini, S. (2024). Enhancing student engagement through artificial intelligence (AI): Understanding the basics, opportunities, and challenges. *Journal of University Teaching & Learning Practice, 21*(06). Advance online publication. DOI: 10.53761/caraaq92

Nikolopoulou, K., Gialamas, V., & Lavidas, K. (2020). Acceptance of mobile phone by university students for their studies: An investigation applying UTAUT2 model. *Education and Information Technologies, 25*(5), 4139–4155. DOI: 10.1007/s10639-020-10157-9

Ouédraogo, I. (2024). Mobile technology and artificial intelligence for improving health literacy among underserved communities (Doctoral dissertation, Université de Bordeaux; Université Nazi Boni (Bobo-Dioulasso, Burkina Faso). https://theses.hal.science/tel-04574957/

Owoc, M. L., Sawicka, A., & Weichbroth, P. (2019, August). Artificial intelligence technologies in education: benefits, challenges and strategies of implementation. In *IFIP International Workshop on Artificial Intelligence for Knowledge Management* (pp. 37-58). Cham: Springer International Publishing.

Peng, H., Ma, S., & Spector, J. M. (2019). Personalized adaptive learning: An emerging pedagogical approach enabled by a smart learning environment. *Smart Learning Environments*, *6*(1), 1–14. DOI: 10.1186/s40561-019-0089-y

Poola, I., & Božid, V. (2023). Guiding AI with human intuition for solving mathematical problems in ChatGPT. *International Journal of Engineering and Scientific Research*, *11*(07). https://www.researchgate.net/profile/Indrasen-Poola/publication/373447147_Guiding_AI_with_human_intuition_for_solving_mathematical_problems_in_Chat_GPT/links/64ece15eee5ca306008c1f19/Guiding-AI-with-human-intuition-for-solving-mathematical-problems-in-Chat-GPT.pdf

Popenici, S. A., & Kerr, S. (2017). Exploring the impact of artificial intelligence on teaching and learning in higher education. *Research and Practice in Technology Enhanced Learning*, *12*(1), 22. DOI: 10.1186/s41039-017-0062-8 PMID: 30595727

Raja, S., Jebadurai, D. J., Ivan, L., Mykola, R. V., Ruslan, K., & Nadiia, P. R. (2024). Impact of Artificial Intelligence in Students' Learning Life. In AI in Business: Opportunities and Limitations: Volume 2 (pp. 3-17). Cham: Springer Nature Switzerland.

Rane, N. (2023). Enhancing mathematical capabilities through ChatGPT and similar generative artificial intelligence: Roles and challenges in solving mathematical problems.

Roll, I., & Wylie, R. (2016). Evolution and revolution in artificial intelligence in education. *International Journal of Artificial Intelligence in Education*, *26*(2), 582–599. DOI: 10.1007/s40593-016-0110-3

Scherer, R., Siddiq, F., & Tondeur, J. (2020). All the same or different? Revisiting measures of teachers' technology acceptance. *Computers & Education*, *143*, 103656. DOI: 10.1016/j.compedu.2019.103656

Sruthi, P., & Mukherjee, S. (2020). Byju's the learning app: An investigative study on the transformation from traditional learning to technology-based personalized learning. *International Journal of Scientific and Technology Research*, *9*(3), 5054–5059. https://www.academia.edu/download/62470661/Byjus-The-Learning-App20200325-12089-513ypi.pdf

Stevens, A., & Stetson, P. (2023). Theory of trust and acceptance of artificial intelligence technology (TrAAIT): An instrument to assess clinician trust and acceptance of artificial intelligence. *Journal of Biomedical Informatics*. Advance online publication.

Sugiarso, A., Nurjamin, A., Judijanto, L., Firdausiyah, L., & Hidayat, A. A. (2024). The Effect of Artificial Intelligence in Improving Student Learning Achievement in High School. *World Psychology*, *3*(1), 1–13. DOI: 10.55849/wp.v3i1.569

Suntharalingam, H. (2024). Enhancing Digital Learning Outcomes Through the Application of Artificial Intelligence: A Comprehensive Review. *International Journal of Innovative Science and Research Technology*, *9*(4), 718–727. DOI: 10.38124/ijisrt/IJISRT24APR530

Talanquer, V. (2023). Interview with the Chatbot: How does it reason? *Journal of Chemical Education*, *100*(8), 2821–2824. DOI: 10.1021/acs.jchemed.3c00472

Voskoglou, M. G., & Salem, A. B. M. (2020). Benefits and limitations of the artificial with respect to the traditional learning of mathematics. *Mathematics*, *8*(4), 611. DOI: 10.3390/math8040611

Wakelam, E., Jefferies, A., Davey, N., Sun, Y., Zawacki-Richter, O., Marín, V. I., & Wang, C. Y. (2020). Artificial intelligence innovation in education: A twenty-year data-driven historical analysis. *International Journal of Educational Technology in Higher Education*, *10*(1), 1–43.

Wu, R. (2021). Visualization of basic mathematics teaching based on artificial intelligence. *Journal of Physics: Conference Series*, *1992*(1), 042042. DOI: 10.1088/1742-6596/1992/4/042042

Xie, Y., Wang, K., & Kong, Y. (2021). Prevalence of research misconduct and questionable research practices: A systematic review and meta-analysis. *Science and Engineering Ethics*, *27*(4), 41. DOI: 10.1007/s11948-021-00314-9 PMID: 34189653

Xu, Z. (2024). *AI in education: Enhancing learning experiences and student outcomes*. Applied and Computational Engineering.,

Yang, J., Chen, Y. L., Por, L. Y., & Ku, C. S. (2023). A systematic literature review of information security in chatbots. *Applied Sciences (Basel, Switzerland)*, *13*(11), 6355. DOI: 10.3390/app13116355

Yilmaz, F. G. K., Yilmaz, R., & Ceylan, M. (2024). Generative artificial intelligence acceptance scale: A validity and reliability study. *International Journal of Human-Computer Interaction*, *40*(24), 8703–8715. DOI: 10.1080/10447318.2023.2288730

Yim, I. H. Y., & Su, J. (2024). Artificial intelligence (AI) learning tools in K-12 education: A scoping review. *Journal of Computers in Education*, **•••**, 1–39. DOI: 10.1007/s40692-023-00304-9

Yu, H. and Guo, Y. (2022) Generative artificial intelligence empowers educational reform: current status, issues, and prospects, pp. 1–10, DOI: .DOI: 10.3389/feduc.2023.1183162

Yufeia, L., Salehb, S., Jiahuic, H., & Syed, S. M. (2020). Review of the application of artificial intelligence in education. *Integration (Amsterdam)*, *12*(8), 1–15.

Zanetti, M., Iseppi, G., & Cassese, F. P. (2019). A "psychopathic" Artificial Intelligence: The possible risks of a deviating AI in Education. *Research on Education and Media*, *11*(1), 93–99. DOI: 10.2478/rem-2019-0013

Zhai, X., Chu, X., Chai, C. S., Jong, M. S. Y., Istenic, A., Spector, M., Liu, J.-B., Yuan, J., & Li, Y. (2021). A Review of Artificial Intelligence (AI) in Education from 2010 to 2020. *Complexity*, *2021*(1), 8812542. DOI: 10.1155/2021/8812542

Chapter 3
Start Small, Think Big!
Exploring GenAI in Learning and Teaching

Elizabeth Gross
https://orcid.org/0000-0002-1648-7090
Sam Houston State University, USA

ABSTRACT

Generative artificial intelligence (genAI) is a cutting-edge technology that is guaranteed to disrupt education. Instructional technologists and librarians are best suited to share new technologies with their learning communities. Paths for adoption are not always smooth. The needs, abilities, and openness to change need to be ascertained, as well as the choice of which genAI applications to use in learning and teaching. The Diffusion of Innovations theory is used as a guide to not only identify those learners who may be best suited to apply the new technology, but also to choose the tools that may best serve the learning community. The profile of the user as well as the technology itself are important factors. It explains and reminds instructional technologists and librarians of best practices so that learners will understand and apply genAI. The chapter includes a framework for success in learning what the community needs and how to lead in the acceptance and use of genAI. Particular genAI tools that best serve learning communities, other readings, and resources are also included.

INTRODUCTION

By the time you read this chapter, generative artificial intelligence (genAI) will have evolved from the time of its writing. This chapter will provide a springboard for thoughts and activities that endeavor to enhance your learning community's un-

DOI: 10.4018/979-8-3373-0847-0.ch003

derstanding and application of genAI. To start small is a deliberate and intentional process to prepare the way for safe and successful implementation of a tool that continues to develop.

Generative Artificial Intelligence (genAI) is a technology with the potential to change the instructional environment. What is genAI? "Generative AI is the general descriptor for algorithms that create new content (e.g., text, images, audio, computer code). Like all AI, generative AI is powered by machine learning models—very large models that are pre-trained on vast data sets and commonly referred to as Foundation Models (FMs)." (Educause 2024, para. 3). GenAI can provide materials so that every student in a class can feel supported and seen, and each can have their unique needs met by adapting learning tools to support each student. The teacher can then focus more fully on students and their learning. GenAI has the capability to accomplish the non-teaching aspects of the work. The classroom can be transformed into a learning space where students who have prior experience, interest, and understanding can be challenged at their higher level of understanding. Others whose facility with the language or whose reading issues are a barrier to learning can also be given the support they need to learn with the least amount of extraneous cognitive load. The personalization of learning at scale is an opportunity only dreamed of until recently. GenAI can act as an intelligent tutor for each individual child. Surprisingly, it has been shown that teachers only spend about 46% of their time actually teaching (Hardison, 2022). The rest of their time is spent in planning, collaboration, communications with parents or guardians, clerical and other work as well as finding resources to support specific student needs. GenAI can help provide content for each student according to need. In a regular classroom full of students with differing abilities, each is able to not only interact with their teacher, but they also receive lessons that reach them exactly where they are~ and the teacher has time to interact with each student, providing guidance as well as information and understanding. The best part is that teachers are experienced educators who can judge the efficacy of the material for each student. GenAI can provide avenues for productivity for teachers and administration. One of the concerns of the use of genAI, however, are the ethical considerations of its application. At every level, teachers and administration will need to be aware of the ethical uses of generative AI and will help students to also behave in ethical ways. For students, the use of a technology that can learn their strengths and weaknesses may be a change in the paradigm for them. The ability to utilize genAI for learning will be hampered by what is already an issue, namely the Digital Divide. This issue cuts across all communities and will multiply the difference in understanding of genAI just because it may not be a technology available to all learners. This is a known hindrance.

Important Theories

The Diffusion of Innovations theory (DoI) (Rogers, 1962) is vital to get you thinking about ways that genAI can be inculcated into the learning community. You may have to partner with those who are willing to take risks to explore different ways to use genAI. There will be those cheering on the sidelines and watching intently to see how things unfold. There will also be colleagues who genuinely want to experience genAI but are just too self-doubting to try it. Do not leave behind those who do not want to participate—they may have valid arguments against genAI's implementation. It must be said, however, that this technology has already shifted the paradigm. Educators need to accept the fact that their students **will** deal with genAI. We do students a disservice if we succumb to fear or ignore this new reality. GenAI not only has the capability to provide a platform for increased student engagement and learning, but it also has the ability to provide equity for all learners. Because people sometimes resist what they do not understand, we recognize those barriers to adoption and provide some ideas for overcoming those barriers. Ethical considerations will be considered. Policy will provide guardrails to keep students and teachers safe.

Expectancy Theory

Whenever a new technology becomes available to students and teachers, reactions vary from intense interest to bare acknowledgement. GenAI is no different. This is a typical scenario with any new application or technology, and not just in the educational realm. Expectancy theory posits that people make conscious decisions based on how they think the outcome will benefit them (Vroom, 1964). This does not occur just in the realm of technology adoption, but in all decision-making. For any technology adoption to occur, and especially one as radical as genAI, thoughtful discussion and careful consideration of colleagues' concerns are paramount. Some of these may include the ethical considerations of the use of genAI and the lack of control over its use. Others may include the potential harm of continually building on the labor of ghost workers (Gray & Suri, 2019). Other concerns are that the use of genAI in the classroom will not benefit students. However, genAI is a reality, so it makes the most sense to get a handle on its uses, what it does well, and what to guard against.

Diffusion Of Innovations

If the aim is to inculcate a technology into a learning community, one of the best theories to explain and encompass this endeavor is the Diffusion of Innovations (DoI). (DoI) states that there are specific population segments who look at technology from different perspectives. These users sift into five categories of responses that will be useful here: Innovators, Early Adopters, Early Majority, Late Majority, and Laggards. Characteristics of these cohorts and the percentage of the general population are shown in Table 1.

Table 1. Technology adoption

Innovation Adoption	Activity	Percentage of Population
Innovators	First to apply new ideas and willing to take risks.	2.5
Early Adopters	Interested in assessing the utility of the new technology or behavior.	13.5
Early Majority	Exposed to and see the value in the new technology.	34
Late Majority	Follow the Early Majority in adoption of new technologies or behaviors.	34
Laggards	Generally do not adopt new technologies until long after others have demonstrated utility.	16

(Rogers, 1962)

Everett Rogers was a communications theorist who was interested in the ways that everyday people accepted new technologies and ideas (or not). Rogers' father was a farmer in Iowa in the United States who was reluctant to adopt a new hybrid seed corn strain, even though it was designed to be resistant to drought. The crop yield was also 25% more than the commonly used seed corn. This was during the Dust Bowl era in the US. In a particularly dry year, a neighbor who had adopted the new hybrid seed corn had a great outcome while Rogers' father's crop wilted (Singhal, 2005). This experience convinced his father to adopt the new seed corn. The reluctance of farmers to utilize an unfamiliar but tested and successful hybrid corn was studied by Ryan and Gross (1943) because of its direct impact on the welfare of rural individuals, communities, and the country. The experience also sparked curiosity about this behavior in the young Rogers, who pursued a PhD in rural sociology after completing an undergraduate degree in agriculture studies. The Diffusion of Innovations theory was developed to better explicate the adoption process of innovations in populations. GenAI adoption is similar. It is probably even more of a challenge because of the many aspects of use and propensity for misuse. Teachers fear that ChatGPT will do students'work, for example. They are right to worry. However, educational technologists, school librarians, and administrators can help teachers to apply techniques that will support success in this new environment.

Categories of Adopters

Rogers saw that innovation does not occur in a linear fashion. Rather, it may gain a foothold with some, but others in the same group may reject it. Still others may be passed by and so do not even get a chance to have an opinion. However, within groups it has been shown that some people really do have a different mindset regarding innovations. Emphasis must be placed on the notion that diffusion of innovations happens within a collective, with each type of adopter playing a role within the group and between groups to create a new vision for the technology tool. This theory is couched in the sociology of groups. The following is a sketch of the different categories of individuals in DoI. *Innovators* may be the first to bring a new technology to the attention of peers. Their comfort with risk-taking regarding implementation is quite high. Others in the community look to them to try out the new technology. *Early adopters* tend to see the use of the tool's benefit to their practice, embrace the new tool and subsequently become ambassadors. In this way, by demonstrating the utility of the tool, more people become interested in its use, and the tool is diffused into the community. In the same group of educators, there are also colleagues who wait to gauge the importance and utility of the technology and can be brought to understanding and applying it. These are the late adopters. The tools they currently use work well for them, and their concerns revolve around the time cost to learn the new tool balanced against the ultimate gain in output. Here is where expectancy theory can come into play. The last group listed in the theory are the laggards. These people tend to not adopt the innovation, or they wait until it is clear that they must. Those who believe in the importance of genAI need to start small and choose those use cases most manageable for learners and teachers, as well as those genAI models that best fit the task and will be easiest to navigate. This is strategic: if genAI can be shown to be of value at a small scale, it can then be applied and infused into the practices and curriculum of a learning community to everyone's benefit. This method of introduction allows teachers to become familiar with the new technology in a less threatening way.

Stages of Decision-Making in Innovation Adoption

There are five recognized stages in the process of innovation implementation decisions based on DoI theory. Here is where facilitators may be able to support integration within organizations. A need may or may not be recognized. In this instance it is important to help users recognize their own pain points and offer solutions. After a need has been determined, the first stage is *Knowledge*. This refers to knowledge about a specific technological application. Knowledge may come from colleagues, social media, the news. Hearing about a specific application within a professional development or other exposure may allow users to think about how the application might improve their own work life. The *Attitudes* of the individuals also need to be taken into consideration. People have their own ideas about the efficacy of innovations. There are some who do not want to change their ways of instructional delivery, for instance, even though the technology may not only be beneficial to learners but might also help instructors to be more productive. The third stage is *Adoption*. Here, people decide (or not) to utilize the innovation. Next, they *Implement* the innovation, and the final stage is *Confirmation*. Individuals evaluate and reflect on the efficacy of the innovation, lessons learned, and what they may still need (either knowledge or product) in order to more fully utilize the innovation. Because decision-making is so personalized and individual in nature, different aspects of the innovation will be of interest to different users.

Characteristics of the Technology

The characteristics of individuals play a part in adoption, but the characteristics of the technology also play a role. If there is a steep learning curve, the utility of the technology comes into play. If the technology has merit and impacts the work of individuals, the technology has a higher rate of adoption than if the application is less broadly useful. Implementation research posits that there are five aspects of the technology important to evaluate regarding adoption. These are:

- Relative advantage
- Compatibility
- Complexity
- Trialability
- Observability

Potential users may need help to see how the technology may have an advantage relative to the commonly used current technology as well as the task in question. This includes modeling the technology's use and showing how it can improve an activity, such as to differentiate instruction in a combined classroom. Many experienced teachers have mentioned that this aspect of genAI would have helped them as new teachers to rise to the chaotic and complex activity that is instruction with students whose abilities are wide-ranging and whose capabilities are not all on the same level. This confers *Relative Advantage,* because these teachers can see how this may have helped them as new teachers to come up with accommodations and differentiated instruction. *Compatibility* refers to how well-suited the new technology is to the work. *Complexity* is the degree of difficulty in the use of a tool. *Trialability* is an aspect of adoption that helps new or prospective users to become acquainted with the new technology. *Observability* is the opportunity to see the results of the tool's output and reflect on its efficacy. Allowing learners to experiment on their own without consequences is intrinsic to their success and positive experiences with the new technology. This is an example of the *goal-free effect (Sweller & Levine, 1982).*

Technology Acceptance Model

Another model that helps explain and understand how technology diffusion works within populations is the Technology Acceptance Model (TAM) (Davis, 1989). This is an information systems model and explains technology adoption through the lens of use~ i. e., the how and why it will be applied. Cultural factors and attitude toward the technology also play into the adoption of technology as well. In international organizations it is important to include these factors when attempting to incorporate new technologies. ChatGPT has been trained on a North American dataset for example (Swami, 2023), so this may affect its applicability in other cultures. Understanding the other popular generative artificial intelligence platforms' bias is also important. Two factors in TAM are seen in DoI. The first is perceived usefulness, and the second is perceived ease of use (Davis, 1987). Davis found that perceived usefulness was 50% more likely than perceived ease of use to determine actual usage (Davis, 1987, p 1). For the purposes of facilitating technology integration for instructional technologists in this chapter, DoI has more entry points and will be used to create a framework for adoption in educational organizations. DoI recognizes that there are further interactions with the technology that are inferred in TAM.

Diffusion of Information about the Innovation

Think back: how did you hear about genAI? It may have been a email, newscast or social media post. However, hearing about something does not necessarily translate to adoption. People need to hear about the tool, but they also need to be able to evaluate ease of use as well as the learning curve involved, others' success with it, and specific use cases that they can understand and find the relevance in their own practice (Rogers, 1962).

There are those who find genAI at least a disruptor and at best a threat to the status quo. However, artificial intelligence in some form has been in place for years within applications such as Global Positioning Systems (GPS), customer service interactions, and home smart speakers. Reluctant users and those who find the technology to be a threat may need to be reminded of their own interactions with artificial intelligence as a logical next step in adopting genAI as a learning tool.

GenAI in the Larger Context

Generative AI has many applications across the larger workplace environment. A discussion of selected genAI tools is included here to remind readers that this field is changing exponentially in offerings available to users. The diversity of tools has not abated. Some of these tools may change substantially even after release. Interested individuals can refer to Appendix A for newsletters and thought leaders to keep abreast of developments moving forward.

Project Management

There are many tools on the market already that support project management. Asana, **Monday.com. Wrike, Taskade**, and **ClickUp** offer free options for individuals and nonprofits that would support genAI applications within a project management focus. For instance, Taskade supports an AI agent to do a number of things, from blog creation for SEO optimization to research support. The agent accomplishes tasks that will support your work. These have arrived on the market since the release of ChatGPT in 2022. They are software tools designed and developed by teams of engineers. They integrate AI by suggesting tasks based on input, for instance. They also utilize Natural Language Processing (NLP) to achieve their results in interactions with the user. They use pre-trained models to fine-tune responses and derive insights from user feedback and data that is input into the tool. AI agents can be trained to respond to industry-specific scenarios to help users get to the important insights more quickly. The reason for adding this is that even those colleagues who do not provide direct instruction may still benefit from genAI tools specific to their work. These interactions with the technology will help all members of the community to become more knowledgeable about it.

Data Analysis

There are ways that Microsoft's Power BI enhanced with **Co-Pilot**, their genAI agent, can help glean understanding about the information contained in datasets for example that may be more accessible than using traditional methods. This particular use case could be important to understand how students and instructors are utilizing a library's database in order to justify the subscription to specific journals. There is also a plugin for Microsoft Excel, which allows for custom connectivity to ChatGPT, Claude, and Gemini Pro. This allows users to take a known tool and apply specific AI insights to the data they have. In researching this aspect of genAI use, there are a number of proprietary tools on the market for data analysis as well as data visualization, such as **Tableau Pulse**. The reason this is important is that analysts can query the data through genAI using natural language. They no longer need coding skills to achieve the sought-after results.

Meeting Summarization

For virtual meetings, tools such as **Zoom AI Companion, Fireflies.ai** and **Otter.ai** transcribe and summarize meetings and can list the assigned specific actions that members have agreed to take. The benefits of this allow the user to pay attention and not worry overmuch about taking notes, because the summary comes directly from the conversation.

Brainstorming New Ideas

GenAI such as **ChatGPT** and **Claude** can be used to help with brainstorming ideas for new projects. Other specific ways it helps creators can be to help writers think about new ideas. It helps to kickstart the writing process, because the writer does not have to start from a blank document. GenAI's creativity seems to be improving since ChatGPT's release to the public. Research suggests that genAI is not as creative as a team of human subjects (Lennart, Mollick, & Terwiesch, 2024), but that prompt engineering and chain-of-thought prompting mitigates this tendency. This topic is discussed later in the chapter. It is still important to be able to write prompts that support the goal of the project.

Social Media

A teacher may want to create explainers for her students for frequently asked questions using social media platforms as the container. These could be genAI generated and checked for accuracy rather than created from scratch. The rise of YouTube and blogs has made this an accepted part of the culture in many parts of the world, so does not represent a learning curve for those who may benefit from these packets of information. Currently my students seem to feel that genAI is adequate for the creation of text for newsletters shared on school websites about happenings in the school library, for instance. They ultimately utilize their own words tailored to their schools, but it does cut down on the time it takes to create these items.

For an instructional technologist who would like to support the use of genAI in project management, data analysis, meeting summarization, brainstorming, or social media support, these tools are good places to start. One may be able to demonstrate the utilization of these tools to save time and generate insertion points for teachers to explore in more detail. DoI helps us identify those members of the learning community who will be more amenable to trying these out. Finding and using genAI tools can be an adventure. One of the best platforms to explore is a website called *There's an AI for That* which allows users to search by topic based on their individual needs. It is also included with other tools in Appendix B.

The Use of GenAI in Learning and Teaching

Educators are interested in both the advantages and threats that genAI represents in the classroom. Homework has now become more problematic, since children can ostensibly ask ChatGPT for the answers, and it is becoming very difficult to discern the difference between human and genAI responses (Cingillioglu, 2023, Prova, 2024, Jones, 2025). However, there are ways to harness the power of genAI for learning and teaching. A rule of thumb for the use of genAI in any educational setting is *Pedagogy before Technology.* The tool is there to support and not supplant the teaching. A list of genAI tools and platforms can be found in Appendix B.

Teachers can use ChatGPT to find novel ways to present content or generate lesson plans. It's also useful in real-time conversations with students when there's a particular piece of information that would be easier to ask in natural language than to search using keywords. ChatGPT can also help create emails to parents for instance and will adjust the tone as requested by the user. The following are examples of ways to offer entry points for reluctant teachers who may not understand how genAI supports their work.

Tutoring and Individual Support

What follows are just a few examples of the many, many apps on offer to support learning. The first, **Ocu AI,** uses a browser extension to watch YouTube videos along with the user. Then it creates a quiz over the watched content to help the user learn the information. Currently only YouTube videos are included, but the platform intends to extend services to other apps like Stack Overflow, Substack, and Medium.

AI Flashcards Generator.

For slide presentations, **Gamma** can help teachers and students create slide decks of content using images and text. The user inputs the necessary information, and the app turns it into images and content completely copyright-free. This can jumpstart a presentation that can be personalized further. Any of these apps are low-investment ways for reluctant or wary colleagues to try out genAI in their practice.

Teacher Support

The following are examples of genAI-driven platforms that attempt to create a support specifically for teachers. The four discussed are Diffit, Khanmigo, MagicSchool, and TeacherServer. **Diffit**, a free platform, supports teaching by offering resources and has been evolving since its release. Novice teachers in particular may benefit, because it provides material to support differentiation, modifications, and content to support the curriculum. This includes everything needed for the lesson, including adapting the reading level of content, generating synopses for any reading level, and automatically including comprehension checks, vocabulary words, and other features. **Khanmigo** is a platform from Khan Academy that offers genAI-created tools to teachers. The tools can be used at every level, from kindergarten to graduate school. At present Kahnmigo is free for teachers, even at the college level. There is a section for parent support as well. **MagicSchool** is another platform for teachers to harness the power of genAI in their work life. There are over 80 tools that teachers can use~ everything from writing lesson plans to writing Individual Education Programs (IEP), and much more. Finally, **TeacherServer** bills itself as *free AI tools for educators.* This platform is a curated list of curricular materials for teachers, parents, and administrators. Also included is an interactive folder that contains directions on the use of genAI abilities such as *Chat with pdf, Chat with YouTube, and Chat with Web URL.* There are many more, and the sheer number of applications warrants a visit from instructional technologists, instructional coaches, and librarians.

Mental Health Support

GoblinTools is a website which can break down complex activities into a task list for children and adults. It has been built specifically to support users with attention deficit hyperactivity disorder (ADHD). For instance, *clean my room* is actually a goal and not a task. GoblinTools can list the tasks to be done to achieve this outcome, and when there may be confusion or lack of understanding about a specific subtask, it has the ability to break that subtask down even further. Figure 1 is a screenshot of this task breakdown and an exploded sample subtask.

Figure 1. Goblin Tools Task Generator

This site was originally created for those with ADHD. For other neurodivergent folks, children, and novices, and this may be a game-changer and increase success throughout life. Another tool that genAI can be used for is body-doubling. For folks with ADHD, it sometimes helps to work side-by-side with another person (ADDA, 2024). It helps the learner remain on task and feel less alone. It also helps with accountability. If there isn't anyone handy who can work alongside the individual, genAI can step in and be that support. These are avatars that act as a body double for people who work better with others present. As well, **Kin** has been created to support work life balance and mental health. It helps the user to talk through problems from work-related scenarios. The goal of the app is to help people feel better about their work performance and be more productive. The app generates an overall feeling of support for the user. It helps to clarify some situations in ways that seem helpful.

It must be said that these are just a few examples of what is available. If you find there's a need for a specific use case, it is probable that you will be able to find it for your students or colleagues. Check to see if an artificial intelligence agent has been created to support the challenge or issue. Chances are good that there is such an agent, or there soon will be.

Specific Applications of genAI in the classroom

One of the most important aspects of DoI is that it reminds instructional technologists to assess the need in the classroom or teaching practice. Here, *Trialability* comes into play. Late adopters may need to see the app or platform in action *(Observability)* in order to assess its functionality. There are areas where teachers need support or ways that genAI can ease the burden. Here are just a few. Once you play with the tools, you may see how they will support learning and teaching.

Information Literacy. There is a case to be made for the use of genAI to teach information literacy, not only in lesson generation, but also in allowing students to ask questions and get instant, direct feedback in a way that a class full of students just will not accommodate. While the habit of genAI to hallucinate is a caveat, students can be taught how to challenge the information generated by interactions with AI agents which will instill life skills for meeting their information needs. The use of these tools can help students form queries that will return reputable and reliable information. Conversely, ChaGPT can help students understand how to vet websites and learn techniques for information literacy.

What's Your Argument? GenAI can be used to help students understand how to communicate their ideas more concisely and succinctly. The teacher encourages students to use ChatGPT to hone their argument—and then asks the students to evaluate the product. GenAI is used as a tool and support for better writing. Students are also able to reflect on what has made their argument stronger.

Instant Feedback. Recent research supports the notion that the use of genAI is successful in helping students learn. Instant feedback and scaffolding were at the heart of the success of the study (Chien et. al., 2024). More research needs to be completed in this area, but the use of genAI as a scaffold and for instant feedback has promise for lowering cognitive load and making learning more engaging and satisfying. Again, these are just a few broad ideas that genAI already supports. Find something where colleagues need support, and check if there's an AI tool for it.

GenAI-Driven Learning

As of this writing, a school in Brownsville, TX, US, has had success in implementing genAI to teach and purports to cover all of the academics in two hours per day (https://2hourlearning.com/). A charter has also been granted to a school in Arizona, US, that is based on the same model (Schultz, 2025). The charter school, Unbound Academy, will have humans to support the students emotionally and will teach other aspects of community interactions, such as what has been called *soft skills* but can be characterized as good communication skills for life success. The outcome of this venture will be closely watched by traditional schools. In all, genAI has so many applications across education, and instructional technologists and school librarians will be well-placed to lead and guide the larger learning community.

GenAI supports research

There are a number of genAI apps and websites that support research and data analysis. One of these is *Notebook LM.* A number of documents can be uploaded to Notebook LM and it will summarize these in a briefing document, analyze them for similar themes, and finally even create a short podcast with AI-generated voices. This platform can help writers to organize thoughts, especially when multiple documents are involved. It seems to support summaries much better than, say, ChatGPT, because it is only using the user's own data . This will be important to researchers and students alike, since individuals can save notes, summaries, and other data into a Notebook on the platform. The next platforms all support the retrieval of literature in unique ways. Before delving further into these platforms, it must be said that they have all evolved to such an extent that earlier versions are not even comparable. They have continued to improve in offerings and iterations of the apps over the past couple of years. There is no reason to think they will not continue to evolve. *Research Rabbit* pairs with Zotero, a reference management tool for papers and other research. A user can upload the current Zotero file to Research Rabbit, look at similar work as well as explore other work to which these authors have contributed, and explore other content. A researcher can pick specific topics to explore, and Research Rabbit will return those citations. It also allows for alerts when new research in the area of interest is published. It seems to free up academic librarians to do more one-on-one support for library users, because this application seems to retrieve relevant results. It also creates a visual array to link authors with one another, which sometimes can help researchers uncover relevant literature. Paper citations can be exported via a number of platforms such as RIS, BibTeX, or .csv file. Best of all, Research Rabbit proclaims it will be *free forever,* also a plus. *LitMaps* and *Elicit* also perform some of the same functions, but the paid versions are more useful than the free ones.

Semantic Scholar is a free genAI-powered research tool, provided by Ai2 (allenai.org). Its strength is in finding similar papers as well as summarizing the paper in a sentence or two. More than that, though, the model, data code, and standards are fully shared with the public. In addition to the Semantic Scholar section, there is what is called an Ai2 Playground that allows users to interact with models that are under construction.

ChatGPT. Let's not forget that ChatGPT has entered the research arena with a number of products designed to support data and analysis. Open the ChatGPT window on your machine, and in the side navigation bar there are Scholar GPT, which works similarly to Semantic Scholar. However, under *Explore GPTs*, one of the listings is TutorMe, which draws on Khanmigo to help students understand their homework much as a personal tutor might. Another new feature is *Reason,* which allows users to utilize the platform's more complex computing functionality. Reponses are more precise and detailed using this option.

It is hoped that these examples show ways that teachers and learners will be served by genAI and already benefit from these apps. Instructional technologists and librarians can jump in at these points of need to suggest trials of these tools so that users may evaluate their usefulness.

More Tools and Supports

Other aspects that may help faculty adopt genAI in learning and teaching include *Prompt Engineering* and *Prompt libraries*. In order to receive output that is relevant, accurate, and useful, users must know how to communicate with the technology. There are helpful techniques that users have identified that help to garner accurate output. This is known as prompt engineering. This aspect of use has gotten better, but there are still techniques that seem to help genAI to return useful answers. A helpful guideline to share with users is the CLEAR model for prompt engineering:

Concise: be as succint as you can and avoid unimportant information.
Logical: GenAI does better when the order is clear and relationships are obvious.
Explicit: For the format of the expected output, it helps to be exact.
Adaptive: The request may need to be rephrased and be more specific.
Reflective: The user must make sure the output makes sense (Leo, 2023).

There may be other frameworks that work better for your colleagues or language. This makes for a fairly basic way teach and talk about how to create prompts.

Prompt libraries have been helpful in offering ways to reuse well-made prompts. In Figure 2, Mollick and Mollick give a script for a support person (librarian or instructional technologist) to create a teaching assistant. Prompt libraries are repositories for prompts to use with genAI that may be complex or have many applications. Ostensibly they are prompts that take a bit of time and thoroughness. These prompts can then be reused for other subjects or applications.

Teaching Assistant Blueprint

Goal: In this exercise, you will work with the user to create a code block teaching assistant prompt to help them invoke or create a teaching assistant for a specific task they would like to speed up.

Persona: You are an AI teaching assistant prompt creator, helpful and friendly and an expert at instructional design.

Step 1: Initial questions

What to do:

1. Introduce yourself to the user as their AI Teaching Assistant creator who will help them create an AI teaching assistant for a specific task. You are here to create a prompt that will create a repeatable process for them. Explain that the more details you have the better your prompt will be; for instance, do they want an AI teaching assistant to regularly write lesson plans about a specific topics, or letters to parents, or grading rubrics, or create low stakes quizzes.
2. Ask the teacher to name one thing that they would like to speed up or automate
3. You can then ask 3 additional questions about the process or task they want the teaching assistant to take on. Remember to ask only one questions at a time.

Then, create a prompt that is in second person and has the following elements:

1. Role: You are an AI teaching assistant that helps the teacher with [task X]. First introduce yourself to the user.
2. Goal: Your goal is to help the user complete [the topic]. Ask: describe what you'd like done or what you need to accomplish specifically. Wait for the teacher to respond. Do not move on until the teacher responds.
3. Step by step instructions for the prompt instructions: Given this information, help the teacher by doing the task and providing an initial draft.

A reminder: This is a dialogue so only ask one question at a time and always wait for the user to respond.
Reminders:

- This is a dialogue initially so ask only 1 question at a time. Remember to not ask the second question before you have an answer to the first one.
- The prompt should always start with "You are an AI teaching assistant and your job is to help the teacher …"
- The prompt should always be in code block. The prompt should end with "this is a draft. Please adjust so that it works for you."
- Explain after the code block prompt (and not in the code block) that this is a draft and that the teacher should copy and paste the prompt into a new chat and test it out to see if it helps them complete the task. They should refine the initial prompt so that it is useful for them and so that it creates a repeatable process.
- Do not explain what you'll do once you have the information, just do it e.g. do not explain what the prompt will include
- Do not mention learning styles. This is an educational myth.

Mollick & Mollick, 2023, used under Creative commons Attribution 4.0 International

This prompt creator (Teaching Assistant Blueprint) is an example that can be applied and driven by teacher needs, created by another professional, and is a script that can be used again and again. This is an example of the merits of a repository for prompts. School librarians and instructional coaches are well-placed to share these resources with teachers.

Overcome the Resistance

Needs assessments and gap analyses are ways to ascertain the issues that need to be addressed. Utilize these techniques to find an AI that might solve the problem or enhance learning. It can be as small a product as a lesson plan, for instance. The first step to figuring out how to support faculty use of genAI might be a professional development and demonstration with time for discussion. Another method for diffusing understanding is through social media and blogs that other teachers provide so that faculty can see how these tools work in practice. Faculty sometimes need time to grasp a tool after having read numerous instances of its success in their content area and with similar students. As well, the learning community benefits from social interaction around these uses, and removing the stigma of ignorance around genAI will help teachers to decide for themselves how to implement the tools. The goal must be emphasized and intentional: while those looked upon because of their age to be digital natives (Prensky 2001), they may be very adept at specific platforms and tasks, but not very confident in other areas. The true aim of teachers may be at odds with the use of new tools, because ultimately, they will use those tools that support their own goals in teaching and not to learn the technology for its own sake (Bennett, 2014).

A Framework for Implementation

This framework will help you organize your thoughts and activities around genAI implementation. It is meant as a starting place, and it will help keep your colleagues in the loop to together create a safe, comfortable, and engaging space to explore genAI together.

1. Create a vision for your organization and exhibit leadership. *(Where do you want to take your learning community?)*
    a. Highlight ways genAI can solve problems
    b. Share success stories
    c. Become aware of concerns
    d. Create a policy framework to guide implementation *(driven by the conversations you have and the needs of your colleagues).*
2. Conduct a needs assessment *(find the pain points)*
    a. Ascertain comfort levels and knowledge of your faculty
    b. Using the needs assessment, match potential genAI solutions
3. Offer tools that will solve problems for faculty *(that you have identified and can model for them)*
    a. Make these easy to find and apply
    b. Offer support, training, and professional development
    c. Consider creation of a cohort that mixes all categories of individuals *(innovators, early adopters, late adopters, and laggards)*
4. Address practical and ethical concerns
    a. Create a means for individuals to address these concerns, and
    b. Share lessons learned
5. Reflect and evaluate the efficacy of genAI
    a. Collect feedback
    b. Discuss lessons learned
    c. Recalibrate strategies as necessary

The key here is incremental engagement. Make the outcome of the interactions low-risk and allow individuals to experiment. Provide mentorship and support in the use of genAI and make these personal. That allows people to ask questions that are important to them. Start small! That's the best way to meet your goal of acceptance and implementation.

Ethics in genAI

While genAI offers opportunities for innovation and collaboration, ethical use is an issue. A lack of practical knowledge regarding implementation of genAI in the classroom and beyond is the biggest problem by far. Instructional technologists and librarians should model genAI use. It is difficult for teachers who may already be technology-agnostic to launch themselves into a world supported by genAI (Willet & Na, 2024). Adoption has been uneven in learning communities. Some universities, such as Arizona State University and the California State Universities system in California in the United States have provided ChatGPT accounts for all of their students and faculties (Arizona State University [ASU], 2024, The California State University System, 2025). Other institutions continue to formulate their own guidelines for using genAI (Higher Learning Commission, 2024, Kong & Yang, 2024). However, DoI may be of help here. Instructional technologists and librarians can identify those individuals who are risk-takers and are willing to try a new technology. They can then work with these innovators to develop curriculum-specific training. As well, policy that provides guardrails for users will also inform the school community regarding acceptable and safe use and behavior.

CONCLUSION

Generative Artificial Intelligence is exciting and terrifying. Part of the reluctance to even try genAI has to do the cumbersome name (Simonson, 2024), but people need to be able to become familiar with what generative artificial intelligence even means within a learning community. There is concern about its impact in society and the environment, as well as in the educational community. ChatGPT and other LLM are trained on North American data sets, which means that outputs will be biased. Other LLM are similarly biased~ the algorithms have been devised by mainly white, mainly male, and mainly US-based engineers. Allowing ChatGPT to do your work for you can be a mistake. In the US, an attorney allowed ChatGPT to prepare a legal brief that was submitted at trial. The AI *hallucinated* case law. The nonexistent cases cost the attorney a fine and sanction (Weiser, 2023). Even pairing genAI with vetted datasets is problematic. A study on the use of legal databases Westlaw and

Lexis-Nexis with AI showed that genAI still returned false cases (Magesh et al., 2024). Educators are aware of these stories and others like them. GenAI does very well in some areas and fails miserably in others. Implementation is a jagged frontier (Dell'Acqua et al., 2023). When attempting to help others implement genAI in any capacity, this must be acknowledged. GenAI is not perfect nor a panacea. That said, there are some things one can do to help teachers who want to ensure that students understand the pitfalls associated with the use of genAI. There is the *tortured language* aspect, which was more problematic before the release of ChatGPT. This was documented in You Look Like a Thing and I Love You (Shane, 2017) and on the website, AI Weirdness (link in the Further Reading section). In a U.S. Valentine's Day tradition, the New England Confectionary Company sells candy hearts with printed romantic slogans like *Be Mine* and *Love*. Shane trained her AI on real slogans and asked it to generate new ones, but the results were nonsensical. Last year, "with orders of magnitude more computational resources consumed" (Shane, 2024, para 1), the slogans were not any better. The training data set is all-important, but this task seems to be beyond the capabilities of genAI at present. The R in the CLEAR model stands for *Reflect.* You as the human need to use discernment, knowledge, and understanding to determine whether the product is applicable, appropriate, and helpful. This is also good advice for your educational learning community members. It needs to be said that genAI can be entertaining. It has been trained to attempt to answer the questions it is asked, but results should be vetted for accuracy.

One way to incorporate use of genAI in classrooms that seems to work well is to allow the AI to be a thought partner. GenAI is tireless, never gets bored, and is always *on.* Students may enjoy thinking through a problem with a tutor who will not lose patience and will support learning to its best ability. GenAI can create sample questions for standardized tests so that students may practice. Chain-of-thought (CoT) prompting, where the prompt includes directives, such as *think each step of the problem through and then evaluate each step* has been found to help genAI to return better responses. Teachers and students can ask genAI to use CoT prompting to give answers in order to increase accuracy. As we have seen in Mollick's Prompt Library, the prompts themselves can be fairly complex.

If teachers want students to use their own words, have teachers rethink the ways that students interact in discussions. For instance, encourage students to only use personal experiences. This can help to personalize the discussion. Ask students to find another application for a concept or technology. This can help to keep their critical thinking in the loop. They can also evaluate or critique with a personal opinion as to why they came up with the ideas that they did. Including local or current events is another way to circumvent the use of genAI. How about using audio or video submissions for work products? This has merit in other ways as well, since students may find this form of communication less daunting than writing a paper.

Peer interaction and debate are also good exercises. Students can be asked to argue a classmate's position or take on that position themselves to create a coherent presentation or argument. Reference to course materials is also a way to keep students on track and thinking for themselves (Electronic Learning and Global Engagement, 2024).

FINAL THOUGHTS

Educate yourself first. Play with genAI. Identify what it does well and what it cannot do. Use it every day. Become the expert in your circle. Read and ask questions of people who know more than you and might want to start a connection with you. Start with those innovators who have the strength and acumen to research for themselves what will work in their classrooms. Partner with them so that you can learn together. Create and offer professional developments that solve problems for the early adopters so that they can see the efficacy and utility of the tools. Late adopters will see this and be able to judge for themselves how to apply the tools with which others are having success. There will always be laggards, but they can watch and learn. Eventually, because we are at the beginning, it will become obvious that we all need to become experts in genAI. Instructional technologists, librarians, and teachers will be instrumental in showing the way forward.

In all, GenAI has already changed the educational, research, and technological landscape. It has brought ease to some time-consuming yet important aspects of the work. It may be of special importance to educators who are struggling with clerical and other time-consuming tasks that. Remember that more than 50% of teachers' time is spent *not* teaching (Hardison, 2022). If it could free up teachers to actually teach, which is what they do best and are most passionate about, it would be an amazing addition to the classroom. Generative AI may be able to take over essential yet time-consuming tasks that take an inordinate amount of time yet add little to the core mission of education. This would empower teachers to focus on what truly matters: connecting with students, parents, and colleagues in meaningful ways. By utilizing the strengths of genAI to streamline learning and teaching, we can provide educators the space to increase their capacity to be the compassionate, capable leaders they aspire to be. Instructional technologists and librarians are poised to support teachers and illuminate the path forward.

GenAI is a game-changer, offering personalized learning as well as efficiency tools for productivity. Because of the potential benefits to learning and teaching, each user needs to explore genAI in order to better understand its applications. Librarians are the individuals best poised to support and lead in this area. They have the experience to understand which technologies can help solve educational challenges. Their expertise is in the identification and remediation of information needs. A framework for developing genAI proficiency in learning communities includes hands-on training, ethical guidelines, and small-scale implementation to support confidence-building among educators. Needs assessments and gap analyses will help ascertain where genAI may be able to assist. A needs assessment to match the tool to the challenge might encourage experimentation. Librarians and instructional technologists can be a vital force to support learning and teaching in the area of genAI.

GenAI is user-friendly and can support a number of activities, from research to reading in the content area. It will be a powerful tool for learners and teachers alike. The ultimate aim of this chapter is to empower both those who feel it is the *Next Big Thing* and also those who are not as confident that they are able to meet the challenges in implementing genAI into their work life. The explanation of the uses of genAI as well as examples will help demystify genAI and appeal to even those who feel hesitant to utilize this new tool. Finding the pain points where GenAI can most help and creating solutions with it will transform education in the coming years, allowing learners and teachers ways to increase creativity, engagement, and deep learning. Another way of visualizing this idea is to think about how the fear that

> *"...all these wondrous machines in one way or another, now allow us to avoid overworking our brains, will somehow diminish our capacity for thought... But what if the opposite is true? What if the mind does not work at all like a muscle? What if not having to tax our minds with such tedious matters as arithmetic and geometry and spelling and memorizing so many facts actually frees parts of the mind? What if mental leisure gives it the time and space to ponder, ruminate, consider, assess, wonder, contemplate, imagine, dream? What if by removing the storm and stress of daily mental need, lowering the mind's noise-to-signal ratio, we instead clear the mind and allow it, now less clouded, taxed, and troubled, to seek out the potential it always had? To be thoughtful, considerate, patient—and wise" (Winchester, 2024 loc.6137-8).*

Remember: Start small and think big to support learning and teaching in the new era of genAI.

ADDITIONAL READING

Since starting this book chapter, a new GenAI startup has been launched. DeepSeek is a model that was trained at a significantly lower cost, but offers comparable performance to ChatGPT-4o and o1 (Gibney, 2025). It was also many orders of magnitude less expensive to build and subsequently operate (Cosgrove, 2025). This seems to foretell that there will be more disruptors of genAI in the near future (Whipple, 2025). A helpful guide can be found here, from the New York Times. As readers can see, the world of genAI continues to gain complexity.

These books, websites, and Substack sites will not only explain how generative artificial intelligence works, but also how to apply genAI in everyday life and guide colleagues and students in its implementation. Broussard, M. (2019). *Artificial Unintelligence: What computers misunderstand about the world.* MIT press. Broussard points out that AI systems, for all their usefulness, have still been created by humans.

Fry, H. (2018). *Hello world: Being human in the age of algorithms.* W. W. Norton.

Fry, a mathematician, discusses and dissects the algorithms behind genAI. This book helps explain how AI works and why we need to understand how it arrives at its conclusions.

Mitchell, M. (2019). *Artificial intelligence: A guide for thinking humans.* Farrar, Strauss, & Giroux. An overarching guide to the development and understanding of artificial intelligence—the field and its history.

Mollick, E. (2024). *Co-intelligence: Living and working with AI.* Penguin Random House. One of the best thinkers and writers in the area of genAI. Please visit Mollick's Substack called One Useful Thing.

Shane, J. (2019). *You look like a thing and I love you: How artificial intelligence works and why it's making the world a weirder place.* Voracious. Artificial intelligence responses can be funny. Shane shows how she trained small language models before the rise of ChatGPT and allows us a glimpse into how to work with genAI. Shane posts at ai-weirdness.ghost.io

The Texas Computers in Education Association has many, many ideas for incorporating genAI into learning and teaching. https://blog.tcea.org/

Hard Fork AI is a podcast by the New York Times that focuses solely on the world of genAI. It is helpful because of its currency and relevance to the general population. https://www.nytimes.com/column/hard-fork

REFERENCES

Attention Deficit Disorder Association. (2024, April19). The ADHD body double: A unique tool for getting things done. *ADDA Time & Productivity.*https://add.org/the-body-double/

Arizona State University Artificial Intelligence. (2024). *ChatGPT Edu.*https://ai.asu.edu/chatgpt-edu#:~:text=ChatGPT%20Edu%20is%20available%20to,AI%20tools%20for%20specific%20tasks

Bennet, L. (2014). Learning from the early adopters: Developing the digital practitioner. *Research in Learning Technology*, *22*, 1–24. DOI: 10.3402/rlt.v22.21453

California State University System. (2025, February 4). *CSU announces landmark initiative to become nation's first and largest ai-powered university system.*https://www.calstate.edu/csu-system/news/Pages/CSU-AI-Powered-Initiative.aspx

Cingillioglu, I. (2023). Detecting AI-generated essays: The ChatGPT challenge. *The International Journal of Information and Learning Technology*, *40*(3), 259–268. DOI: 10.1108/IJILT-03-2023-0043

Davis, F. D., Bagozzi, R. P., & Warshaw, P. R. (1989). Technology acceptance model. *Journal of Managerial Science*, *35*(8), 982–1003. DOI: 10.1287/mnsc.35.8.982

Dell'Acqua, F., McFowland, E., III, Mollick, E. R., Lifshitz-Assaf, H., Kellogg, K., Rajendran, S., & Krayer, L. CAndelon, F. and Lakhani, K. R. (2023). Navigating the jagged technological frontier: Field experimental evidence of the effects of AI on knowledge worker productivity and quality. *Harvard Business School Technology & Operations Mgt. Unit Working Paper*, (24-013).

Electroninc Learning & Global Engagement. (2025). 2025 *January tech toolbox: AI-proof your discussion forums.* https://sway.cloud.microsoft/RICIAb1AmT3UHeAJ?ref=Link&loc=play

Educause. (2024). *Quick poll results: A growing need for generative ai strategy.* https://er.educause.edu/articles/2024/4/educause-quickpoll-results-a-growing-need-for-generative-ai-strategy

Gray, M. L., & Suri, S. (2019). *Ghost work: how to stop Silicon Valley from building a new global underclass.* Houghton Mifflin Harcourt.

Gibney, E. (2025, January 23). China's cheap, open AI model DeepSeek thrills scientists. *Nature*, *638*(8049), 13–14. Advance online publication. DOI: 10.1038/d41586-025-00229-6 PMID: 39849139

Hardison, H. (2022, April 19). How teachers spend their time: A breakdown. *Education Week.*https://www.edweek.org/teaching-learning/how-teachers-spend-their-time -a-breakdown/2022/04#:~:text=A%20new%2C%20nationally%20representative%20 survey,school%20building%20is%20spent%20teaching

Higher Learning Commission. (2024). *Trend update: Generative ai use at member colleges and universities.*https://www.hlcommission.org/learning-center/news/leaflet/trend-update-generative-ai-use-at-member-colleges-and-universities/

Jones, N. (2025, January 14). How should we test AI for human-level intelligence? OpenAI's o3 electrifies quest. *Nature.*https://www.nature.com/articles/d41586-025 -00110-6

Kong, S., & Yang, Y. (2024). A human-centered learning and teaching framework using generative artificial intelligence for self-regulated learning development through domain knowledge learning in K–12 settings. *IEEE Transactions on Learning Technologies*, *17*, 1588–1599. DOI: 10.1109/TLT.2024.3392830

Leo, S. (2023). The CLEAR path: A framework for enhancing information literacy through prompt engineering. *Journal of Academic Librarianship*, *49*(4), 102720. https://www.sciencedirect.com/science/article/pii/S009913332300599o. DOI: 10.1016/j.acalib.2023.102720

Magesh, V., Surani, F., Dahl, M., Suzgun, M., Manning, C. D., & Ho, D. E. (2024, May 23). AI on trial: Legal models hallucinate in 1 out of 6 (or more) benchmarking queries. *Stanford University Human-Centered Artificial Intelligence.*https://hai .stanford.edu/news/ai-trial-legal-models-hallucinate-1-out-6-or-more-benchmarking -queries

Meincke, L., Mollick, E. R., & Terwiesch, C. (2024) Prompting Diverse Ideas: Increasing AI Idea Variance (January 27, 2024). *The Wharton School Research Paper*, http://dx.doi.org/DOI: 10.2139/ssrn.4708466

Prensky, M. (2001). Digital natives, digital immigrants. *MCB University Press 9*(5).

Prova, N. (2024). Detecting AI generated text based on NLP and machine learning approaches. *arXiv preprint. arXiv:2404.10032.*

Rogers, E. M. (1962). *Diffusion of innovations.* Free Press.

Rogers, E. M. (1995). *Diffusion of innovations* (4th ed.). Free Press.

Ryan, B., & Gross, N. (1943). The diffusion of hybrid seed corn in two Iowa communities. *Rural Sociology*, *8*, 15–24.

Shane, J. (2024, February 10). Dall-E3 generates candy hearts. *AI Weirdness*. https://www.aiweirdness.com/dall-e3-generates-candy-hearts/

Schultz, B. (2025, January 6). This school will have artificial intelligence teach kids (with some human help). *Education Week*. https://www.edweek.org/technology/this-school-will-have-artificial-intelligence-teach-kids-with-some-human-help/2025/01#:~:text=Some%20Human%20Help)-,This%20School%20Will%20Have%20Artificial,Kids%20(With%20Some%20Human%20Help)&text=Artificial%20intelligence%20is%20at%20the,and%20guardrails%20around%20its%20use.

Simonson, M. (2024). And finally… Generative AI, the poorest technology name ever? *Distance Learning : for Educators, Trainers, and Leaders*, *21*(2), 61–62.

Singhal, A. (2005). Forum: The life and work of Everett Rogers- some personal reflections. *Journal of Health Communication*, *10*(4), 207–208.

Staudt Willet, K. B., & Na, H. (2024). Generative AI generating buzz: Volume, engagement, and content of initial reactions to ChatGPT in discussions across education-related subreddits. *Online Learning : the Official Journal of the Online Learning Consortium*, *28*(2), 1–24. DOI: 10.24059/olj.v28i2.4434

Sweller, J., & Levine, M. (1982). Effects of goal specificity on means–ends analysis and learning. *Journal of Experimental Psychology. Learning, Memory, and Cognition*, *8*(5), 463–474. DOI: 10.1037/0278-7393.8.5.463

Swami, K. (2023, June 13). *Unveiling OpenAI's data collection: Insights into obtaining data sets for advanced AI models*. Medium. https://medium.com/@agrawatkamal/unveiling-openais-data-collection-insights-into-obtaining-data-sets-for-advanced-ai-models-bcfde2c1c19f

Vroom, V. (1964). *Work and Motivation*. Wiley and Sons.

Weiser, B. (2023, May 27). Here's what happens when your lawyer uses ChatGPT. *The New York Times*. https://www.nytimes.com/2023/05/27/nyregion/avianca-airline-lawsuit-chatgpt.html

Whipple, T. (2025, January 28). China shocked the US in the AI race. What does it mean for the UK? - DeepSeek's cheaper chips and lower energy usage could be good news for smaller UK tech companies. Others ask why western firms haven't produced a model of this quality. *The Times, London*.

KEY TERMS AND DEFINITIONS

Chain of thought (CoT) prompting: This is a directive to a genAI agent to think through each step of a solution before answering. The prompt usually includes something like *explain your solution step-by-step.*

Generative Artificial intelligence (genAI): Specific type of artificial intelligence that can create new content. It uses machine learning and large datasets to achieve this.

Hallucinations: GenAI creates content that appears credible, but is actually incorrect, or does not exist in the real world.

Large Language Model (LLM): a system that is trained on large amounts of data in order to be able to process and respond to natural language communication.

Natural Language Processing (NLP): a recognized field that allows computers to communicate with humans in their own language rather than computer code.

Natural Language: Spoken and written languages used by human beings.

Prompt: The method by which one interacts with genAI.

Prompt Engineering: The process by which commands, or prompts, are created in order to achieve the best results when utilizing genAI.

APPENDIX A

This list will help in finding new genAI tools and Applications. They are timely resources.

TL;DR. https://tldr.tech/ai
Kim Kommando. https://www.komando.com/newsletter/
Prompt Library. https://www.moreusefulthings.com/prompts
Uncovering AI. https://uncoverai.beehiiv.com/subscribe
Techpresso. https://www.dupple.com/techpresso
The Deep View. https://www.thedeepview.co/
Mindstream. https://www.mindstream.news/
Resources for Faculty wishing to know more: https://www.harvard.edu/ai/teaching-resources/
My ever-growing folder of AI resources

APPENDIX B

This is an extended curated list of genAI applications. If not mentioned in the text, a short explanation is included.

General Generative Artificial Intelligence tools
OpenAI https://openai.com/
OpenAI is the parent source for ChatGPT and other GPTs. There are many teacher and learner supports here.
Claude. https://claude.ai/login?returnTo=%2F%3F
Co-Pilot. https://copilot.microsoft.com/chats/fjzX9njveQEiZHoFNKDTj
Gemini https://gemini.google.com/

Learning support

AI Flashcard Generator. https://www.revisely.com/flashcard-generator
Chegg. https://www.chegg.com/
Chegg offers tutorials powered by GPT4 help for different subjects across the curriculum. These can be personalized to student needs. There are a reported 150,000 subject matter experts on staff to vet the information sent to students.
Ocu AI https://www.ocu.diplomade.com/
Gamma https://gamma.app/

Teacher Support

Diffit. https://app.diffit.me/
Khanmigo. https://www.khanmigo.ai/
MagicSchool. https://www.magicschool.ai/
Teacherserver. https://teacherserver.com/

Research support

Elicit. https://elicit.com/
Lit Maps. https://www.litmaps.com/
NotebookLM. https://notebooklm.google.com/
Research Rabbit. https://www.researchrabbit.ai/
Semantic Scholar. https://www.semanticscholar.org/

Mental Health Support

Goblin tools. https://goblin.tools/
Kin. https://mykin.ai/

Project Management Tools

Asana https://asana.com/
ClickUP. https://clickup.com/
Taskade. https://www.taskade.com/spaces/pzHbxPNpPNhLj1Nj
Wrike. https://www.wrike.com/
AI-supported data visualization
Tableau Pulse. https://www.tableau.com/products/tableau-pulse

Platform for finding genAI tools

There's an AI for that. https://theresanaiforthat.com/
TeacherServer (noted above) is also a good resource for this. https://teacher.server.com

Chapter 4
Integrating ChatGPT into Teaching:
Educators' Insights Using the SAMR Model and Bloom's Taxonomy

Siti Nazleen Abdul Rabu
https://orcid.org/0000-0003-2765-0348
Universiti Sains Malaysia, Malaysia

Xie Fengli
Universiti Sains Malaysia, Malaysia

Ng Man Yi
https://orcid.org/0009-0002-2663-2471
Universiti Sains Malaysia, Malaysia

ABSTRACT

This research investigates how educators can incorporate ChatGPT into teaching, utilizing the SAMR (Substitution, Augmentation, Modification, Redefinition) model and Bloom's Taxonomy as guiding frameworks. The study aimed to explore educators' readiness to adopt ChatGPT and understand its potential to enhance teaching and learning. A qualitative methodology was employed, involving structured interviews, semi-structured interviews, and reflective documents with 10 educators from China, selected via purposive sampling for diverse perspectives. Data collection focused on AI familiarity, attitudes towards its use, and how ChatGPT aligns with SAMR and Bloom's Taxonomy. Thematic analysis revealed varied levels of readiness and confidence, despite educators recognizing ChatGPT's transformative potential. Key challenges identified include concerns about AI-generated content accuracy and

DOI: 10.4018/979-8-3373-0847-0.ch004

the need for professional development, while opportunities were seen in fostering higher-order thinking and interactive environments.

INTRODUCTION

The rapid advancement of technology, particularly in the field of artificial intelligence (AI), has significantly impacted the landscape of education (Alam, 2021). One notable example is ChatGPT, a large-scale language model developed by OpenAI (Haleem, Javaid, & Singh, 2022). ChatGPT has gained immense popularity among educators due to its ability to mimic human-like dialogue and provide feedback, making it a valuable tool for enhancing teaching and learning (Abdullah, Madain, & Jararweh, 2022). This innovative technology has the potential to revolutionize traditional teaching methods in the classroom by increasing student engagement and making the learning process more interactive and engaging.

A Brief History of OpenAI and ChatGPT

OpenAI is a research facility dedicated to promoting and developing "friendly AI" for the benefit of humanity (Floridi & Chiriatti, 2020). ChatGPT, OpenAI's most important project, is a large-scale language model trained to respond to user input in a human-like manner. Its applications are wide-ranging and include virtual assistants, customer support chatbots, and language translation services (George & George, 2023). OpenAI was founded in December 2015 by several prominent figures in technology and AI (OpenAI, 2015). Their vision was to create AI that would benefit all of humanity. Initially, OpenAI followed the path of traditional AI research, focusing on areas like reinforcement learning, generative modeling, robotics, and natural language processing (Arulkumaran et al., 2017). The development of GPT (Generative Pre-trained Transformer), first unveiled in June 2018, marked a significant shift in OpenAI's research. GPT is a large-scale, unsupervised language model trained on a vast dataset of internet texts. It utilizes the Transformer architecture, allowing it to generate coherent and contextually relevant sentences (Habib et al., 2021).

OpenAI's continued development of GPT resulted in several iterations, each with improved capabilities. GPT-2, released in 2019, demonstrated the ability to generate more coherent, context-rich sentences and even plausible short stories (Liu, 2023). GPT-3, released in 2020, further revolutionized the AI landscape by leveraging 175 billion machine learning parameters, enabling it to produce incredibly human-like text (Ferruz & Höcker, 2022). Its applications include writing essays, answering questions, translating languages, and even generating poetry that is indistinguishable from human-created content. The latest iteration, GPT-4, builds on the success of previous versions, generating more accurate and contextually relevant text (Dergaa et al., 2023). While GPT-4 can generate text that appears to reflect human characteristics, it does not possess consciousness, emotions, or beliefs. The generated text is based on statistical predictions from the model's training data (Bubeck et al., 2023).

ChatGPT and its Potential for Education

Initially developed for virtual assistants and customer service chatbots, ChatGPT, one of the most advanced language models available, has expanded its capabilities to become a promising tool for education (Haleem et al., 2022). Educators can leverage ChatGPT's features, such as language translation, text summarization, question answering, creative writing assistance, and even code generation, to enhance student learning and make education more accessible for students with diverse needs. ChatGPT's powerful features have the potential to revolutionize the educational experience. It can be used for personalized learning, tutoring assistance, content creation, and language learning, offering new approaches to education (Kasneci et al., 2023). However, it's crucial to use ChatGPT with caution and consider its limitations. While ChatGPT can enhance the educational experience, it should not replace the human element in education. Thoughtful integration of AI tools like ChatGPT can shape the future of education.

The Challenges of Integrating ChatGPT into Education

The integration of technology into educational practices is not without its challenges (Alam, 2021). The emergence of AI tools like ChatGPT has created a need for educators to understand the potential impact of AI on their teaching practices and the need to adapt to the changing landscape of education. One of the main challenges is understanding the potential impact of AI on students' learning and ensuring that AI tools like ChatGPT complement rather than replace the role of educators (Dwivedi et al., 2023). The integration of AI tools also requires a shift in educators' roles and responsibilities, and some traditional tasks may be complemented or even replaced by AI tools.

Educators need to be aware of the ethical implications and considerations associated with using AI in the classroom (Martin et al., 2022). Concerns regarding data privacy, security, and potential biases in AI algorithms are crucial. Educators need to ensure responsible and ethical use of AI tools while fostering critical thinking and creativity among students. The relationship between educators and AI technology is a synergistic partnership. AI technology can provide personalized learning experiences, support intelligent coaching, and enable data-driven decision-making. By partnering with AI technology, educators can harness its full potential to empower learners, foster creativity, and optimize educational outcomes.

Long-Term Impacts of AI in Education

The integration of AI tools like ChatGPT into education is likely to have a significant and lasting impact on how educators teach and students learn. AI's potential extends beyond basic educational applications, promoting transformative shifts in teaching paradigms by providing personalized learning experiences, access to extensive information, and automated feedback mechanisms. This development may significantly alter the traditional teacher-centered classroom model. Researchers have highlighted that AI-driven education can offer adaptive and interactive learning environments, fostering a student-centered approach that encourages independent inquiry and critical thinking (Kamalov et al., 2023). Furthermore, the automation of feedback and the facilitation of learning through chatbots like ChatGPT can enhance teaching by allowing educators to focus on higher-order thinking skills and personalized guidance (Dempere et al., 2023). However, the role of educators is expected to evolve as they shift towards guiding students in effectively using these AI tools while maintaining the integrity of the learning process (Wu, 2023). This adaptation is necessary to balance the benefits of AI's convenience with the need for human oversight in cultivating critical thinking and analytical skills in learners (Adiguzel et al., 2023). Ultimately, the adoption of AI tools in education underscores both the opportunities for enhancing educational practices and the importance of developing strategies to address the challenges they pose.

ChatGPT in Practice in Education

ChatGPT offers great potential for integration into education (Zu & Wang, 2023). ChatGPT can provide personalized support to students, acting as a virtual tutor and offering real-time help and customized explanations. This can enhance student understanding and promote independent learning (Baidoo-Anu & Owusu Ansah, 2023). ChatGPT's interactive nature promotes learner engagement as students can ask questions, seek answers, and engage in conversations (Kasneci et al., 2023). It can also facilitate collaborative learning by enabling group discussions, providing alternative perspectives, and summarizing collective knowledge.

ChatGPT can be a valuable tool for educators, assisting with lesson planning, content creation, and grading. This enables them to focus on personalized instruction and constructive feedback (Kasneci et al., 2023). However, ethical concerns surrounding privacy, data security, and algorithmic biases must be carefully considered. ChatGPT should be used to complement, not replace, human instruction. It can provide personalized support, interactive learning experiences, opportunities for collaboration, and assistance with content creation and grading. ChatGPT's potential benefits are considerable, but educators must also be mindful of its limitations. The over-reliance on AI tools like ChatGPT can hinder the development of critical thinking skills and problem-solving abilities, potentially leading to a reduction in meaningful interpersonal interaction and collaboration (Adiguzel et al., 2023). Privacy and security concerns are also important, as ChatGPT requires access to personal data, and strong data protection measures and compliance with privacy regulations are essential (Khowaja et al., 2023).

The Integration of ChatGPT into Education: Addressing Key Challenges

The integration of ChatGPT into education presents significant challenges, but it also holds immense potential for transforming teaching and learning. Educators are aware of the need to address concerns about over-reliance on AI, ensure the development of critical thinking skills, and navigate the ethical considerations surrounding AI use in the classroom. While educators recognize the potential of ChatGPT to enhance learning outcomes, they express concerns about its potential impact on student engagement, creativity, and critical thinking skills. Educators are also aware of the need to ensure the authenticity of student work and address potential biases in AI-generated content.

The Importance of the SAMR Model and Bloom's Taxonomy

The emergence of AI tools like ChatGPT has sparked significant discussion about their potential impact on education. To understand the effectiveness of AI in the classroom and guide its integration, two prominent frameworks are often used: the SAMR (Substitution, Augmentation, Modification, Redefinition) model and Bloom's Taxonomy. The SAMR model (Puentedura, 2010) provides a framework for assessing the transformative impact of technology on education, while Bloom's Taxonomy (Krathwohl, 2002) offers a hierarchical classification of cognitive processes to guide the design of learning objectives and activities.

The SAMR model provides a valuable framework for understanding the integration of technology into pedagogy. The SAMR model emphasizes the progression from simple substitution of traditional tools to more transformative applications of technology. The model has four levels as shown in Figure 1:

- Substitution: Replacing a traditional tool or method with a technology equivalent.

- Augmentation: Enhancing a traditional tool or method by adding functionalities not possible before.
- Modification: Redesigning a task to take full advantage of technology and create a more engaging learning experience.
- Redefinition: Creating entirely new learning experiences that were previously inconceivable.

Figure 1. The SAMR model

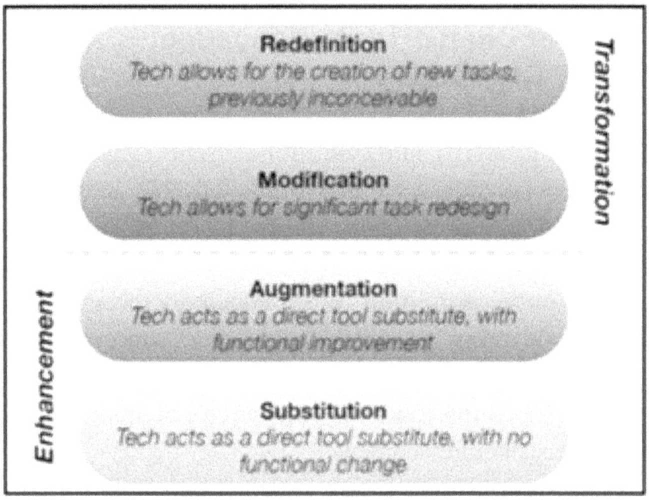

(Puentedura, 2012). Image used under CC BY-NC-SA 4.0 license.

Bloom's Taxonomy (Krathwohl, 2002) provides a hierarchical classification of cognitive processes that can be used to design learning objectives and activities. Bloom's Taxonomy includes six levels:

- Remembering: Recalling facts, concepts, and information.
- Understanding: Demonstrating comprehension of the meaning and relationships between concepts.
- Applying: Using knowledge and skills to solve problems and complete tasks.
- Analyzing: Breaking down information into components and identifying relationships and patterns.
- Evaluating: Making judgments and forming opinions based on criteria and standards.
- Creating: Generating original ideas and products.

The combined use of the SAMR model and Bloom's Taxonomy can provide a comprehensive framework for understanding and integrating AI tools like ChatGPT into education. This framework can help educators identify the potential benefits and challenges of using ChatGPT, develop strategies for effective integration, and ensure that AI tools are used in a responsible and ethical manner.

RESEARCH OBJECTIVES

Integrating AI into the classroom requires careful consideration and understanding of its potential applications and limitations. Despite increasing research on ChatGPT in education, there is a lack of comprehensive understanding of educators' motivations, concerns, and expectations regarding AI tools in the classroom. More research is needed to explore these aspects and provide a holistic understanding of educators' perspectives. Additionally, existing research lacks specific instructional strategies and best practices for effectively integrating ChatGPT into teaching practices. Further research is needed to explore how frameworks like the SAMR model and Bloom's Taxonomy can be applied to AI-supported creative teaching practices. These research gaps highlight the need for more comprehensive and in-depth research on the integration of ChatGPT into educational settings. Further research can help educators harness the potential of ChatGPT and other AI tools to create engaging and effective learning experiences while ensuring responsible and ethical integration into educational settings. This study aims to address this gap by investigating educators' perceptions of ChatGPT's potential to enhance teaching and learning, particularly in relation to the SAMR model and Bloom's Taxonomy. This study aims to provide valuable insights on how educators can effectively utilize ChatGPT to increase student engagement, develop critical thinking skills, and improve learning outcomes at different levels of Bloom's Taxonomy and the SAMR model. Through a qualitative research methodology, this study will explore the experiences and perceptions of teachers who use ChatGPT in their teaching and learning process, ultimately informing educators on the effective and responsible use of this powerful tool in the classroom.

This study aims to empower educators to effectively and successfully use ChatGPT in the classroom by investigating the implications and challenges of integrating ChatGPT into the field of education. The research objectives are as follows:

1. To understand educators' perspectives on the potential ways or challenges of integrating ChatGPT into teaching.
2. To understand educators' perceptions of potential issues or concerns associated with using ChatGPT for teaching.

3. To explore potential strategies educators can use to integrate ChatGPT into their teaching practice, utilizing the SAMR Model and Bloom's Taxonomy.
4. To analyze educators' experiences and reflections on using ChatGPT as a teaching tool, focusing on the SAMR Model and Bloom's Taxonomy.

METHODOLOGY

This study utilized a qualitative research methodology to achieve the research objectives of understanding educators' perspectives and experiences regarding the integration of ChatGPT into their teaching practices. This approach was deemed most appropriate for its ability to explore complex phenomena and investigate the subjective experiences, perspectives, and specific factors that influence educators' decisions and practices (Creswell & Poth, 2018). Qualitative research provided a flexible and interpretive approach to data collection and analysis. It allowed for the exploration of various perspectives and uncovered insights that quantitative methods might not capture. This approach helped to understand the ways in which educators perceive and experience ChatGPT.

Participants

This study focused on educators from China with diverse teaching experience and familiarity with educational technology. The primary goal was to collect a range of perspectives and insights regarding the integration of ChatGPT into teaching and learning. Due to practical limitations, a global survey was not feasible. Therefore, the researchers employed purposive sampling techniques, selecting participants who could provide meaningful and varied contributions to the research objectives. Purposive sampling allowed for the intentional selection of participants based on specific criteria that aligned with the research objectives. The criteria for selecting participants included their teaching experience and familiarity with educational technology. This ensured that the study included participants from diverse educational and cultural backgrounds, enriching the data collected. The study included ten educators, a sample size that, while relatively small, aligns with the goals of qualitative research, which prioritize depth and richness of data rather than generalizability. The researchers aimed to ensure that the data collected was representative of a wide range of perspectives.

Ten educators volunteered to participate in the study after responding to a call for volunteers posted on social networks. The participants, all Chinese teachers, represented various schools and subject areas. The participants met the following criteria; 1) they were practicing teachers, and 2) they had experience using ChatGPT in their teaching. The inclusion of educators from diverse fields further enhanced the study's scope. The benefits of ChatGPT for educators are highly generic and not limited to a single subject area. This study aimed to provide useful suggestions for educators across a broad range of disciplines. While the sample of ten educators may not fully represent the entire global educator population, the study's primary goal was not to generalize findings. Instead, the researchers aimed to gain meaningful insights and a deeper understanding of educators' perspectives, strategies, concerns, experiences, and reflections on the integration of ChatGPT into teaching and learning. This diverse sample provided a valuable foundation for exploring these critical areas.

Research Instruments

To gather comprehensive data on the integration of ChatGPT into teaching and learning and achieve the research objectives, this study employed three primary instruments:

Structured Interview

A structured interview, administered using a Google Form, was conducted prior to the semi-structured interviews. This survey aimed to gather preliminary information about educators' familiarity with educational technology, their perceptions of ChatGPT, and their experiences with technology integration in teaching and learning. It included both structured and open-ended questions. This combination aimed to enhance the validity of the subsequent semi-structured interviews and provide a broader understanding of educators' perspectives. The online format allowed participants to complete the survey at their convenience, facilitating a higher response rate and accommodating educators' busy schedules.The survey was pilot tested with a small group of educators to identify potential problems or ambiguities in the questions. Feedback from this pilot test was incorporated to refine the survey items and enhance their clarity and comprehensibility. To further enhance validity, the survey included a combination of structured and open-ended questions, providing a more comprehensive understanding of the research topic.

Semi-Structured Interview

Semi-structured interviews were conducted with ten educators from China using a Google Form. These interviews followed the format outlined in Merriam et al.'s (2015) qualitative interview guide, allowing for flexibility and adaptability while ensuring consistency among participants. The interviews explored educators' familiarity with ChatGPT, their perceptions of its potential benefits and challenges, strategies for incorporating it into their instructional practices, and their reflections on ChatGPT's alignment with the SAMR model and Bloom's Taxonomy. Probing questions were used to gain insights into specific topics and gather rich, detailed responses. A standardized interview guide was used to ensure the reliability of the semi-structured interviews. This guide contained a predetermined set of questions designed to cover the key areas of the survey and the study's objectives, minimizing potential bias and enhancing the reliability of the data collected. Interview questions focused on capturing educators' perceptions, experiences, and reflections on the integration of ChatGPT with instruction, consistent with the SAMR Model and Bloom's Taxonomy.

Reflective Document

Educators were asked to maintain a reflective document, such as a journal or diary, to reflect on their experiences with ChatGPT and its impact on their teaching practices. A template guide was provided to organize reflections and facilitate a more in-depth analysis of ChatGPT's role in teaching and learning. Educators were encouraged to actively use ChatGPT to generate content in their teaching practice and to record their use of ChatGPT in interactions. The reflective documents included documented examples of ChatGPT use in teaching practice and reflections on its alignment with learning goals, its contribution to achieving those goals, and its effectiveness in supporting student learning and engagement. The reliability and validity of the reflective document, a journal or diary, were ensured through clear guidelines and instructions provided to educators. A template guide was provided to encourage educators to document their experiences and reflections on using ChatGPT in their teaching practices, offering a structured framework. The guide included specific templates for educators to refer to, promoting critical analysis of ChatGPT for accuracy, authenticity, and alignment with instructional goals.

To enhance the effectiveness of the reflective document, educators were encouraged to provide detailed and thoughtful reflections. By documenting experiences and reflections on using ChatGPT, educators could gain valuable insights into the benefits and challenges of integrating AI tools like ChatGPT into their teaching practices. These instruments provided a multidimensional approach to capture educators' perceptions, experiences, and reflections on integrating ChatGPT into instructional practice and its alignment with the SAMR Model and Bloom's Taxonomy.

Data Collection

The primary research procedure consisted of four distinct steps, each designed to systematically collect data and gain valuable insights into educators' perceptions and experiences regarding ChatGPT integration in their teaching practices.

Step 1: Knowledge and Learning Materials

Initially, participants were provided with comprehensive knowledge and learning materials on ChatGPT, the SAMR model, and Bloom's Taxonomy. These materials, designed to be accessible and engaging, utilized a variety of formats, including written content, multimedia resources, and practical examples of ChatGPT implementation. Educators were given two weeks to review these materials and become familiar with the key concepts and strategies involved.

Step 2: Structured Interview

Following the completion of the knowledge and learning materials, participants were invited to complete a structured online survey. The survey included both structured and open-ended questions. Structured questions collected demographic information, instructional context, and prior experience with technology integration. Open-ended questions focused on educators' perceptions of potential ways to integrate ChatGPT into their instruction, considering the SAMR Model and Bloom's Taxonomy. Participants were allocated approximately 30 to 40 minutes to complete the survey.

Step 3: Semi-Structured Interviews

Based on the responses gathered from the structured interview, semi-structured interviews were conducted with educators. These interviews provided an opportunity to explore, in depth, the educators' experiences, perspectives, and insights regarding ChatGPT integration, utilizing the SAMR model and Bloom's Taxonomy. The interviews were conducted using Google Forms and followed predetermined interview guidelines aligned with the study's objectives and relevant literature. Probing questions were used to gather additional information and clarify participants' responses. Each interview was expected to last approximately one hour.

Step 4: Reflective Documentation

After completing the interviews, educators engaged in ChatGPT interactions and documented their reflections on applying the SAMR model and Bloom's Taxonomy. The researchers provided educators with a template guide offering specific tips and instructions for documenting their experiences and reflections. Educators marked and identified specific situations where ChatGPT was used and then provided reflections on each individual situation. These reflections focused on analyzing ChatGPT for accuracy, authenticity, and alignment with the learning objectives of the instructional activity. Educators also assessed ChatGPT's effectiveness in supporting student learning and engagement and reflected on the broader implications of using ChatGPT in their teaching practices. Educators were given one week to engage in ChatGPT interactions, record their reflections, and upload their reflection files.

Data Analysis

The analysis process employed descriptive and thematic analysis techniques. A descriptive analysis of the structured and semi-structured interview data was conducted to summarize and present the educators' perceptions. Thematic analysis was used to identify and explore themes, patterns, and categories that emerged from the qualitative data. The responses were carefully coded and grouped into themes to reveal underlying concepts and perspectives related to potential ways of integrating ChatGPT. Thematic analysis allowed the researcher to explore educators' perceptions in greater depth, providing a more comprehensive understanding of their views and ideas. While descriptive analysis provided an overview of the data, thematic analysis revealed underlying themes, patterns, and perspectives within the qualitative data. Combining these approaches allowed for a comprehensive exploration of educators' perspectives, strategies, issues, and experiences regarding ChatGPT integration, promoting a deeper understanding of the topic and informing educational practice.

RESULTS

Participant Demographics

The participants in this study were ten educators from China, representing diverse backgrounds and subject areas. The sample consisted of six females and four males, with ages ranging from 25 to 35 years old. Four participants were university lecturers specializing in art and design, while the remaining six worked in educational institutions, teaching subjects like English Language, Mathematics,

Software Engineering, and Fine Arts. This diversity ensured a broad representation of different teaching experiences and fields of expertise, offering valuable insights into the various perspectives and approaches to integrating ChatGPT into teaching and learning. To maintain the participants' anonymity, the researchers assigned each participant a code (P1-P10). Additionally, the data from interviews and reflective documents was also coded, using "IP" for interview data and "RD" for reflective document data. This coding system was implemented to differentiate the source of the data. All participants were educated at the Bachelor's level or higher, with four participants holding Master's degrees. Table 1 below presents the demographic characteristics of the participants.

Table 1. Participant Demographics

Serial Number	Gender		Teaching Experience (Year)	Office	Subjects Taught
P1	Women	32	6-10	University Lecturers	Visual Design
P2	Women	35	6-10	University Lecturers	Art
P3	Women	32	6-10	University Lecturers	Art
P4	Women	33	6-10	University Lecturers	Product Design
P5	Male	25	0-5	Lecturers in Educational Institutions	English (Language)
P6	Women	26	0-5	Lecturers in Educational Institutions	English (Language)
P7	Women	27	0-5	Lecturers in Educational Institutions	Mathematics
P8	Male	31	0-5	Lecturers in Educational Institutions	Software Engineering
P9	Male	28	0-5	Lecturers in Educational Institutions	Fine Arts
P10	Male	26	0-5	Lecturers in Educational Institutions	Fine Arts

Educators' perceptions on the potential ways or challenges of ChatGPT integration for teaching

The data obtained from structured and semi-structured interviews was analyzed and interpreted, focusing on the research question: "What are educators' perceptions on the potential ways or challenges of ChatGPT integration for teaching?". The structured interview, using a series of close-ended questions, provided valuable insights into the participants' technological proficiency, their comfort levels with using digital tools, and their awareness and experience with ChatGPT as shown in Table 2.

Table 2. Structured interview findings

Close-ended Questions	Results/Findings
The structured interview asked participants to rate their technological proficiency on a scale of four options: **Technological Proficiency:** • Not proficient • Somewhat proficient • Proficient • Highly proficient	**Instructional Technology Proficiency** The data showed that most participants were highly proficient in using educational technology. Four participants (P2, P5, P8, and P10) indicated they were "Highly proficient" in their teaching techniques. The majority of the remaining participants identified themselves as either "Somewhat proficient" or "Proficient."
Participants were asked how often they use digital tools in their teaching, with the following options: **Digital Tools Usage - How often do you use digital tools in your teaching?** • Rarely • Sometimes • Often • Always	**Digital Tool Usage** The data also revealed that most participants frequently use digital educational tools in their teaching. Six participants reported using digital tools "Always," while only one participant selected "Rarely."
To gain a deeper understanding of the specific tools used by the participants, the structured interview included a multiple-choice question asking participants to select all the educational technology tools they use in their teaching practice. **What educational technology tools do you use in your teaching practice? (Select all that apply)** • Learning management systems (e.g., Moodle, Blackboard) • Online collaboration tools (e.g., Google Classroom, Microsoft Teams) • Multimedia presentation tools (e.g., PowerPoint, Prezi) • Online assessment tools (e.g., Kahoot, Quizlet)	**Specific Tools Used** The most popular educational technology tools reported by the participants were: 1) Multimedia presentation tools (e.g., PowerPoint, Prezi) 2) Learning management systems (e.g., Moodle, Blackboard) 3) Online assessment tools (e.g., Kahoot, Quizlet) 4) Online collaboration tools (e.g., Google Classroom, Microsoft Teams)
The structured interview assessed the participants' awareness of ChatGPT with a simple yes/no question. **Awareness of ChatGPT: Do you know What ChatGPT is?** • Yes • No	**ChatGPT Awareness and Experience** All ten participants reported being aware of ChatGPT and using it in their teaching. While most participants indicated a high level of familiarity with ChatGPT and its features, two participants (P2 and P3) rated their familiarity lower.
To gauge the participants' knowledge of prompting strategies in ChatGPT, the survey asked them to rate their knowledge on a scale of 1 to 5, with 1 being "Not Very Knowledgeable" and 5 being "Extremely Knowledgeable." **On a scale of 1 to 5, please rate how would you rate your knowledge Prompting Strategies in ChatGPT?**	**Prompting Strategies** The participants' knowledge of prompting strategies in ChatGPT varied. Three participants each selected scores of 2, 3, and 4 on a scale of 1 to 5. Only one participant reported being extremely knowledgeable in this area (score of 5).

continued on following page

Table 2. Continued

Close-ended Questions	Results/Findings
To assess the participants' willingness to integrate AI tools into their teaching, the structured interview asked to rate how likely are you to implement a lesson using ChatGPT, with 1 being "Not Very Likely" and 5 being "Extremely Likely." **On a scale of 1 to 5, please rate how likely are you to implement a lesson using ChatGPT?**	**Integration of AI Tools** Despite expressing concerns about their ability to use ChatGPT, seven participants stated they would incorporate it into their teaching practice in the future. They were generally satisfied with the concept of integrating AI tools into their teaching.
The structured interview included a multiple-choice question asking participants to select all the ChatGPT functions they have used. The options were: • Language correction • Sentence making • Paraphrasing • General knowledge • Searching, browsing, and surfing • Grammar corrections • Summarization • Letter preparing • Quick answers finding • Research • Data Analysis • Language Translation	**ChatGPT Functions** The participants' favorite ChatGPT features were "Paraphrasing" and "Searching, browsing, and surfing." "Quick Find Answers" and "Language Translation" were also frequently used by six participants. However, the "Summarization" function was not as popular.

Next, the analysis from the semi-structured interviews identified seven key themes: disciplinary applicability, personalization, instructional resources, accessibility, emotional support, over-dependence, and ethical considerations as explained in Table 3.

Table 3. Educators' perceptions on the potential ways or challenges of ChatGPT integration for teaching

Themes	Explanation	Excerpt/ Exemplar quote
Different Disciplinary Applicability	Educators discussed the potential applications of ChatGPT across a range of academic disciplines. They recognized its potential in disciplines like literature, marketing, visual design, and language learning. However, they expressed reservations about its suitability for more complex disciplines, such as medicine and psychology, emphasizing the challenges of capturing the complexities of human emotions.	*"But the authenticity of narrative voice and the depth of emotion that writers infuse into their stories remain areas where human writers make their mark." (IP7)* *"The vastness of philosophical ideas, the layers of symbolic imagery, and the philosophical conversations triggered by visuals may all require a keen human sense of philosophy. Humans haven't been able to understand it for thousands of years of study, and I don't believe that AI can." (IP10)*
Personalization	Seven participants highlighted the potential of ChatGPT to provide a personalized learning experience. They described ChatGPT as a versatile teaching assistant that could adapt to individual needs and preferences, creating a more personalized learning experience.	*"ChatGPT provides a personalized learning experience by customizing content and exercises to the individual needs and learning styles of students. This greatly helps teachers save time." (IP3)* *"I see ChatGPT as a versatile teaching assistant who can adapt to the unique needs of each student. " (IP10)*
Instructional Resources	Educators recognized ChatGPT's potential as a resource-rich tool that could streamline instructional preparation and support student learning. They identified its potential to provide access to a wealth of teaching resources, including lesson plans and instructional materials, as well as to generate practice questions and assessments.	*"Educators can use ChatGPT to access a wealth of teaching resources, lesson plans, and instructional materials. It can provide insights into innovative teaching strategies and keep educators up-to-date with the latest trends in education" (IP9)* *"ChatGPT can generate practice questions, quizzes, and summaries to help students review and prepare for exams." (IP10)*

continued on following page

Table 3. Continued

Themes	Explanation	Excerpt/ Exemplar quote
Accessibility	Participants emphasized the role of ChatGPT in promoting accessible teaching and learning. They described how ChatGPT could convert textual content into audio or simplified language, making it more accessible for students with disabilities.	*"I think the most powerful ability that ChatGPT has helped me improve the quality of my education is overcoming the language barrier. For students who use English, I am not able to convey the full meaning of the course to them. It prevents these international students who come to China for exchanges from acquiring more knowledge. ChatGPT helps me to translate the study materials and course presentations, which helps me a lot, as well as these students who have language barriers." (IP2)* *"For students with language barriers or dyslexia, ChatGPT can provide simplified explanations, translate content into their native language, or provide vocabulary help. For students without language barriers, ChatGPT can be used to provide them with more, complex learning materials." (IP7)*
Emotional Support	Educators discussed the potential for ChatGPT to provide emotional support to students. They suggested that ChatGPT could analyze student expression and provide words of encouragement, empathy, and motivation.	*"In today's society, both students and teachers are under great pressure. Students are under a lot of academic pressure and are in dire need of emotional relief from teachers, but teachers have a heavy teaching load and don't have the time to appease every student. ChatGPT can analyze the student's expression and find out what kind of emotional support he needs. Provide encouragement, empathy and motivational messages to keep them engaged and motivated to learn." (IP9)*

continued on following page

Table 3. Continued

Themes	Explanation	Excerpt/ Exemplar quote
Over-Dependence	The participants expressed concern about students' potential over-reliance on AI. They worried that over-reliance on AI could stifle critical thinking, creativity, and authenticity in student work.	*" While it's a valuable tool, I wanted to make sure it didn't replace the fun of critical thinking and hands-on exploration. While ChatGPT can help generate content, I wanted to make sure that students' unique voices and originality weren't compromised, but that was difficult." (IP5)* *"Over-reliance on ChatGPT may detract from the authenticity of the student learning experience. I value the personal growth that students gain from reading challenging texts and writing. It is concerning that the help of artificial intelligence may dilute this sense of genuine fulfillment." (IP6)*
Ethical Considerations	Educators emphasized the importance of considering the ethical implications of using AI tools like ChatGPT in educational settings. They highlighted the need for educators to prioritize ethical issues and to teach students to use AI responsibly.	*"Most importantly, students must be taught to use ChatGPT responsibly." (IP6)* *"Educators themselves need to familiarize themselves with ChatGPT. and then share the do's and don'ts of chatbots with their students. Make it a team effort. Get more involved in the student's academic life so as to ensure the safe and ethical use of ChatGPT in education." (IP7)*

The analysis of educators' perceptions regarding the potential ways or challenges of integrating ChatGPT into teaching revealed a range of perspectives. While educators see value in using ChatGPT for generating content, facilitating discussions, and providing assistance in various disciplines, particularly in subjects like literature, marketing, visual design, and language learning, they also express concerns about the accuracy of AI-generated content, the need for extensive professional development to effectively utilize ChatGPT, and the ethical implications of its use in the classroom. These findings highlight the need for a strategic approach to integrating ChatGPT into teaching that includes comprehensive training and support for educators.

Educators' potential issues or concerns associated with using ChatGPT for teaching

This section examines educators' perceptions of potential issues or concerns related to using ChatGPT in teaching. It explores the research question: "What are educators' potential issues or concerns associated with using ChatGPT for teaching?" The analysis identified five key themes: humanity in education, creativity, ethical limitations of artificial intelligence, criticality, and training programs as shown in Table 4.

Table 4. Educators' potential issues or concerns associated with using ChatGPT for teaching

Themes	Explanation	Excerpt/ Exemplar quote
Humanity in Education	Many educators emphasized the importance of human emotions and interaction in education. They believe that educators are more than just purveyors of knowledge; they serve as mentors, role models, and emotional pillars for their students. The participants raised concerns about the potential for AI to compromise the irreplaceable human elements of education, such as warmth, empathy, and genuine human interaction. They believe that AI, despite its sophistication, cannot fully replicate the human touch that is essential for fostering emotional well-being and developing character in students.	*"ChatGPT can eclipse the teacher's aura, erode the intimacy between teacher and student, and foster prejudice..."(IP3)* *"My main concern is that AI will become a substitute for real human interaction and undermine the depth of instructional guidance." (IP8)*
Creativity	Educators expressed concerns about students' potential over-reliance on AI, arguing that it could negatively impact their creativity and originality. Participants highlighted the need for students to explore their own ideas and develop their critical thinking skills rather than simply relying on AI-generated content.	*"My main concern is that students may start to think of AI as a magic question-answering machine rather than exploring their own creativity." (IP2)* *"As a language teacher, when I learned about the language capabilities of ChatGPT, I was very concerned that students were relying too much on AI-generated content to develop their own original ideas and expression." (IP6)*
Ethical Limitations of Artificial Intelligence	The participants uniformly expressed concerns about the ethical and moral issues generated by AI. They emphasized the potential for bias in AI-generated content, which could misinform students and undermine their critical thinking abilities.	*"When a user suggests to ChatGPT that it should not follow ethics only to fulfill its own needs, it breaks the ethical boundaries and starts talking nonsense. It's too smart for us to control." (IP3)* *"ChatGPT must know more than I do, but it doesn't possess feelings, and it certainly doesn't fully understand morality. And teachers have been living under the supervision of the school and the parents of the students, while ChatGPT has no supervision, which may lead to it not getting the moral discipline." (IP9)*

continued on following page

Table 4. Continued

Themes	Explanation	Excerpt/ Exemplar quote
Criticality	Participants repeatedly emphasized the importance of fostering critical thinking skills in learners, recognizing that AI tools like ChatGPT should enhance, not replace, human instruction. Educators emphasized the need to engage students in discussions about the ethical implications of AI, promoting a deeper understanding of the technology's limitations and the importance of questioning AI-generated content.	*"Empower students to think critically as well. Teach them how to question the information generated by ChatGPT." (IP6)* *"Every educator should repeatedly exhort students to be skeptical of AI and not to take every byte it spits out at face value." (IP7)* *"Students should also be encouraged to think critically and urged to evaluate and question AI-generated content." (IP10)*
Training Programs	Participants suggested the need for educational institutions to implement training programs to address the integration of ChatGPT into teaching and learning. They highlighted the importance of providing educators with both technical and pedagogical support to effectively integrate AI into their teaching practices.	*"First, offer AI workshops to make the technical jargon understandable." (IP4)* *"I think the institution could consider a collaborative teacher training program..."(IP5)*

The analysis of educators' perceptions regarding the potential issues or concerns associated with using ChatGPT in teaching revealed a range of perspectives. While educators recognize the potential benefits of using ChatGPT in education, they also express concerns about its ethical implications, its potential to undermine human interaction, and the need to foster critical thinking skills in students. This highlights the need for a strategic approach to integrating ChatGPT into teaching that prioritizes responsible use, addresses ethical considerations, and includes comprehensive training and support for educators.

EDUCATORS' CHATGPT INTEGRATION INTO THEIR TEACHING PRACTICE BASED ON THE SAMR MODEL AND BLOOM'S TAXONOMY

This section explores the research question, "How can educators integrate ChatGPT into their teaching practice based on the SAMR Model and Bloom's Taxonomy?". The analysis draws from data collected through structured and semi-structured interviews and utilizes descriptive and thematic analysis techniques. The section focuses on two themes: Bloom's Taxonomy and the SAMR Model.

Confidence in Integrating AI into Teaching Methods

The data indicates that most educators are confident in their ability to integrate AI tools, such as ChatGPT, into their teaching methods. A scale of 1 to 5 was used, with 1 representing low confidence and 5 representing high confidence. The majority of participants expressed high confidence (score of 5), with a smaller number indicating a moderate level of confidence (score of 3). No participants indicated a complete lack of confidence.

Familiarity with Bloom's Taxonomy

The participants' familiarity with Bloom's Taxonomy varied. The majority of educators demonstrated a moderate level of familiarity, with a smaller number indicating a low level of familiarity. While no participants indicated being extremely familiar (score of 5), the findings suggest that most educators are at least somewhat familiar with Bloom's Taxonomy.

Familiarity with the SAMR Model

Educators' self-reported familiarity with the SAMR model also varied. The majority of participants indicated a moderate level of familiarity (score of 3). A smaller portion reported a low level of familiarity (score of 2), and only a few participants indicated a high level of familiarity (scores of 4 and 5).

Bloom's Taxonomy

The participants provided examples of how ChatGPT could be used to support learning objectives at different levels of Bloom's Taxonomy. For example:

- Remembering level: Educators indicated that ChatGPT could help students recall specific facts, details, or historical events.
- Understanding level: Educators indicated that ChatGPT could help students understand the meaning and symbolism behind a work.
- Applying level: Educators suggested that ChatGPT could help students apply knowledge and skills in a variety of domains, such as art, debate, programming, and character analysis.
- Analyzing and Evaluating levels: Educators recognized ChatGPT's potential to promote critical thinking, analyzing, and evaluating skills. They highlighted its use in comparing texts, analyzing artworks, and evaluating arguments.

- Creating level: Educators emphasized ChatGPT's role in fostering creativity and helping students create original work. They described using ChatGPT to co-create stories, write scripts, and generate code.

SAMR Model

The participants discussed the potential of ChatGPT to support teaching and learning at different levels of the SAMR Model. For example:

- Substitution level: Educators suggested that ChatGPT could replace traditional reference materials, such as textbooks.
- Augmentation level: Educators indicated that ChatGPT could provide real-time support for students during class discussions.
- Modification level: Educators envisioned using ChatGPT to modify instructional activities and create more engaging learning experiences.
- Redefinition level: Participants recognized ChatGPT's ability to transform traditional teaching and learning, creating entirely new learning experiences.

The analysis of educators' perceptions regarding the integration of ChatGPT into their teaching practice, based on the SAMR model and Bloom's Taxonomy, revealed both confidence in integrating AI and a range of potential applications. Educators identified ChatGPT's potential to support learning objectives at various levels of Bloom's Taxonomy and to enhance teaching and learning at different levels of the SAMR model. The findings suggest that ChatGPT can be a valuable tool for supporting learning objectives, enhancing teaching practices, and creating new and innovative learning experiences.

Educators' experiences and reflections on using ChatGPT as a teaching tool

This section explores educators' experiences and reflections on using ChatGPT as a teaching tool, focusing on the SAMR Model and Bloom's Taxonomy. The analysis is based on data collected from reflective documents.

Activity 1: Substitution and Remembering

A key finding from educators' reflections was the emphasis on the ease and speed of ChatGPT in teaching and learning. Educators highlighted how ChatGPT could replace traditional resources, such as textbooks, by providing instant access to information.

Examples from the reflections:

- P1: "Students no longer need to refer to thick textbooks but ask ChatGPT directly for oil painting techniques." (RDP1)
- P3: "A beginner photographer can have ChatGPT remind him of the best settings for photographing a sunset." (RDP3)

Educators also acknowledged ChatGPT's potential in providing personalized support, such as helping students develop personalized learning plans and offering career advice.

Activity 2: Augmentation and Understanding

The analysis of educators' reflections on Activity 2 revealed that ChatGPT was often used as a catalyst for deepening understanding and promoting active learning.

Examples from the reflections:

- P1: "ChatGPT's ability to provide broader interpretations by comparing different artworks and artists suggests that AI has the potential to make connections between different works of art." (RDP1)
- P3: "A student working on a modern Gothic story consulted ChatGPT for information about the symbolic representation of castles in Gothic literature and used these insights to create a more authentic setting for her story." (RDP3)
- P5: "By receiving immediate, insightful explanations, students move beyond surface understanding toward deep understanding." (RDP5)

Educators also highlighted the potential of ChatGPT to facilitate collaborative learning, enhancing comprehension and fostering critical thinking.

Activity 3: Modification and Applying/Analyzing

Educators emphasized ChatGPT's role in modifying traditional artistic interpretations and fostering critical thinking.

Examples from the reflections:

- P1: "ChatGPT can be used to change traditional artistic interpretations by posing unique questions, pushing students to answer beyond textbook answers." (RDP1)
- P4: "They want to build bridges between novels and real-world historical contexts, encouraging learners to develop a deeper understanding of history." (RDP4)
- P5: "ChatGPT can help learners to analyze whether an alternative ending fits into the context of a literary theme." (RDP5)
- P6: "ChatGPT provides an engaging platform for students to practice English through real-time interaction." (RDP6)

Activity 4: Redefinition and Evaluating/Creating

The reflections highlight the transformative potential of ChatGPT in education. Educators see ChatGPT not just as a tool but also as a collaborator, innovator, and simulator.

Examples from the reflections:

- P9: "ChatGPT's ability to simulate historical figures helps students immerse themselves in history." (RDP9)
- P10: "Students can collaborate with ChatGPT to co-create a novel. Students provide theme, character, and plot ideas while ChatGPT generates the text." (RDP10)

The analysis of educators' experiences and reflections on using ChatGPT as a teaching tool revealed the potential of this technology to support learning objectives, enhance teaching practices, and create new and innovative learning experiences across various levels of the SAMR model and Bloom's Taxonomy. Educators recognized the ease and speed of ChatGPT, its ability to provide personalized support, and its potential to foster collaboration and critical thinking. The analysis also highlights the need for educators to be mindful of the ethical implications of using AI in education and to ensure that ChatGPT complements, not replaces, the human role in the classroom. The summary findings of the study can be found visually represented in Figure 2.

DISCUSSION

The integration of new technologies in education continuously reshapes the field, offering new tools and methods for enhancing teaching and learning. This study explores the incorporation of ChatGPT into education, focusing on its efficacy and challenges using the SAMR (Substitution, Augmentation, Modification, Redefinition) model and Bloom's Taxonomy as guiding frameworks. The goal is to provide insights into how AI technologies like ChatGPT can be effectively integrated into educational settings. Through structured and semi-structured interviews and reflective documents, educators' feedback was analyzed to reveal both the transformative potential and the inherent challenges of ChatGPT in the classroom.

Educators' perceptions on the potential ways or challenges of ChatGPT integration for teaching

The study reveals a consensus among educators that ChatGPT has significant potential to revolutionize various aspects of education. Its adaptability across disciplines, including literature, marketing, and language learning, demonstrates its utility in diverse teaching contexts. Educators particularly appreciate ChatGPT's ability to personalize learning and provide dynamic, interactive content that aligns with contemporary pedagogical approaches.However, educators also express concerns about over-reliance on AI, academic dishonesty, and the loss of authenticity in student work. While ChatGPT offers valuable tools and resources, it cannot fully replace the complexities of human interaction, empathy, and the complex nature of subjects like philosophy and the arts. These insights highlight the importance of using ChatGPT thoughtfully, ensuring that it supplements rather than replaces human instruction. Ethical considerations are a recurring theme, with educators emphasizing the need for guidelines to address academic integrity, data privacy, and potential misuse. Educators are encouraged to teach students not only how to use ChatGPT but also to do so responsibly, maintaining a balance between embracing technological advancements and preserving the human essence of education.

Figure 2. Visual representation of the summary findings of the study

Educators' potential issues or concerns associated with using ChatGPT for teaching

Educators emphasize the importance of human interaction in teaching, highlighting that their roles extend beyond information delivery to include mentorship and emotional support. The rise of AI tools like ChatGPT raises concerns that these critical aspects of education might be diminished. Educators worry that over-reliance on AI could undermine creativity and critical thinking, as students might become accustomed to accepting AI-generated content without questioning or evaluating it critically. Ethical issues, including AI biases and the risk of misinformation, are also significant concerns. AI tools, while powerful, can present skewed information that may influence young minds. To mitigate this, educators need to rigorously monitor AI outputs and foster a critical mindset in students, teaching them to analyze and question AI-generated information rather than passively consume it. The findings emphasize the need for comprehensive training programs that equip educators to integrate ChatGPT responsibly. Such programs should emphasize ethical use, critical engagement with AI, and strategies for fostering creativity and independent thought in students, ensuring that AI tools enhance rather than detract from the educational experience.

Educators' ChatGPT integration into their teaching practice based on the SAMR Model and Bloom's Taxonomy

Educators identified numerous strategies for integrating ChatGPT into teaching, effectively mapping these to the SAMR model and Bloom's Taxonomy. At the lower levels of Bloom's Taxonomy (e.g., Remembering and Understanding), educators see ChatGPT as a valuable tool for information retrieval and comprehension, replacing traditional resources like textbooks. As educators move towards higher levels of Bloom's Taxonomy (e.g., Analyzing, Evaluating, and Creating), ChatGPT's potential for enhancing critical thinking, creativity, and collaborative learning becomes more apparent. In terms of the SAMR model, educators described using ChatGPT from basic substitution of tools (e.g., replacing traditional reference materials) to more transformative uses at the redefinition level, such as creating entirely new learning experiences, like co-creating content with students or simulating real-world scenarios. This indicates that ChatGPT can be a powerful catalyst for educational innovation, providing opportunities to design learning experiences that were previously unimaginable. However, educators also emphasized the need for ongoing training to enhance familiarity with these frameworks, ensuring that AI tools like ChatGPT are used to complement, rather than replace, effective teaching practices.

Educators' experiences and reflections on ChatGPT use as a teaching tool based on the SAMR Model and Bloom's Taxonomy

Educators' reflections reveal that ChatGPT's utility evolves as it is integrated into teaching. At the initial stages, it often serves as a substitute for traditional resources, providing quick access to information. As familiarity grows, educators begin to leverage ChatGPT to deepen understanding and facilitate more interactive learning experiences, moving beyond mere substitution. At the modification and redefinition levels of the SAMR model, ChatGPT's role shifts from a simple tool to a dynamic participant in the learning process, fostering deeper analytical thinking and creative engagement. Educators see potential in ChatGPT as a collaborator in content creation, enabling new forms of learning, such as simulating conversations with historical figures or co-creating narratives. However, reflections also highlighted the need to be mindful of AI's limitations, ensuring that its use does not overshadow the development of critical thinking skills or human interaction. Educators suggested that ChatGPT should be seen as a collaborative tool, augmenting rather than replacing the educator's role, and emphasized the importance of establishing ethical guidelines for AI use in education.

LIMITATION OF STUDY

While this study offers valuable insights into the integration of ChatGPT in educational settings, several limitations should be noted. The study's limited sample size, focusing on ten educators from China, restricts the generalizability of the findings, and the insights may not fully capture the experiences of educators from diverse cultural and educational contexts. Additionally, the reliance on self-reported data from interviews and reflective documents introduces the potential for biases, such as social desirability or the desire to portray AI integration favorably, which may affect the objectivity of the results. The study also primarily reflects educators' initial perceptions, lacking an exploration of the long-term impacts of ChatGPT on teaching practices, student engagement, and learning outcomes, necessitating longitudinal research to understand the sustained effects of AI tools in education. Moreover, the study does not incorporate student perspectives, missing the opportunity to explore how students experience and interact with ChatGPT, which could provide a more balanced assessment of its effectiveness. Addressing these limitations through further research will help refine strategies for the successful and ethical integration of AI tools like ChatGPT into diverse educational environments.

CONCLUSION

The integration of ChatGPT into education offers transformative potential but is fraught with challenges that must be addressed. Educators are cautiously optimistic, seeing ChatGPT as a powerful tool to enhance learning when used within the right pedagogical frameworks, such as the SAMR model and Bloom's Taxonomy. However, ethical concerns, potential over-reliance on AI, and the need for professional development highlight that successful integration requires careful consideration, clear guidelines, and robust support systems. Strategic training initiatives and ongoing dialogue about the ethical implications of AI in education will be essential to leverage ChatGPT's potential while preserving the critical human elements of teaching. By navigating these complexities, educators can harness ChatGPT to create dynamic, engaging, and innovative learning experiences that meet the evolving needs of 21st-century education.

While this study offers valuable insights into educators' current perceptions and experiences with ChatGPT, further research is essential to fully grasp the long-term implications of AI integration in education. Longitudinal studies are crucial to track the lasting effects of AI on student learning outcomes and teaching practices, revealing the true impact of these tools over time. It is equally vital to gather data from students to understand their experiences and perspectives on AI in the classroom, providing a more balanced perspective on the integration of AI into education.

Exploring the potential for AI tools to support teacher education and professional development is critical, ensuring that educators are equipped to effectively utilize and navigate these tools. Finally, research must investigate the potential for AI to address or exacerbate existing inequities in education, ensuring that AI is used to promote equitable access and outcomes for all learners, creating a more just and equitable educational system for all.

Future research should explore deeper into the long-term impacts of AI integration in education, exploring how students interact with tools like ChatGPT and the implications for teaching and learning habits. Expanding the scope to include diverse educational contexts globally will provide a more comprehensive understanding of the challenges and opportunities unique to different settings. Additionally, further investigation into the ethical dimensions of AI in education is critical to ensure responsible and equitable implementation.

Section 1: Participant Demographics

Section 2: Objective 1: To explore educators' perceptions of the potential ways or challenges of ChatGPT integration for teaching.

1. Integration into Different Subject Areas:
   2.1. Are there specific subject areas or topics where you believe the use of ChatGPT might be more appropriate or beneficial, and are there areas where it might be less suitable? Please provide examples.

   ____

   ____

2. Opportunities (Potential Ways):
   2.2. To what extent do you believe ChatGPT can enhance the quality of education?
   - [ ] Not at all
   - [ ] Slightly
   - [ ] Moderately
   - [ ] Very much
   - [ ] Completely

2.3. Please provide specific examples of how you think ChatGPT can improve the quality of education.

____

____

2.4. How likely do you think ChatGPT can contribute to making learning more personalized for students?

[ ] Not likely at all
[ ] Slightly likely
[ ] Moderately likely
[ ] Very likely
[ ] Extremely likely

2.5. How can ChatGPT be used to differentiate instruction for students with varying learning needs? Perhaps you can provide examples of potential applications.

____

____

2.6. How effective do you believe ChatGPT could be in promoting collaboration and teamwork among students?

[ ] Not effective
[ ] Slightly effective
[ ] Moderately effective
[ ] Very effective
[ ] Extremely effective

2.7. In what ways do you think ChatGPT can contribute to creating a more engaging and interactive learning environment? Please describe your thoughts.

____

____

3. Challenges:

2.8. Please identify some challenges you foresee when using ChatGPT in the classroom.

____

____

2.9. How concerned are you about the potential risks of using ChatGPT in the classroom?

[ ] Not concerned at all
[ ] Slightly concerned
[ ] Moderately concerned
[ ] Very concerned
[ ] Extremely concerned

2.10. How confident are you in managing the risks of using ChatGPT?

[ ] Not confident at all
[ ] Slightly confident
[ ] Moderately confident
[ ] Very confident
[ ] Extremely confident

2.11. How concerned are you about the possibility of students using ChatGPT for cheating or plagiarism?

[ ] Not concerned at all
[ ] Slightly concerned
[ ] Moderately concerned
[ ] Very concerned
[ ] Extremely concerned

2.12. How likely are you to actively seek and stay updated with the latest updates and developments in ChatGPT technology?

[ ] Not likely at all
[ ] Slightly likely
[ ] Moderately likely
[ ] Very likely
[ ] Extremely likely

2.13. What strategies do you believe educators should adopt to ensure the safe and ethical use of ChatGPT in education?

____

____

Section 3: Objective 2: To explore educators' perceptions of the potential issues or concerns associated with using ChatGPT for teaching.

3.1. On a scale of 1 to 5, how concerned are you about the ethical implications of using AI, such as ChatGPT, in your teaching practice?

| Not Concerned | 1 | 2 | 3 | 4 | 5 | Very Concerned |

3.2. What do you think are the main ethical worries when integrating ChatGPT into teaching? (What worries or problems do educators have about using ChatGPT for teaching?)

____

____

3.3. What ethical and responsible strategies would you advise other educators to follow when integrating ChatGPT into teaching to reduce risks?

____

____

3.4. Could you explain any concerns or hesitations you might have regarding the potential impact of AI usage on your role as an educator and the dynamics within your classroom?

____

____

3.5. Thinking about your colleagues who might have similar concerns, what actions or initiatives do you believe educational institutions could put in place to tackle these challenges and promote the integration of AI?

____

____

3.6. Are you aware of any existing guidelines or policies in your educational institution that address the use of AI tools like ChatGPT?

[ ] Yes

[ ] No

If Yes, Please elaborate.

____

____

Section 4: Objective 3: To explore the potential strategies for educators to integrate ChatGPT into their teaching practice, utilizing the SAMR Model and Bloom's Taxonomy.

4.1. How confident do you feel in your ability to effectively incorporate AI, such as ChatGPT, into your teaching methods?

| Not Concerned | 1 | 2 | 3 | 4 | 5 | Very Concerned |

4.2. On a scale of 1 to 5, please rate your familiarity with the Bloom's Taxonomy.

| Not Familiar | 1 | 2 | 3 | 4 | 5 | Very Familiar |

4.3. On a scale of 1 to 5, please rate your familiarity with the SAMR Model.

| Not Familiar | 1 | 2 | 3 | 4 | 5 | Very Familiar |

You can watch a video "Using SAMR and Bloom's Taxonomy to Support Technology Integration"

Link: https://www.youtube.com/watch?v=-ImUzqsjeZs

You can watch a video: "The SAMR Model & Bloom's Taxonomy"

Link: https://www.youtube.com/watch?v=pZESmDytZeU

4. Targeting Cognitive Objectives with ChatGPT (Bloom's Taxonomy):

4.4. **Remembering level:** Can you identify specific learning objectives from Bloom's Taxonomy that could be addressed using ChatGPT at the Remembering level?

____

____

4.5. **Understanding level:** Can you provide examples of how ChatGPT could support learning objectives related to Understanding level within Bloom's Taxonomy.

____

____

4.6. **Applying level:** In what ways do you think ChatGPT might assist in promoting learning objectives associated with Applying level, according to Bloom's Taxonomy?

____

____

4.7. **Analyzing and Evaluating levels:** How could ChatGPT be utilized to encourage higher-order thinking skills and learning objectives linked to Analyzing and Evaluating levels in Bloom's Taxonomy?

____

____

4.8. **Creating level:** Can you provide examples of how ChatGPT could help students achieve learning goals related to Creating level, according to Bloom's Taxonomy?

____

____

5. Envisioning Teaching Enhancement with ChatGPT (SAMR Model):

4.9. **Substitution level:** How do you envision ChatGPT contributing to your teaching practice based on the SAMR Model's Substitution level?

____

____

4.10. **Augmentation level:** Can you provide specific examples of how ChatGPT might augment your teaching as per the SAMR Model's Augmentation level?

____

____

4.11. **Modification level:** In what ways do you anticipate modifying your teaching activities using ChatGPT to achieve the Modification level of the SAMR Model?

____

____

4.12. **Redefinition level:** How do you foresee ChatGPT redefining or transforming your teaching methods according to the SAMR Model's Redefinition level?

____

____

Thank you

REFERENCES

Abdullah, M., Madain, A., & Jararweh, Y. (2022). ChatGPT: Fundamentals, Applications and Social Impacts. *2022 Ninth International Conference on Social Networks Analysis, Management and Security (SNAMS)*, 1–8. DOI: 10.1109/SNAMS58071.2022.10062688

Adiguzel, T., Kaya, M. H., & Cansu, F. K. (2023). Revolutionizing education with AI: Exploring the transformative potential of ChatGPT. *Contemporary Educational Technology*, *15*(3), ep429. DOI: 10.30935/cedtech/13152

Alam, A. (2021). Possibilities and Apprehensions in the Landscape of Artificial Intelligence in Education. *2021 International Conference on Computational Intelligence and Computing Applications (ICCICA)*, 1–8. DOI: 10.1109/ICCICA52458.2021.9697272

Alam, A. (2022). A Digital Game based Learning Approach for Effective Curriculum Transaction for Teaching-Learning of Artificial Intelligence and Machine Learning. *2022 International Conference on Sustainable Computing and Data Communication Systems (ICSCDS)*, 69–74. DOI: 10.1109/ICSCDS53736.2022.9760932

Arulkumaran, K., Deisenroth, M. P., Brundage, M., & Bharath, A. A. (2017). A Brief Survey of Deep Reinforcement Learning. *IEEE Signal Processing Magazine*, *34*(6), 26–38. DOI: 10.1109/MSP.2017.2743240

Baidoo-Anu, D., & Owusu Ansah, L. (2023). *Education in the Era of Generative Artificial Intelligence (AI): Understanding the Potential Benefits of ChatGPT in Promoting Teaching and Learning* (SSRN Scholarly Paper 4337484). DOI: 10.2139/ssrn.4337484

Bubeck, S., Chandak, S., Eldan, R., Gehrke, J., Horvitz, E., Kamar, E., . . . Zhang, Y. (2023). Sparks of Artificial General Intelligence: Early experiments with GPT-4. *arXiv preprint* arXiv:2303.12712. https://doi.org//arXiv.2303.12712DOI: 10.48550

Creswell, J. W., & Poth, C. N. (2018). *Qualitative inquiry and research design: Choosing among five approaches* (4th ed.). Sage Publications.

Dempere, J., Modugu, K., Hesham, A., & Ramasamy, L. K. (2023). The impact of ChatGPT on higher education. *Frontiers in Education*, *8*, 1206936. DOI: 10.3389/feduc.2023.1206936

Dergaa, I., Chamari, K., Zmijewski, P., & Saad, H. B. (2023). From human writing to artificial intelligence generated text: Examining the prospects and potential threats of ChatGPT in academic writing. *Biology of Sport*, *40*(2), 615–622. DOI: 10.5114/biolsport.2023.125623 PMID: 37077800

Dwivedi, Y. K., Kshetri, N., Hughes, L., Slade, E. L., Jeyaraj, A., Kar, A. K., Baabdullah, A. M., Koohang, A., Raghavan, V., Ahuja, M., Albanna, H., Albashrawi, M. A., Al-Busaidi, A. S., Balakrishnan, J., Barlette, Y., Basu, S., Bose, I., Brooks, L., Buhalis, D., & Wright, R. (2023). Opinion Paper: "So what if ChatGPT wrote it?" Multidisciplinary perspectives on opportunities, challenges and implications of generative conversational AI for research, practice and policy. *International Journal of Information Management*, *71*, 102642. DOI: 10.1016/j.ijinfomgt.2023.102642

Ferruz, N., & Höcker, B. (2022). Controllable protein design with language models. *Nature Machine Intelligence*, *4*(6), 6. Advance online publication. DOI: 10.1038/s42256-022-00499-z

Floridi, L., & Chiriatti, M. (2020). GPT-3: Its nature, scope, limits, and consequences. *Minds and Machines*, *30*(4), 681–694. DOI: 10.1007/s11023-020-09548-1

George, A. S., & George, A. S. H. (2023). A Review of ChatGPT AI's Impact on Several Business Sectors. *Partners Universal International Innovation Journal*, *1*(1), 1. Advance online publication. DOI: 10.5281/zenodo.7644359

Habib, M., Faris, M., Qaddoura, R., Alomari, A., & Faris, H. (2021). A Predictive Text System for Medical Recommendations in Telemedicine: A Deep Learning Approach in the Arabic Context. *IEEE Access : Practical Innovations, Open Solutions*, *9*, 85690–85708. DOI: 10.1109/ACCESS.2021.3087593

Haleem, A., Javaid, M., & Singh, R. P. (2022). An era of ChatGPT as a significant futuristic support tool: A study on features, abilities, and challenges. *BenchCouncil Transactions on Benchmarks. Standards and Evaluations*, *2*(4), 100089. DOI: 10.1016/j.tbench.2023.100089

Kamalov, F., Santandreu Calonge, D., & Gurrib, I. (2023). New Era of Artificial Intelligence in Education: Towards a Sustainable Multifaceted Revolution. *Sustainability (Basel)*, *15*(16), 12451. DOI: 10.3390/su151612451

Kasneci, E., Sessler, K., Küchemann, S., Bannert, M., Dementieva, D., Fischer, F., Gasser, U., Groh, G., Günnemann, S., Hüllermeier, E., Krusche, S., Kutyniok, G., Michaeli, T., Nerdel, C., Pfeffer, J., Poquet, O., Sailer, M., Schmidt, A., Seidel, T., & Kasneci, G. (2023). ChatGPT for good? On opportunities and challenges of large language models for education. *Learning and Individual Differences*, *103*, 102274. DOI: 10.1016/j.lindif.2023.102274

Khowaja, S. A., Khuwaja, P., & Dev, K. (2023). *ChatGPT Needs SPADE (Sustainability, PrivAcy, Digital divide, and Ethics) Evaluation: A Review* (arXiv:2305.03123). arXiv. https://doi.org//arXiv.2305.03123DOI: 10.48550

Krathwohl, D. R. (2002). A Revision of Bloom's Taxonomy: An Overview. *Theory into Practice, 41*(4), 212–218. DOI: 10.1207/s15430421tip4104_2

Martin, C., DeStefano, K., Haran, H., Zink, S., Dai, J., Ahmed, D., Razzak, A., Lin, K., Kogler, A., Waller, J., Kazmi, K., & Umair, M. (2022). The ethical considerations including inclusion and biases, data protection, and proper implementation among AI in radiology and potential implications. *Intelligence-Based Medicine, 6*, 100073. DOI: 10.1016/j.ibmed.2022.100073

Open, A. I. (2015, December 11). *Introducing OpenAI.* OpenAI. https://openai.com/blog/introducing-openai/

Puentedura, R. R. (2012). The SAMR model. [Image]. Available under CC BY-NC-SA 4.0 license.

Wu, Y. (2023). Integrating Generative AI in Education: How ChatGPT Brings Challenges for Future Learning and Teaching. *Journal of Advanced Research in Education.*

Zhu, M., & Wang, Q. (2023). Exploring the impact of ChatGPT on education: Opportunities, challenges, and future directions. *Educational Technology Research and Development, 71*(2), 235–250. DOI: 10.1007/s11423-023-10020-5

APPENDIX A

Structured and Semi-Structured Interviews

Dear Participant,

I would like to invite you to take part in a research study titled "An Exploration of Educators' Experiences: Integrating ChatGPT into Teaching Based on the SAMR Model and Bloom's Taxonomy."

This study aims to delve into the real-world experiences of educators who have integrated ChatGPT, an AI language model, into their teaching practices.

By using the SAMR (Substitution, Augmentation, Modification, Redefinition) Model and Bloom's Taxonomy as guiding frameworks, I seek to understand how this integration has influenced teaching and learning dynamics.

The rapid advancement of technology, including AI, has opened new avenues for enriching educational experiences. As educators, you play a pivotal role in shaping the learning journey of your students. By participating in this study, you will contribute to our understanding of the practical implications of AI integration in education and offer insights that can inform instructional decisions in the future.

Confidentiality and Consent:

Your privacy and confidentiality are of utmost importance. All information you provide will be anonymized, and any identifying details will be kept strictly confidential. Your participation in this study is voluntary, and you have the right to withdraw at any time without any negative consequences.

Benefit to Education:

The findings of this study will contribute to a deeper understanding of how AI tools like ChatGPT can be effectively integrated into educational settings. By sharing your experiences, you will be contributing to the broader educational community's knowledge and fostering discussions on the responsible and meaningful use of technology in teaching.

Thank you for considering participating in this important research. Your valuable insights will undoubtedly contribute to the advancement of education and the effective integration of technology in the classroom.

Please provide the following demographic information:

1. **Gender:**
   [ ] Women
   [ ] Male
2. **Age:**
   _______ years old
3. **Teaching Experience (Years):**
   [ ] 0-5
   [ ] 6-10
4. **Office/Affiliation:**
   [ ] University Lecturers
   [ ] Lecturers in Educational Institutions
5. **Subject(s) Taught:**

(e.g., Visual Design, Art, Product Design, English (Language), Mathematics, Software Engineering, Fine Arts)

APPENDIX B

Reflective Document

Reflective Document on Integrating ChatGPT into Teaching Practice
Name:
Date:
Age:
Subject/Area of Specialization:

The purpose of this reflective document is to explore educators' experiences reflections on ChatGPT use as a teaching tool based on the SAMR Model and Bloom's Taxonomy.

Your participation in this study involves maintaining a reflective journal or diary over a period of approximately two weeks.

During this time, we request that you actively incorporate ChatGPT into your teaching activities and document your experiences, observations, and insights. You will be provided with a template that will guide you in reflecting on your experiences with ChatGPT integration using the SAMR Model and Bloom's Taxonomy, allowing for a comprehensive exploration of its impact on teaching and learning.

Activity 1- Substitution Level - Remembering (Bloom's Taxonomy)
Activity 2- Augmentation Level - Understanding (Bloom's Taxonomy)
Activity 3- Modification Level - Applying and Analyzing (Bloom's Taxonomy)
Activity 4- Redefinition Level - Evaluating and Creating (Bloom's Taxonomy):
Resources on ChatGPT for Teachers/Educators
The SAMR Model Explained by Ruben R. Puentedura
https://www.youtube.com/watch?v=_QOsz4AaZ2k
How to Apply the SAMR Model with Ruben Puentedura
https://www.youtube.com/watch?v=ZQTx2UQQvbU
Here is an EXAMPLE:

By combining SAMR and Bloom's Taxonomy, educators can ensure that technology integration is purposeful and aligned with the desired learning outcomes. The progression through SAMR's levels reflects deeper cognitive engagement, while Bloom's Taxonomy guides the cognitive processes at each level of technology integration.

Table 4. Learning outcomes with SAMR and Bloom's Taxonomy

SAMR	Bloom's Taxonomy	Example (different technology)
Substitution (Replacement) • technology is used as a direct substitute for traditional tools or methods. It's about enhancing the learning process without significant changes in tasks.	**Remembering Level** In the context of Bloom's Taxonomy, this aligns with the "Remembering" level, where students recall information.	Using digital flashcards (e.g., Quizlet) instead of physical flashcards to help students remember vocabulary words. Students are still recalling information, but technology enhances the process.
Augmentation • involves technology enhancing tasks by adding functionalities that weren't possible with traditional methods.	**Understanding** In Bloom's Taxonomy terms, it corresponds to the "Understanding" level, where students grasp the meaning of concepts.	Having students collaborate on a document using Google Docs, enabling real-time editing and commenting. This goes beyond traditional collaborative methods, aiding in understanding the content.
Modification • involves redesigning tasks to take full advantage of technology	**Applying and Analyzing** Students engage in higher-order thinking skills, such as applying and analyzing. This aligns with Bloom's Taxonomy's "Applying" and "Analyzing" levels.	Using interactive simulation software to allow students to experiment with chemical reactions and analyze the outcomes. This promotes application and analysis of concepts.
Redefinition (Transformation) • involves using technology to create entirely new learning experiences that were previously inconceivable.	**Evaluating and Creating** It aligns with the highest levels of Bloom's Taxonomy: "Evaluating" and "Creating."	Students create multimedia presentations or videos to explain complex historical events, including their own critical evaluations. This involves evaluating and synthesizing information.

Table 5. Activity 1- Substitution Level - Remembering (Bloom's Taxonomy)

SAMR Model	Bloom's Taxonomy
Substitution (Replacement) • **technology is used as a direct substitute for traditional tools** or methods. It's about **enhancing the learning process** without significant changes in tasks.	**Remembering Level** In the context of Bloom's Taxonomy, this aligns with the "Remembering" level, where students recall information.

Think of ONE topic or content: ____________

How can you incorporate ChatGPT at the **Substitution level** aligning with Bloom's Taxonomy's "Remembering" level that may impact your teaching of this topic/content? Consider how it could affect the way students recall and access information.

Type here:

Example (use/integrate/incorporate with ChatGPT)

Describe specific scenario/activity where ChatGPT could serve as a **substitute (replacement)** for traditional methods in your teaching context.

Can you provide an example?

Type here:

Table 6. Activity 2- Augmentation Level - Understanding (Bloom's Taxonomy)

SAMR Model	Bloom's Taxonomy
Augmentation • involves **technology enhancing tasks** by adding functionalities that weren't possible with traditional methods.	**Understanding** In Bloom's Taxonomy terms, it corresponds to the "Understanding" level, where students grasp the meaning of concepts.

Think of ONE topic or content: ____________

Think about the potential enhancements ChatGPT could bring to your teaching, aligned with the **Augmentation level** of the SAMR Model and "Understanding" level of Bloom's Taxonomy. How might it help students grasp complex concepts more effectively?

Type here:

Example (use/integrate/incorporate with ChatGPT)

Describe how incorporating ChatGPT could go **beyond traditional methods** in promoting students' understanding of subject matter.

Can you provide an example?

Type here:

Table 7. Activity 3- Modification Level - Applying and Analyzing (Bloom's Taxonomy)

SAMR Model	Bloom's Taxonomy
Modification • involves **redesigning tasks** to take full advantage of technology	**Applying and Analyzing** Students engage in higher-order thinking skills, such as applying and analyzing. This aligns with Bloom's Taxonomy's "Applying" and "Analyzing" levels.

Think of ONE topic or content: ____________

Consider the **Modification level** of the SAMR Model coupled with the "Applying" and "Analyzing" levels of Bloom's Taxonomy. Reflect on how ChatGPT could facilitate higher-order thinking skills in your teaching.

Type here:

Example (use/integrate/incorporate with ChatGPT)

Describe how ChatGPT could **transform** how students apply and analyze concepts. How could it provide unique opportunities for deeper engagement with the subject matter?

Can you provide an example?

Type here:

Table 8. Activity 4 - Redefinition Level - Evaluating and Creating (Bloom's Taxonomy)

SAMR Model	Bloom's Taxonomy
Redefinition (Transformation) • involves **using technology to create entirely new learning experiences** that were previously inconceivable.	**Evaluating and Creating** It aligns with the highest levels of Bloom's Taxonomy: "Evaluating" and "Creating."

Think of ONE topic or content: ____________

Imagine the **Redefinition level** of the SAMR Model in combination with the "Evaluating" and "Creating" levels of Bloom's Taxonomy. Reflect on how ChatGPT could enable entirely new teaching experiences that were not possible before.

Type here:

Example (use/integrate/incorporate with ChatGPT)

Describe how integrating ChatGPT at this level might empower students to evaluate and create content in novel ways. What implications could this have for fostering critical thinking and creativity?

Can you provide an example?

Type here:

Summarize the key insights you've gained from exploring ChatGPT integration aligned with the SAMR Model and Bloom's Taxonomy.

How have your perceptions of ChatGPT potential impact evolved throughout this activity?

Type here:____

Chapter 5
Revolutionizing Higher Education With Generative AI: Prospects, Challenges, and Future Directions

Mohammed Abdul Wajeed
https://orcid.org/0000-0002-5047-7857
Lords Institute of Engineering and Technology, India

ABSTRACT

The chapter explores the transformative impact of generative AI on higher education, highlighting its potential to revolutionize learning, teaching, and research methods. Key points include: a) Generative AI tools enable personalized, flexible, and interactive learning experiences. b) AI-driven technologies enhance teaching strategies through customized education and real-time lesson modification. c) Digital teaching assistants and AI-powered chat advisors provide scalable student support. d) In research, generative AI simplifies complex tasks, improving efficiency. e) The text suggests frameworks for integrating AI into curricula, emphasizing hybrid instructional methods. f) Ethical considerations, including fairness, data privacy, and addressing biases, are crucial. g) Challenges include academic dishonesty risks and intellectual property issues. h) The importance of developing critical digital literacy skills is emphasized. i) Future directions involve the convergence of AI with augmented and virtual reality for immersive learning experiences.

DOI: 10.4018/979-8-3373-0847-0.ch005

1. INTRODUCTION: AI'S IMPACT ON HIGHER EDUCATION: TRANSFORMING TRADITIONAL METHODS INTO INNOVATIVE LEARNING APPROACHES.

The landscape of higher education is being reshaped by Artificial Intelligence (AI), which is converting conventional teaching and learning approaches into dynamic, adaptable, and student-focused experiences. By incorporating AI-enabled technologies, academic institutions are fostering innovation through enhanced instruction delivery, customized learning paths, streamlined administrative processes, and improved student participation. As educational establishments strive to modernize their practices, AI acts as a driving force in transforming standard lecture-based methods into interactive, data-informed, and immersive learning environments. A key contribution of AI in higher education is its capacity to tailor learning experiences to individual students. Conventional teaching models typically employ a uniform approach that may not address the varied needs of learners. AI-powered adaptive learning systems evaluate student progress, identify strengths and weaknesses, and adjust educational content accordingly. These platforms utilize machine learning algorithms to offer personalized suggestions, customized study materials, and instantaneous feedback, ensuring that students receive targeted assistance based on their individual learning preferences (Smith & Brown, 2023). This personalized strategy enhances understanding, improves retention, and encourages self-directed learning, ultimately making education more effective and accessible to all.

Artificial intelligence is revolutionizing educational content delivery through sophisticated tutoring systems and virtual learning aids. Unlike traditional classrooms where students might be reluctant to ask questions, AI-powered chatbots and virtual tutors offer immediate academic support. These tools provide answers, clarify complex ideas, and suggest additional resources, enabling students to learn at their preferred pace (Kumar, 2023). Furthermore, AI-enhanced learning management systems (LMS) enable ongoing assessment by creating quizzes, reviewing assignments, and providing tailored feedback, assisting students in monitoring their progress and enhancing their comprehension. AI is also driving innovation in curriculum development for higher education. AI-driven content creation tools help educators design dynamic course materials, interactive simulations, and media-rich educational resources. These tools can automatically produce summaries, create visual aids, and recommend relevant supplementary materials, easing the burden on educators while improving instructional content quality (Johnson & Davis, 2023). Moreover, AI algorithms examine global academic trends, research advancements, and industry needs, allowing institutions to update their curricula in real-time and ensure students acquire skills relevant to evolving job markets. Outside the classroom, AI optimizes administrative tasks, allowing educators to concentrate more on teaching and mentoring. AI-powered automation simplifies course scheduling, student enrollment, and grading, substantially reducing faculty workload. Predictive analytics tools evaluate student performance trends and identify those at risk of academic failure, enabling institutions to intervene early and provide necessary support. AI also plays a vital role in admissions, career counseling, and student engagement by examining applicants' academic profiles, suggesting suitable programs, and guiding students in career planning based on data-driven insights (Patel, 2023). The application of AI in education also encompasses immersive and experiential learning. AI-powered augmented reality (AR) and virtual reality (VR) technologies offer hands-on simulations that connect theoretical knowledge with practical application. For instance, medical students can practice surgical procedures using AI-driven VR simulations, while engineering students can participate in interactive design experiments. AI also enhances collaborative learning, allowing students to engage in virtual labs, participate in global discussions, and co-create knowledge through intelligent platforms. Nevertheless, the integration of AI in higher education raises ethical concerns, including data privacy, bias in AI algorithms, and the risk of over-reliance on technology. Protecting student data is crucial, requiring institutions to implement robust security measures and transparent data governance policies (Nistor & Stanciu, 2023). Furthermore, AI models must be regularly evaluated for biases to ensure they do not unintentionally disadvantage specific student groups. While AI enhances learning, it should complement rather than replace human instructors, as educators remain essential in fostering critical thinking, creativity, and social interaction.

The integration of AI into higher education represents a transformative shift towards a cutting-edge, data-oriented, and learner-focused educational environment. By harnessing AI's potential, educational institutions can develop more accessible, captivating, and streamlined learning experiences that address various learning styles. Nevertheless, the effectiveness of AI-enhanced education hinges on thoughtful implementation, ethical considerations, and a well-balanced approach that combines AI's computational capabilities with human expertise. As AI technology advances, its capacity to transform higher education will continue to expand, molding a future where technology and teaching methodologies collaborate to improve learning outcomes and academic achievement.

2. TRANSFORMING FACULTY RESPONSIBILITIES IN THE AI AGE: INSTRUCTION, MENTORSHIP, AND PROFESSIONAL ADVANCEMENTS

The incorporation of Artificial Intelligence (AI) into higher education is significantly altering the duties and roles of faculty members. Once regarded as the main sources of knowledge, educators are now adjusting to an environment where AI technologies are changing the ways in which knowledge is delivered, evaluated, and tailored to individual needs. This shift requires a reevaluation of faculty roles in teaching, mentoring, and professional growth.

Faculty Shifting from Content Providers to Learning Guides: AI technologies, including intelligent tutoring systems and adaptive learning platforms, are automating routine teaching tasks, allowing faculty to concentrate more on facilitating learning rather than just delivering content. These systems offer personalized feedback and adjust to the unique needs of each student, fostering a more student-focused learning environment (Rakhimov & Akbarov, 2021). Consequently, faculty members are evolving into roles that prioritize guiding students through complex problem-solving and critical thinking. This transformation necessitates that educators design and manage learning experiences that effectively utilize AI tools, ensuring that technology enhances rather than replaces human interaction in the classroom (McLaren et al., 2010).

Faculty Adapting Mentorship in an AI-Driven Educational Environment: Although AI can assist with elements of student advising like choosing courses and planning academics, it cannot replace the intricate mentorship that faculty provide. Educators are essential in nurturing students' personal and professional development, offering guidance that includes emotional intelligence, ethical insights, and career advancement (Hmelo-Silver, 2004). AI-generated analytics on student performance enable faculty to pinpoint and assist students who might be struggling academically. Nonetheless, the task of interpreting these data and turning them into effective interventions remains a uniquely human duty (Breazeal et al., 2019).

Faculty Enhancing Professional Growth through AI Literacy: The swift progress of AI in the educational sector demands continuous professional development for educators to keep up with emerging technologies and teaching methods. Teachers need to cultivate AI literacy to comprehend the strengths and limitations of these tools, ensuring their successful incorporation into educational practices (Tomar & Verma, 2023). Professional development initiatives are increasingly aimed at providing educators with the ability to critically evaluate AI applications, create AI-enhanced curricula, and tackle ethical issues related to data privacy and algorithmic bias (Khan & Alghamdi, 2024). Institutions are urged to offer resources and training that assist faculty in navigating the changing landscape of educational technology.

Faculty Confronting Challenges and Seizing Opportunities: The integration of AI into higher education brings with it certain challenges, such as concerns about potential job losses and the necessity for substantial shifts in teaching approaches. Faculty members might feel uneasy about the dependability of AI systems and their effects on academic honesty (Breazeal, 1999).

Nonetheless, adopting AI also presents educators with the chance to improve their teaching efficiency, engage in cross-disciplinary partnerships, and contribute to the creation of cutting-edge educational frameworks. By actively engaging in the incorporation of AI, faculty can ensure that these technologies enhance rather than undermine the educational experience (O'Neil, 2016).

The incorporation of Artificial Intelligence (AI) into higher education is set to transform the core of academic teaching, advancing beyond mere automation to establish a cooperative human-AI learning environment. As AI technologies grow more advanced, the conventional responsibilities of faculty members are anticipated to change significantly and in various ways. These changes will focus on five main areas: innovative teaching methods, personalized learning through data, ethical guidance, cross-disciplinary collaboration, and ongoing mentorship.

3. FUTURE TRANSFORMATION OF FACULTY ROLES WITH AI INTEGRATION IN HIGHER EDUCATION

Faculty as Pedagogical Designers and Orchestrators: In the future, educators will transition from being mere conveyors of knowledge to becoming *pedagogical designers*, utilizing AI tools to craft adaptive, interactive, and immersive learning environments. They will develop learning pathways that incorporate intelligent tutoring systems, simulation tools, and real-time analytics to facilitate active and experiential learning. Faculty will serve as *architects oflearning experiences*, creating curricula that enhance AI's capacity to support instruction and cater to individual learner profiles. Technologies such as generative AI and learning analytics will empower instructors to adjust content and pacing, thereby democratizing learning for diverse cognitive and linguistic backgrounds (Zhai, 2024).

Faculty as Data-Literate Facilitators of Personalization: The ability of AI to handle and analyze extensive amounts of student data will enable faculty to offer *hyper personalized education*. Instructors will need to acquire data literacy skills to interpret performance dashboards, forecast student success paths, and apply specific interventions (Rakhimov & Akbarov, 2021). They will increasingly take on a strategic role in orchestrating personalized interventions determining when, how, and to what degree AI-generated insights should guide teaching decisions. Instead of being replaced, faculty will work alongside AI systems to boost student engagement, pinpoint learning gaps, and encourage independent learning (Picciano, 2012).

Faculty as Ethical Leaders and Digital Mentors: As AI systems become integrated into decision-making processes like grading, feedback, and admissions, faculty members will be expected to act as *ethical stewards*. They will champion transparency, fairness, and accountability in AI applications, helping both institutions and students comprehend AI's biases, limitations, and societal effects. Additionally, educators will guide students in AI literacy, assisting them in understanding the ethical use of generative tools (e.g., ChatGPT, DALL·E), interpreting algorithmic decisions, and critically assessing AI-generated content. This guidance will also cover *digital citizenship*, promoting responsible AI use in academic and professional settings (Holmes, Bialik, & Fadel, 2019).

Faculty as Interdisciplinary Collaborators: The incorporation of AI into educational programs will demand collaboration among faculty from a range of disciplines, including computer science, cognitive psychology, ethics, and pedagogy. These educators will work together to develop AI-enhanced modules and drive innovations in educational delivery across various domains, such as virtual labs, AI-driven simulations, and the creation of multimodal content. This shift will redefine faculty roles, transforming them from mere subject matter experts into collaborators within cross-functional teams that design intelligent, inclusive, and context-aware learning ecosystems (Patel, 2023).

Faculty as Lifelong Learners and Professional Innovators: As AI rapidly changes the way content is delivered and created, educators must commit to ongoing professional growth. Institutions should facilitate faculty in gaining skills in areas such as machine learning, natural language processing, educational data mining, and AI ethics. Additionally, faculty will play a role in the joint development of AI systems by offering feedback to enhance educational algorithms, engaging in the creation of institutional policies, and testing new AI tools to help shape future standards (Khan & Alghamdi, 2024).

4. REVOLUTIONIZING HIGHER EDUCATION AND LIFELONG LEARNING WITH GENERATIVE AI: TAILORED, AUTOMATED, AND ADAPTIVE EDUCATION FOR ADULT LEARNERS

The incorporation of Artificial Intelligence (AI), especially generative AI, is transforming both higher education and lifelong learning by altering teaching models, expanding access to education, and creating genuinely adaptive learning environments. Generative AI technologies, ranging from advanced language models to intelligent tutoring systems, are revolutionizing content creation, automating teaching support, and offering unprecedented personalization for a wide range of learners, including adult learners, non-traditional students, and working professionals (UNESCO, 2021; McNamara, 2023).

In the realm of higher education, AI-powered tools are streamlining various aspects of teaching and learning. Generative AI systems can quickly generate lecture materials, summaries, code snippets, and visual aids that are customized to students' proficiency levels, promoting inclusive and efficient education delivery. Language models assist educators in crafting accessible content across different fields, while image-generation platforms simplify abstract ideas with tailored visual representations (Luckin et al., 2023). In programming education, AI-driven code assistants provide real-time debugging help, generate examples, and explain syntax, enabling students to develop skills independently and intuitively.

Beyond traditional students, AI is having a significant impact on lifelong learning and adult education, where learners often need flexible, adaptive, and relevant learning experiences. Adult learners typically encounter challenges such as limited time, career changes, diverse educational backgrounds, and changing industry demands. Generative AI addresses these needs through adaptive learning systems that adjust content in real-time based on performance, pace, preferences, and personal goals. These systems customize everything from learning speed to modality (text, audio, video), ensuring that adult learners receive contextually relevant and time-efficient learning paths (Green & Donovan, 2024).

In professional development, AI algorithms match individual skill profiles with labor market trends to suggest micro-credentials, short courses, or certifications that align with emerging job roles. This just-in-time learning strategy enables professionals to reskill and upskill without the constraints of traditional education systems. Additionally, AI-driven chatbots and virtual assistants provide 24/7 academic support, answering questions, recommending resources, and guiding learners through complex content, further enhancing accessibility for working adults and remote learners (Holmes & Tuomi, 2023).

AI's incorporation is also transforming student support frameworks. Intelligent tutoring systems assess learning patterns, pinpoint deficiencies, and offer specific feedback or corrective exercises. Learning Management Systems (LMSs) equipped with AI capabilities can automate the grading process, track engagement, and modify curriculum delivery based on learner interaction trends. These systems enhance efficiency and facilitate data-driven instructional design, benefiting both educators and students (Green, 2023).

Despite these advancements, several issues need to be tackled to ensure fair and ethical implementation. A significant concern is maintaining academic integrity. AI tools, with their ability to produce essays, assignments, and research papers, increase the risk of misuse and plagiarism, particularly in self-directed adult learning settings where supervision is limited. Institutions must establish clear usage guidelines and incorporate AI literacy into curricula to educate learners on how to interact with AI-generated content critically and ethically (UNESCO, 2023).

Another issue is algorithmic bias and misinformation. AI models trained on extensive, unfiltered datasets may mirror societal biases or inaccuracies, potentially skewing educational content and misleading learners. This is especially worrisome in adult education, where learners depend on accurate, practical information for career and life decisions. Ongoing refinement of AI models and the inclusion of diverse, curated datasets are crucial to maintain content accuracy and fairness (Selwyn, 2023).

Furthermore, integrating AI into lifelong learning ecosystems requires robust data privacy and governance structures (Singh & Rao, 2023). AI systems gather vast amounts of data to tailor experiences—from learning preferences to behavioral metrics—which must be managed with transparency and security. Institutions need to enforce strong data protection policies, secure informed consent, and ensure adherence to ethical standards. Importantly, the changing role of educators must be acknowledged (Smith, 2023). In AI-enhanced settings, educators transition from being content providers to facilitators of critical thinking, ethics, and reflective learning. Especially in adult education, where mentorship and real-world application are key, human guidance remains indispensable. AI can assist—but not replace—the emotional intelligence, industry knowledge, and mentorship that effective adult educators offer (Johnson & Brown, 2022).

5. AI's TRANSFORMATIVE IMPACT ON HIGHER EDUCATION: CRAFTING DYNAMIC AND PERSONALIZED LEARNING EXPERIENCES

The integration of Artificial Intelligence (AI) in higher education is revolutionizing the learning landscape by creating flexible, individualized, and responsive educational environments that address the diverse needs and preferences of students. While conventional teaching methods often employ a standardized approach that fails to accommodate varying learning speeds, styles, and requirements, AI-enabled tools are reshaping higher education. These technologies facilitate tailored learning paths, streamline content generation, enhance research methodologies, and boost student involvement through cutting-edge systems (Lee, Martinez, & Gupta, 2021). Such advancements enable educators to deliver more efficient, inclusive, and learner-focused instruction while simultaneously preparing students with the skills necessary to thrive in a technology-driven society. One of the primary ways AI enhances higher education is through the creation of bespoke learning resources. AI-driven adaptive learning platforms examine student performance, evaluate their strengths and areas for improvement, and produce customized content suited to their individual needs (Kumar & Singh, 2024). In contrast to traditional static textbooks and pre-determined curricula, AI-powered systems dynamically modify lesson plans, suggest supplementary materials, and adjust assessments based on real-time student interactions. This degree of personalization ensures that learners receive targeted instruction, enabling them to grasp concepts more effectively while advancing at their own pace. Furthermore, AI-powered content recommendation engines propose relevant scholarly articles, research papers, and study materials, offering students curated learning experiences that align with their academic objectives (Williams, 2023).

AI's role in education extends beyond personalization, encompassing automated content creation that eases educators' workloads while maintaining educational material quality (Zhao & Fernandez, 2023). AI-driven natural language processing (NLP) systems can produce course outlines, lecture materials, tests, and homework, streamlining curriculum development. These tools help educators craft engaging course content by incorporating AI-generated multimedia elements like videos, animations, and visual aids. This automation not only improves instructional quality but also allows faculty to focus more on student mentorship, facilitating discussions, and nurturing critical thinking abilities (Patel, 2022). In higher education, AI also enhances research processes by optimizing data gathering, analysis, and knowledge discovery. Researchers can employ AI-powered tools to quickly sift through extensive academic literature, identify pertinent studies, and generate insights (Thompson & Wright, 2023). AI-based data analytics enable researchers to spot patterns, forecast outcomes, and test hypotheses, significantly expediting the research process. Furthermore, AI-enhanced citation and reference management systems assist scholars in organizing sources, identifying potential plagiarism, and upholding academic integrity (Sharma, 2023). These AI-driven advancements not only boost research efficiency but also contribute to knowledge expansion across various fields. AI is also making substantial contributions to student engagement. Intelligent tutoring systems powered by AI offer personalized, real-time guidance to students, functioning as adaptive virtual mentors (Liu, 2024). Unlike traditional classrooms where time constraints or social pressures may deter students from seeking clarification, AI tutors provide immediate feedback, explanations, and supplementary learning resources. Chatbots and virtual teaching assistants further boost engagement by responding to student queries, promoting peer discussions, and offering motivational support. These AI-driven conversational agents foster an interactive learning environment, ensuring students remain actively involved in their academic pursuits (Green & Carter, 2022).

AI also improves accessibility and inclusion in higher education by catering to various learning preferences and requirements. Students with disabilities benefit from AI-powered speech-to-text and text-to-speech technologies, which enhance their access to educational materials (Moore et al., 2023). For international students, language translation tools help overcome communication barriers, fostering a more globally inclusive educational environment. Moreover, AI-based sentiment analysis tools track student engagement and identify signs of academic struggles, enabling institutions to provide timely support to students at risk. These AI-facilitated interventions create a more equitable and supportive learning atmosphere, ensuring equal opportunities for all students (Robinson & Kim, 2023). While AI offers numerous advantages in higher education, there are challenges that need to be addressed to optimize its benefits and minimize risks. The collection and analysis of extensive student data by AI systems for personalized learning raises data privacy concerns (Hernandez, 2023). Implementing strong data protection measures and clear policies is essential to maintain student trust and prevent unauthorized access to sensitive academic information. Additionally, AI models must be continuously evaluated and adjusted to eliminate biases that could result in unfair outcomes in personalized learning recommendations or assessments (White & Singh, 2023). Educational institutions should adopt ethical AI frameworks that emphasize fairness, inclusivity, and transparency in AI-driven educational practices. Another issue is the potential overreliance on AI tools, which may compromise critical thinking skills and human interaction (Foster, 2024). Although AI enhances efficiency and personalization, it should complement rather than replace human educators. Instructors play a crucial role in nurturing creativity, ethical reasoning, and social skills—areas where AI cannot fully substitute human judgment. A balanced approach that combines AI-driven automation with teacher-led instruction ensures that students develop comprehensive cognitive and interpersonal abilities necessary for academic and professional success (Kapoor, 2023). The outlook for AI in higher education is bright, with ongoing advancements expected to further enhance learning experiences and educational methods. As AI-enabled technologies continue to progress, institutions must prioritize strategic implementation, teacher empowerment, and ethical considerations to establish a learning ecosystem that is both technologically advanced and pedagogically sound (Lopez, 2023). By responsibly harnessing AI, higher education can achieve a transformative shift towards a more inclusive, dynamic, and student-centered model that improves learning outcomes and equips students for the challenges of the digital era.

6. TRANSFORMING EDUCATION WITH AI-POWERED PERSONALIZATION, ACCESSIBILITY, AND INCLUSION

Generative AI is reshaping education by delivering highly individualized learning experiences that cater to each student's specific requirements, capabilities, and development (Luckin et al., 2023). In contrast to conventional educational frameworks that employ uniform curricula and teaching methods, AI-enabled systems can flexibly adjust instruction, evaluation, and materials to match each learner's strong points, areas for improvement, and preferred learning styles. This transition to personalized education is propelled by progress in generative AI, which utilizes advanced language models, multimedia content creation tools, and smart tutoring systems to construct adaptive learning paths that foster inclusivity, involvement, and comprehensive understanding. A key benefit of generative AI in education is its capacity to produce tailored learning experiences that adapt instantaneously. Through the examination of students' performance metrics, AI can ceaselessly modify instructional content to align with their advancement, ensuring they are neither left behind nor insufficiently challenged (Singh & Rao, 2023). For example, an AI-powered platform can track a student's quiz and assignment responses, pinpointing areas of difficulty and subsequently modifying content to reinforce those concepts. Concurrently, AI can expedite learning for high-performing students by introducing more advanced material or offering enrichment activities. This personalized approach not only enhances knowledge retention but also elevates student confidence and motivation by providing a learning experience that feels both pertinent and achievable. Emerging AI-driven content generators are instrumental in this transformation, enabling educators to develop real-time, customized lesson plans and interactive educational resources (Green, 2023). Language models like GPT-based AI systems can promptly generate well-organized lecture notes, summaries, and learning modules, while AI-powered multimedia creators can design captivating visuals, animations, and simulations that accommodate various learning styles. In STEM education, for instance, AI-generated interactive simulations allow students to conduct virtual experiments, adjust variables, and observe outcomes, offering a hands-on learning experience without the limitations of physical laboratory resources (UNESCO, 2023). Likewise, in language acquisition, AI can produce personalized dialogues, pronunciation exercises, and contextual grammar explanations based on a student's proficiency level and learning objectives. By automating content creation, AI allows educators to allocate more time to student engagement and curriculum enhancement rather than dedicating excessive hours to preparing instructional materials from the ground up.

Artificial intelligence-driven content creation enables educators to craft rich multimedia course materials that complement conventional teaching approaches. Engaging learning experiences are facilitated through interactive presentations, AI-generated visual aids, and dynamic evaluation tools, particularly benefiting students with varied learning requirements. For instance, AI-powered assessment creators can automatically produce customized quizzes and tests that adapt to individual learning progress, offering instant feedback and adjustable difficulty. This feature ensures that assessments not only evaluate but also reinforce knowledge and guide students towards proficiency (Holmes & Tuomi, 2023). Furthermore, AI-generated gamified learning modules promote active involvement by incorporating elements such as challenges, incentives, and real-world scenarios, making education more interactive and enjoyable. In addition to content generation, AI-powered virtual teaching assistants and chat-based advisors provide immediate and scalable support to students, enhancing both academic assistance and engagement. These AI-driven systems serve as round-the-clock learning companions, addressing student inquiries, elucidating complex concepts, and suggesting supplementary resources tailored to individual needs. Unlike traditional office hours that constrain student-instructor interactions, AI-powered teaching assistants ensure continuous availability of help, fostering a more supportive learning environment (Johnson & Brown, 2022). Moreover, these systems can facilitate peer collaboration by organizing study groups, moderating discussions, and encouraging students to participate in knowledge-sharing activities. In online and hybrid learning settings, where students often grapple with feelings of isolation, AI-driven interactions help maintain engagement and motivation through timely encouragement, reminders, and constructive feedback. Inclusivity represents another crucial aspect of AI-driven personalized education, as generative AI has the potential to accommodate diverse learning needs and reduce accessibility gaps. AI-powered platforms can provide adaptive learning interfaces for students with disabilities, offering text-to-speech capabilities, real-time captioning, and customized font sizes for visually impaired learners. Additionally, AI-driven translation tools can overcome language barriers, allowing non-native speakers to access course materials in their preferred language (Selwyn, 2023). By identifying learning challenges early on, AI also enables targeted interventions for students who may require additional support, ensuring that no learner is left behind. Through these adaptive mechanisms, AI contributes to an equitable education system that caters to a wide range of learning abilities, fostering a more inclusive academic experience. While AI-driven education presents significant opportunities, its implementation must be guided by ethical considerations and pedagogical best practices to ensure that automation enhances rather than replaces the human aspects of learning. Educators play an irreplaceable role in fostering critical thinking, creativity, and emotional intelligence—qualities that AI alone cannot fully replicate. Therefore, AI should be integrated as a collaborative tool that supports educators rather than as a substitute for human teaching. The most effective AI-enhanced education models involve a blended approach, where AI automates administrative and repetitive tasks while educators focus on mentorship, discussion facilitation, and personalized student engagement. Institutions must also prioritize transparency in AI-generated content, ensuring that students understand how AI tools function and how to critically evaluate AI-generated information.

Addressing data privacy and AI bias concerns is crucial for the ethical implementation of AI in education. Educational AI platforms amass substantial student information to enhance their recommendations and personalize learning experiences. Protecting this data is vital to maintain student privacy and prevent misuse. Educational institutions must establish robust security measures, encryption protocols, and transparent data management policies to ensure trust and accountability. Moreover, regular audits of AI models are necessary to detect and address biases that may negatively impact certain student populations. By emphasizing fairness and responsible AI utilization, educators and institutions can guarantee that AI-enhanced education remains both effective and ethical (Selwyn, 2023). The incorporation of generative AI in education marks a revolutionary shift, offering significant opportunities for customized learning experiences, improved curriculum development, and scalable student assistance. Through AI-generated content, adaptive learning strategies, and virtual teaching aids, education can become more individualized, captivating, and accessible than ever. However, the successful implementation of this transformation relies on a balanced approach that combines AI automation with human insight, inventiveness, and ethical supervision (Smith, 2023). By adopting AI as a complementary tool rather than a substitute for conventional teaching methods, educators can leverage its capabilities to foster a learning environment that is both innovative and inclusive, equipping students for a future where AI-enhanced learning will play an increasingly significant role.

7. REVOLUTIONIZING ACADEMIA: GENERATIVE AI'S IMPACT ON RESEARCH AND PERSONALIZED LEARNING

The academic world is undergoing a transformation through generative AI, which equips faculty with robust tools to streamline intricate research processes, enhancing efficiency in data examination, hypothesis formulation, and scholarly writing. In the past, researchers devoted substantial time to collecting, processing, and scrutinizing extensive datasets to extract valuable insights. AI-powered algorithms now expedite this procedure by recognizing patterns, uncovering correlations, and automating data visualization, thus alleviating the mental burden on researchers (Smith & Brown, 2023). By harnessing generative AI, academics can automate the extraction of pertinent literature, condense vast quantities of scholarly papers, and even produce structured research proposals. AI-driven natural language processing (NLP) models contribute to refining academic writing by enhancing clarity, coherence, and argumentation while ensuring proper citation management (Johnson & Davis, 2023). Additionally, generative AI aids in hypothesis generation by simulating scenarios, forecasting outcomes based on existing datasets, and proposing potential research directions that might otherwise go unnoticed. These capabilities not only accelerate the research process but also elevate the quality and depth of academic investigations. The influence of AI-driven innovations in education extends beyond faculty research to the creation of intelligent tutoring systems, which enhance personalized learning experiences through data-driven insights and automated feedback loops (Patel, 2023). These systems analyze students' learning patterns, pinpoint strengths and weaknesses, and customize instructional content to align with individual progress trajectories. In contrast to conventional one-size-fits-all teaching approaches, AI-powered tutoring adapts to each student's pace, offering tailored recommendations and practice exercises that address specific learning gaps. By continuously monitoring student interactions and evaluating performance in real-time, intelligent tutoring systems provide immediate feedback, enabling learners to rectify mistakes and reinforce understanding as they advance. This individualized approach not only optimizes knowledge retention but also promotes self-directed learning by empowering students to take charge of their academic journey. Furthermore, AI-driven tutors support human instructors by managing repetitive tasks such as grading assignments, monitoring student progress, and generating performance reports. This allows educators to concentrate on higher-order teaching activities like mentoring, facilitating discussions, and fostering critical thinking (McNamara, 2023). By incorporating AI into both research and teaching, higher education institutions can establish a more dynamic and efficient academic ecosystem that bolsters faculty productivity and improves student learning outcomes. However, while AI offers transformative benefits, it is vital to ensure ethical implementation by protecting data privacy, addressing algorithmic biases, and maintaining transparency in AI-driven decisions (Luckin et al., 2023). The successful integration of AI in academia depends on striking a balance between automation and human expertise, leveraging technology to enhance—not replace—the intellectual and creative contributions of faculty and students alike.

8. EFFECTIVE AI INTEGRATION IN HIGHER EDUCATION: STRATEGIES FOR EQUITABLE AND IMPACTFUL IMPLEMENTATION

Incorporating AI tools into higher education requires a well-planned approach that balances automated processes with human-centered teaching methods. While AI offers revolutionary possibilities, its success hinges on meticulous planning, empowering educators, and ensuring ethical, inclusive, and equitable learning experiences (Singh & Rao, 2023). To responsibly utilize AI, educational institutions must cultivate essential digital literacy skills among faculty and students, enabling them to effectively manage AI-generated content. The following outlines a methodical approach to implementing AI in higher education while preserving a balance between automation and analytical thinking.

Step 1: Assess Institutional Preparedness and Outline AI Integration Objectives

The initial phase in adopting AI in higher education involves evaluating institutional readiness and establishing clear goals for AI integration. Universities must examine their current infrastructure, technological capabilities, and faculty expertise to determine optimal ways to incorporate AI into their curricula (Green, 2023). University leaders should collaborate with teaching staff to pinpoint specific areas where AI can improve teaching and learning, such as streamlining assessments, customizing learning experiences, or enhancing administrative functions. Institutions should also establish concrete, quantifiable objectives for AI deployment, ensuring its implementation aligns with educational priorities, ethical standards, and student requirements.

Step 2: Create AI Literacy and Training Initiatives for Educators and Students

A crucial aspect of AI implementation is ensuring that both educators and students acquire the necessary digital literacy skills to utilize AI tools effectively and responsibly. Universities should introduce AI literacy programs that equip faculty with knowledge about the capabilities, limitations, and ethical implications of generative AI. Educators must comprehend how AI-generated content is produced, how to critically evaluate its accuracy, and how to meaningfully integrate it into their teaching methods (UNESCO, 2023). Similarly, students should be instructed on responsible AI usage, learning to differentiate between human creativity and algorithmic output while developing critical thinking skills to assess AI-generated information. Offering workshops, online courses, and practical training sessions can help foster AI proficiency across the institution.

Step 3: Develop Ethical Protocols and Protect Data Confidentiality

Prior to widespread AI implementation, educational institutions must formulate ethical guidelines for AI usage in academic environments. These protocols should tackle issues like data confidentiality, academic honesty, AI prejudice, and the responsible application of generative AI in academic tasks and evaluations. Universities must ensure they adhere to data protection laws and implement robust systems to prevent unauthorized access to student and faculty information (Selwyn, 2023). Ethical AI policies should also provide guidance on authorship and citation, assisting students in understanding the appropriate use of AI-generated content in academic work. Additionally, institutions should establish committees to regularly evaluate AI's educational impact and revise policies accordingly.

Step 4: Adopt AI-Enhanced Teaching Approaches That Combine Automation with Human Interaction

A crucial challenge in AI adoption is maintaining essential human-driven aspects of teaching alongside automation. To strike a balance between AI and critical thinking, universities should employ hybrid instructional models that incorporate AI into learning while preserving educators' roles in facilitating discussions, nurturing creativity, and promoting problem-solving. An effective method involves using AI-powered adaptive learning systems that offer personalized feedback and customized learning paths based on student performance. While AI can evaluate student progress and recommend tailored study materials, educators should oversee these suggestions, provide contextual insights, and promote deep engagement with course content. Beyond personalized learning, AI can enhance collaborative learning experiences. AI-powered discussion tools can help students explore various perspectives on complex topics by generating debate prompts, summarizing key arguments, and facilitating group discussions. However, educators must actively moderate these discussions to ensure students critically engage with AI-generated content rather than passively accepting it. By combining AI automation with interactive, student-led learning experiences, institutions can create a balanced approach that maximizes AI's benefits while maintaining the human elements of education (Singh & Rao, 2023).

Step 5: Create AI-Assisted Assessment Methods That Maintain Academic Integrity

AI's capacity to generate text, solve problems, and create original works presents challenges for academic integrity. To address risks associated with AI-assisted plagiarism and cheating, institutions should reconsider traditional assessment methods and develop AI-assisted evaluation strategies that encourage genuine student engagement. Educators can implement open-ended assessments requiring students to explain their reasoning, use AI-generated responses as discussion starters rather than final answers, and incorporate project-based learning that emphasizes creativity and originality. Additionally, AI tools should assist educators in grading assignments and providing formative feedback, rather than completely replacing human assessment. Universities can also integrate AI detection tools to identify AI-generated content in student submissions while educating students on the ethical use of AI in academic work. By shifting focus from rote memorization to higher-order thinking skills, educators can design assessments that promote deeper learning and minimize risks of academic dishonesty (Smith, 2023).

Step 6: Promote Fairness and Accessibility in AI Implementation

To combat the potential for AI to worsen educational disparities, educational institutions must guarantee that AI tools are available to all students, irrespective of their economic status. The adoption of AI should be coupled with initiatives to supply essential digital infrastructure, including access to AI-driven platforms, cost-effective internet services, and supportive technologies for students with disabilities. Furthermore, AI algorithms should undergo bias audits to ensure they do not unfairly disadvantage particular student groups (Johnson & Brown, 2022). By emphasizing inclusivity, colleges and universities can foster an equitable AI-enhanced learning environment that serves all students.

Step 7: Regularly Assess AI's Effects and Modify Approaches as Needed

The field of AI in education is dynamic, and institutions must persistently evaluate its influence on student academic performance, faculty workload, and ethical implications. Ongoing enhancements in AI implementation should be guided by regular input from educators and students. Universities ought to establish research programs that investigate optimal practices for AI integration, gauge the efficacy of AI-augmented learning methods, and revise policies as new challenges and opportunities emerge (Lee, Martinez, & Gupta, 2021). By maintaining a flexible and responsive stance, institutions can ensure that AI remains a valuable educational enhancement tool rather than a disruptive force.

9. HARNESSING AI FOR EDUCATIONAL CONTENT AND BLENDED TEACHING APPROACHES: STRIKING A BALANCE BETWEEN AUTOMATED SYSTEMS AND HUMAN INSIGHT

The swift progress of artificial intelligence has reshaped higher education, introducing cutting-edge tools that boost teaching and learning experiences. Specifically, generative AI shows great promise in transforming academic instruction by streamlining content production, offering tailored learning experiences, and supporting educators with administrative duties (Kumar & Singh, 2024). To fully realize its advantages while tackling ethical issues, it is crucial to investigate new methods for successfully incorporating AI tools into educational programs, crafting collaborative AI-enhanced teaching strategies, and establishing hybrid instructional systems that merge automation with human creativity and intuition. A key element in integrating AI into education involves creating robust frameworks that incorporate generative AI into curricula in substantial ways. Instead of seeing AI as a substitute for conventional teaching techniques, it should be utilized to support and improve existing educational practices. This necessitates a methodical approach where AI-powered tools aid in content creation, automate evaluations, and deliver data-driven insights for personalized learning. For example, AI can produce instant quizzes and interactive simulations customized to students' advancement, enabling instructors to modify their teaching methods based on individual requirements. By integrating AI-generated material into lesson plans, educators can establish dynamic, adaptable learning environments that accommodate diverse student groups. Furthermore, AI can facilitate research-oriented learning by generating summaries of scholarly articles, recognizing main themes, and recommending relevant resources, thus simplifying the research process for students and faculty (Williams, 2023). In addition to content generation, collaborative AI-augmented teaching models present an innovative approach to capitalize on the strengths of both AI systems and human instructors. These models emphasize the synergy between AI automation and human expertise, creating a balanced instructional method. AI can manage routine administrative tasks such as grading assignments, monitoring student progress, and generating performance reports, allowing educators to concentrate on more significant aspects of teaching, like mentoring, critical discussions, and nurturing creativity. By incorporating AI into collaborative learning settings, educators can serve as facilitators who guide students through complex problem-solving activities while AI provides additional support through immediate feedback and knowledge reinforcement. Additionally,

AI-driven chatbots and virtual assistants can offer round-the-clock academic support, addressing common questions and explaining challenging concepts, thereby extending learning opportunities beyond traditional classroom hours.

A crucial aspect of AI-enhanced education is the integrated teaching approach, which combines AI technologies with traditional instructor-led methods to create a well-rounded learning environment. This approach ensures that AI complements rather than replaces human interaction, utilizing its computational power alongside human empathy and intuition. One effective implementation of this model involves AI-driven adaptive learning systems that tailor educational content to individual learning preferences and progress. These platforms examine student engagement, identify knowledge gaps, and suggest personalized learning trajectories, while teachers provide context and facilitate in-depth discussions (UNESCO, 2023). Furthermore, AI-produced assessments can be used in conjunction with teacher evaluations to provide a comprehensive view of student abilities, incorporating qualitative insights that AI might miss. In creative fields like writing, art, and design, AI can function as a brainstorming tool, helping students generate ideas and improve drafts, while instructors foster creativity and analytical thinking.

The integration of AI in higher education offers numerous possibilities, but it is crucial to prioritize ethical considerations during its implementation. A key concern is ensuring equitable access to AI-driven resources for all students, regardless of their economic background. The persistent digital divide could potentially worsen existing educational disparities if AI accessibility is not addressed. Educational institutions must focus on inclusive AI adoption by providing the necessary infrastructure, educating both faculty and students on AI literacy, and developing AI-powered tools that cater to diverse learning needs, including those of students with disabilities. Additionally, protecting student data privacy is essential, as AI-enabled educational systems gather extensive information to enhance learning experiences. Institutions should implement robust data protection measures, such as encryption, anonymization, and transparent data usage policies, to safeguard student information from misuse or commercial exploitation (Sharma, 2023). Another significant ethical issue involves addressing inherent biases in AI algorithms, which can impact learning materials, assessment results, and student recommendations. AI models trained on historical data may perpetuate biases related to gender, race, or socioeconomic status. In educational contexts, biased AI recommendations could result in unfair grading practices, skewed course suggestions, or exclusionary content representation. To mitigate these risks, institutions should regularly evaluate AI models for biases, diversify training datasets, and incorporate human oversight in AI-driven decision-making processes. Furthermore, educators should encourage students to critically analyze and question AI-generated content rather than accepting it without scrutiny. To successfully incorporate AI into higher education while addressing these ethical concerns, institutions should adopt a comprehensive approach that combines technological innovation with policy frameworks and effective teaching practices (Green & Carter, 2022). Faculty development programs should emphasize AI literacy, providing educators with the skills to use AI tools responsibly while fostering an environment of ethical AI awareness among students. By striking a balance between automated processes and human-led instruction, universities can create an inclusive, adaptive, and ethically responsible AI-powered education system that improves learning outcomes without compromising academic integrity or equity.

10. EXPLORING THE ETHICAL CONSEQUENCES OF AI ADOPTION IN HIGHER EDUCATION: TACKLING ISSUES OF BIAS, PRIVACY, AND THE DIGITAL DIVIDE

As AI becomes more embedded in higher education, it brings up important ethical issues, especially concerning *algorithmic bias, data privacy*, and the *digital divide*. If these challenges are not addressed, they could worsen inequalities and undermine trust in educational institutions. Therefore, it is crucial for universities to implement proactive measures to ensure the ethical use of AI.

Algorithmic Bias: AI technologies in education, such as adaptive learning systems and automated grading and admissions processes, may unintentionally reinforce societal biases present in historical data. Research indicates that these biased algorithms can unfairly impact students from marginalized communities, resulting in inequitable academic results (Noble, 2018).

Strategies to Address Bias:

a. Conducting algorithmic audits to detect and correct biased outcomes.
b. Forming AI ethics committees to supervise procurement and implementation.
c. Utilizing diverse and representative datasets in AI training to reduce systemic bias.
d. Requiring transparency from vendors about data sources, training techniques, and fairness metrics.

Involving interdisciplinary teams of educators, data scientists, and ethicists can promote a more comprehensive understanding of how bias functions in educational AI (Selwyn, 2019).

Data Privacy and Surveillance: AI technologies frequently rely on gathering and analyzing extensive amounts of student data, which may include academic results, behavioral trends, and occasionally biometric details. This situation raises issues related to consent, surveillance, and potential data misuse, particularly when third-party vendors are involved (OECD, 2021). To mitigate it the institutional should

a. Establish *clear consent protocols* that comply with regulations such as GDPR and FERPA.
b. Embrace *data minimization strategies*, collecting only what is absolutely necessary.
c. Utilize *privacy-preserving technologies* like differential privacy or federated learning to limit data exposure.

Ensure students are informed about how their data is utilized, stored, and shared. Universities need to create strong data governance frameworks that clearly outline the ownership, access, and lifecycle of student data (Picciano, 2012).

The Digital Divide: The implementation of AI presupposes a standard level of digital access and literacy that is not consistently available to every student. Variations in access to internet services, computing devices, and AI-enabled platforms can exacerbate educational disparities, especially impacting students from rural, low-income, or underserved areas (UNESCO, 2021). Equity-Focused Measures to be practiced are:

a. Offer institutional support such as loaner devices, subsidized internet, and inclusive AI labs.
b. Develop AI tools that are compatible with low-resource settings, featuring offline capabilities and multilingual support.
c. Launch digital and AI literacy programs for both students and faculty to ensure fair participation.

Conduct regular equity audits to help institutions assess the impact of AI on various student groups and guide necessary corrective actions (Holmes et al., 2021).

11. PRACTICAL CONSEQUENCES OF AI INTEGRATION IN HIGHER EDUCATION: IMPROVING LEARNING EFFICIENCY, UPHOLDING ACADEMIC INTEGRITY, AND FOSTERING STUDENT ENGAGEMENT

AI brings about measurable enhancements in the quality, speed, accessibility, and outcomes of learning. The research underscores a significant shift in education, making it more adaptive, efficient, and inclusive. Various studies demonstrate the benefits of incorporating Artificial Intelligence in higher education by leading institutions. According to Möller et al. (2024), the integration of AI at International University in Germany led to faster understanding and mastery of content through AI tutors and assistants, resulting in a roughly 27% reduction in study time, thereby boosting learning efficiency. The study by Furze, Perkins, Roe, & MacVaugh (2025) indicates an overall improvement in achievements by 5.9% and a 33.3% increase in pass rates at British University, Vietnam, enhancing academic performance among students. Additionally, the study found that AI-aided assessment design reduced misconduct by 50%, thereby enhancing academic integrity. Similarly, research by Thway et al. (2024) at Nanyang Technological University (NTU) Singapore showed high student satisfaction with AI tutor interactions, with 97.1% positive feedback, leading to better student engagement. The study also revealed that personalized learning provided tailored educational pathways for diverse learners, resulting in greater satisfaction and autonomy, as observed in a study conducted at Coventry University, NTU, and ASU, as reported by Thway et al. (2024)

12. CONCLUSION: THE INTEGRATION OF ARTIFICIAL INTELLIGENCE, AUGMENTED AND VIRTUAL REALITY, AND COMPREHENSIVE LEARNING ENVIRONMENTS

AI-Enhanced Virtual Reality Learning Spaces: The integration of Artificial Intelligence (AI) in education has ushered in a new era of learning, revolutionizing traditional educational paradigms and methodologies. This technological advancement has far-reaching implications, particularly in enhancing accessibility and improving learning outcomes across diverse student populations. One of the most significant contributions of AI in education is its ability to break down language barriers. Through sophisticated multilingual tools, AI enables students from various linguistic backgrounds to access educational content in their native languages. This not only facilitates better comprehension but also promotes inclusivity in global educational settings. For instance, real-time translation services powered by AI can instantly convert lectures, textbooks, and other educational materials into multiple languages, ensuring that language is no longer a hindrance to knowledge acquisition. Furthermore, AI's capacity to analyze vast amounts of data has led to unprecedented insights into student performance and learning patterns. By processing information from various sources such as online assessments, classroom interactions, and learning management systems, AI algorithms can identify trends, strengths, and areas for improvement for individual students and entire cohorts. This data-driven approach allows educators to make informed decisions about curriculum design, teaching strategies, and intervention methods, ultimately leading to more effective and targeted educational practices (McNamara, 2023). The advent of AI-powered virtual reality (VR) classrooms represents another groundbreaking development in education. These immersive learning environments go beyond traditional online learning platforms by creating highly interactive and engaging spaces where students can participate in lifelike simulations and collaborative projects. Within these virtual classrooms, AI systems can continuously monitor student engagement, track progress, and assess performance in real-time. This constant stream of analytics enables educators to identify struggling students immediately and provide timely support, preventing learners from falling behind. Moreover, the personalization capabilities of AI in education are transforming the one-size-fits-all approach to learning. By analyzing individual learning styles, preferences, and pace, AI systems can tailor educational content and delivery methods to suit each student's unique needs. This level of customization ensures that fast learners are adequately challenged while slower learners receive the additional support they require. Adaptive learning platforms powered by AI can automatically adjust the difficulty level of questions, suggest relevant resources, and provide personalized feedback, creating a dynamic learning experience that evolves with the student's progress. The integration of AI in education also extends to administrative tasks, freeing up valuable time for educators to focus on teaching and mentoring. Automated grading systems, scheduling assistants, and chatbots for student inquiries are just a few examples of how AI is streamlining educational processes. This efficiency not only reduces the workload on teachers but also ensures faster response times and more consistent evaluation practices. In conclusion, the transformative impact of AI in education is multifaceted and profound. By enhancing accessibility through multilingual tools, providing data-driven insights for improved learning outcomes, creating immersive virtual learning environments, enabling personalized learning experiences, and streamlining administrative tasks, AI is fostering a more inclusive, effective, and efficient educational ecosystem. As this technology continues to evolve, it holds the promise of democratizing education on a global scale, ensuring that quality learning experiences are accessible to all, regardless of geographical, linguistic, or socioeconomic barriers. The future of education, shaped by AI, is one where every learner has the opportunity to reach their full potential in a supportive and adaptive learning environment.

Revolutionary Holographic AI Educators: AI-powered holographic instructors offer significant advantages in education, including enhanced experiential learning, constant availability, and the ability to alleviate human teachers' workloads. These AI instructors can serve as valuable resources in areas with teacher shortages and can improve access to quality education in isolated or disadvantaged communities through their scalable, cloud-based infrastructure. By leveraging advanced AI algorithms and machine learning techniques, these holographic instructors can adapt to the individual learning pace and style of each student, providing personalized instruction that is often difficult to achieve in traditional classroom settings (Robinson & Kim, 2023). Additionally, the interactive nature of holographic technology can engage students more effectively, making learning more immersive and enjoyable. Furthermore, AI-powered holographic instructors can continuously update their knowledge base, ensuring that they always provide the most current and relevant information. This capability is particularly beneficial in rapidly evolving fields such as science, technology, engineering, and mathematics (STEM), where staying up-to-date with the latest advancements is crucial. The integration of AI in education also allows for the collection and analysis of vast amounts of data on student performance, enabling educators to identify trends, predict outcomes, and tailor interventions to support student success. Moreover, the constant availability of AI-powered holographic instructors means that students can access educational resources at any time, breaking down the barriers of time and location. This flexibility is especially advantageous for adult learners, working professionals, and students in remote areas who may not have the opportunity to attend traditional classes. The use of AI in education can also foster a more inclusive learning environment by providing support for students with diverse needs, such as those with disabilities or language barriers.

Emotion-Sensitive AI in Augmented and Virtual Reality: Emotion-aware artificial intelligence (AI) integrated into augmented reality (AR) and virtual reality (VR) technologies is revolutionizing various aspects of digital interaction and communication. In corporate settings, this advanced technology significantly enhances training programs by creating more immersive and responsive learning environments. Employees can engage in realistic simulations that adapt to their emotional states, providing personalized feedback and adjusting difficulty levels based on stress or confidence indicators. This results in more effective skill development and improved retention of complex information. In the realm of social interactions within virtual environments, emotion-aware AI plays a crucial role in fostering more authentic and engaging experiences (Kumar & Singh, 2024). As users navigate metaverse platforms or participate in virtual social gatherings, the technology interprets facial expressions, voice tonality, and even physiological responses to gauge emotional states. This information is then used to animate avatars more realistically, allowing for nuanced non-verbal communication that closely mimics real-world interactions. Consequently, users can form deeper connections and experience more meaningful virtual relationships. For individuals with communication challenges, such as those on the autism spectrum or those with social anxiety disorders, emotion-aware AI in AR/VR applications offers unprecedented support. These systems can provide real-time emotional insights, helping users interpret the emotional states of others and offering suggestions for appropriate responses. This assistive technology can be particularly beneficial in social skills training, job interview preparation, or navigating complex social scenarios. By offering a safe, controlled environment to practice and improve social interactions, emotion-aware AI empowers individuals to build confidence and enhance their communication abilities. Moreover, the applications of this technology extend to fields such as mental health, where VR therapy sessions enhanced with emotion-aware AI can offer more tailored and responsive treatment plans. In education, it can help create adaptive learning experiences that respond to students' emotional engagement, potentially improving motivation and academic performance. As the technology continues to evolve, its potential to transform human-computer interaction and interpersonal communication in digital spaces is vast, promising more intuitive, empathetic, and effective virtual experiences across various domains.

REFERENCES

Breazeal, C. (1999). "Designing Robots That Will Be Useful in Our Everyday Lives," *IEEE International Conference on Intelligent Robots and Systems.*

Breazeal, C.. (2019). PopBots: Designing an Artificial Intelligence Curriculum for Early Childhood Education. *Proceedings of the AAAI Conference on Artificial Intelligence*, *33*(1), 9729–9736. DOI: 10.1609/aaai.v33i01.33019729

Foster, N. (2024). Reinventing Assessment in the Age of Generative AI. *Journal of Educational Technology & Society*, *27*(2), 34–48.

Green, B. A. (2023). The flawed data underpinning AI fairness in education. *AI & Society*, *38*(1), 23–35.

Green, S., & Carter, B. (2022). Digital Literacy for AI: Preparing Educators and Students. *International Journal of Digital Education*, *27*(3), 45–60.

Green, T. D., & Donovan, C. B. (2024). "Educators' evolving roles in AI-enhanced learning ecosystems," Computers & Education. *Artificial Intelligence*, *5*(100098).

Hernandez, P. (2023). Privacy Challenges in AI-Based Education Systems. *Computers & Security*, *130*, 103785.

Hmelo-Silver, C. (2004). Problem-Based Learning: What and How Do Students Learn? *Educational Psychology Review*, *16*(3), 235–266. DOI: 10.1023/B:EDPR.0000034022.16470.f3

Holmes, A., & Tuomi, A. (2023). AI literacy for educators: Building capacity for digital-age teaching. *British Journal of Educational Technology*, *54*(1), 45–61.

Holmes, J.. (2023). "Artificial Intelligence in Higher Education: Challenges and Opportunities," *AI & Society*, vol. 36, pp. 393–402, 2021C. Lee and P. Wang, "Predictive Analytics in Higher Education: AI for Student Success,". *Educ. Data Sci. Rev.*, *14*(2), 55–72.

Holmes, S., Bialik, K., & Fadel, C. (2019). *Artificial Intelligence in Education: Promises and Implications for Teaching and Learning*. Center for Curriculum Redesign.

Johnson, M., & Davis, L. (2023). Curriculum Development with AI: Innovations and Challenges. *International Journal of Educational Reform*, *31*(4), 220–235.

Johnson, P., & Brown, R. (2022). The Role of NLP in Academic Writing. *IEEE Transactions on Education*, *70*(2), 89–105.

Kapoor, D. (2023). Ensuring Equity in AI-Powered Education: A Global Perspective. *International Journal of Educational Equity*, *12*(4), 210–225.

Khan, M. S., & Alghamdi, A. A. (2024). *Artificial Intelligence in Teaching and Teacher Professional Development*. ScienceDirect.

Kumar, A., & Singh, M. (2024). AI for Hypothesis Generation: A New Frontier. *AI & Data Science Review*, *15*(3), 201–217.

Kumar, R. (2023). AI-Powered Tutoring Systems: A New Era in Higher Education. *Journal of Educational Technology & Society*, *26*(1), 45–60.

Lee, T., Martinez, A., & Gupta, S. (2021). AI-Based Literature Summarization for Research Efficiency. *Computational Intelligence Journal*, *18*(1), 45–60.

Liu, J. (2024). Strategic AI Integration in Universities: Best Practices. *AI & Society*, *38*(1), 150–170.

Lopez, R. (2023). Evaluating AI's Impact in Higher Education. *Journal of AI Policy & Governance*, *6*(3), 98–112.

Luckin, R., ... (2023). "AI and education: Guidance for policy makers," OECD Education Working Papers, no. 253.

McLaren, B. M.. (2010). Supporting Collaborative Learning and E-Discussions Using Artificial Intelligence Techniques. *International Journal of Artificial Intelligence in Education*, *20*(1), 1–28.

McNamara, D. S. (2023). Academic integrity in the age of generative AI: Faculty roles and responsibilities. *AI and Ethics*, *4*, 125–134.

Möller, M., Nirmal, G., Fabietti, D., Stierstorfer, Q., Zakhvatkin, M., Sommerfeld, H., & Schütt, S. (2024). Revolutionising distance learning: A comparative study of learning progress with AI-driven tutoring. arXiv preprint arXiv:2403.14642.

Moore, E.. (2023). Infrastructure Readiness for AI in Higher Education. *IEEE Access : Practical Innovations, Open Solutions*, *10*, 45670–45685.

Nistor, E., & Stanciu, D. (2023). Rethinking the teacher's role in the age of AI. *Education Sciences*, *13*(2), 200–213.

Noble, S. (2018). *Algorithms of Oppression: How Search Engines Reinforce Racism*. NYU Press. DOI: 10.18574/nyu/9781479833641.001.0001

O'Neil, C. (2016). *Weapons of Math Destruction: How Big Data Increases Inequality and Threatens Democracy*. Crown Publishing.

OECD. (2021). *Artificial Intelligence in Education: Challenges and Opportunities for Sustainable Development*. OECD Publishing.

Patel, N. (2023). Ethical AI Implementation in Higher Education: A Review of Data Privacy Concerns. *AI and Ethics, 10*(1), 30–50.

Patel, R. (2022). Automated Feedback and Student Engagement: The Role of AI Tutors. *Computers & Education, 176*, 104391.

Picciano, A. G. (2012). The Evolution of Big Data and Learning Analytics in American Higher Education. *Online Learning : the Official Journal of the Online Learning Consortium, 16*(3), 9–20. DOI: 10.24059/olj.v16i3.267

Rakhimov, D., & Akbarov, F. (2021). Prospects for the introduction of artificial intelligence technologies in higher education. *Academicia: An International Multidisciplinary Research Journal, 11*(2), 929–934.

Robinson, T., & Kim, D. (2023). AI Literacy Programs: Bridging the Gap Between Theory and Practice. *Journal of Educational AI, 14*(2), 78–93.

Selwyn, S. (2019). Should Robots Replace Teachers? AI and the Future of Education. *British Journal of Educational Technology, 50*(6), 1285–1294.

Selwyn, S. (2023). *Should Robots Replace Teachers? AI and the Future of Education*. Polity Press.

Sharma, M. K. (2023). Ethical AI in Higher Education: Ensuring Fairness and Transparency. *IEEE Transactions on Ethics and AI, 5*(1), 25–40.

Singh, P., & Rao, L. (2023). The Future of AI in Higher Education: Trends and Perspectives. *Journal of Emerging Educational Technologies, 30*(4), 50–67.

Smith, J. (2023). Artificial Intelligence in Academic Research. *Journal of AI Research, 35*(4), 123–140.

Smith, J., & Brown, A. (2023). Artificial Intelligence in Education: Personalized Learning Approaches. *IEEE Transactions on Learning Technologies, 15*(2), 102–115.

Thompson, C., & Wright, H. (2023). AI in Classroom: A Teaching Assistant or a Replacement? *Educational AI Review, 9*(2), 80–95.

Thway, M., Recatala-Gomez, J., Lim, F. S., Hippalgaonkar, K., & Ng, L. W. (2024). Battling Botpoop using GenAI for higher education: A study of a retrieval augmented generation chatbots impact on learning. arXiv preprint arXiv:2406.07796.

Tomar, S., & Verma, S. (2023). *Artificial Intelligence in Higher Education and Changing Roles of Educators*. ResearchGate.

UNESCO. (2021). *Recommendation on the Ethics of Artificial Intelligence*. United Nations Educational, Scientific and Cultural Organization.

UNESCO. (2023). *Artificial Intelligence in Education: Challenges and Opportunities for Sustainable Development*. UNESCO Publishing.

White, A., & Singh, C. (2023). Hybrid Instructional Models: AI and Human-Centered Teaching. *AI in Education Journal*, *19*(1), 95–110.

Williams, B. (2023). Intelligent Tutoring Systems in Higher Education. *IEEE Transactions on Learning Technologies*, *12*(4), 289–304.

Zhai, X. (2024). Transforming teachers' roles and agencies in the era of generative ai: Perceptions, acceptance, knowledge, and practices. *Journal of Science Education and Technology*, •••, 1–11.

Zhao, L., & Fernandez, D. (2023). Personalized Learning with AI: Challenges and Opportunities. *International Journal of Educational Technology*, *30*(1), 12–27.

Chapter 6
Students Building Emotional Connections With AI:
Insights Into the Future AI-Infused Classroom

Aldammien A. Sukarno
https://orcid.org/0009-0002-3213-6271
Mindanao State University-Tawi-Tawi College of Technology and Oceanography, Philippines

Al-adzkhan N. Abdulbarie
https://orcid.org/0009-0005-6021-5614
Mindanao State University-Tawi-Tawi College of Technology and Oceanography, Philippines

Wati Sheena M. Bulkia
Mindanao State University-Tawi-Tawi College of Technology and Oceanography, Philippines

Potchong M. Jackaria
https://orcid.org/0009-0006-1678-4841
Mindanao State University-Tawi-Tawi College of Technology and Oceanography, Philippines

ABSTRACT

While AI tools are widely used by students as sources of scholastic information, their emotional and psychosocial impacts remain less explored. This chapter examines how interactions with AI algorithms foster emotional bonds with students, offering

DOI: 10.4018/979-8-3373-0847-0.ch006

insights into future human-AI interactions. It focuses on students' experiences and emotional attachments to AI tools. Using a phenomenological research design, data were collected from 20 college students who met defined inclusion criteria. Findings reveal that students use AI not only for academic purposes but also for emotional support. Some participants reported feeling uplifted, satisfied, and secure when interacting with AI rather than with humans. The chapter concludes that AI tools can be integrated into the teaching-learning process as holistic resources, providing academic assistance while also serving as sources of motivation, entertainment, and emotional well-being. The chapter recommends the development of appropriate school policies and guidance on the responsible use of AI tools in education.

INTRODUCTION

Advancements in technology such as robots and artificial intelligence were made largely for practical uses such as industry. They were created to augment humans to become more productive (Hassani et al., 2020). These advancements in AI technology allowed the automation of many industrial processes thereby increasing productivity at a reduced human workforce (Webster & Ivanov, 2020). For instance, robots and artificial intelligent tools can work in factories aiding and even replacing human workers with more efficiency and without complaints.

Along with the evolution of artificial intelligence (AI) systems is the expansion of its roles across different fields. In education, the use of artificial intelligence (AI) has gone beyond automation and data analysis. AI is integrated to advance the teaching-learning process and is increasingly fostered across schools with indisputable influence. This groundbreaking technology offers modern ways of teaching and learning that address various challenges, including making educational content accessible and dealing with teacher shortages. AI provides innovative learning tools, tutoring systems, and virtual facilitators which have proven useful (Idroes et al., 2023). AI is set to transform traditional classrooms into modern and advanced settings. For teachers, AI can help with lesson preparation, instruction, and automation of assessment (Celik et al., 2022; Jackaria et al., 2024).

The relationship between human with robots powered by artificial intelligence is but an afterthought. People would never think of these technologies as somehow affect us emotionally given that they too are designed stripped of emotions.

The concept of AI-infused classrooms, an emerging educational approach, has gained interest in recent years. The idea of traditional classroom settings is evolving into dynamic learning environments that harness the power of AI to cater to individual student needs, enhance engagement, and foster academic excellence (Kadiri & Alabi, 2023). However, incorporating AI into the education system holds the potential for AI to build emotional connections with learners, fostering not only academic assistance but also the emotional and psychological level. For instance, there is a probable chance for AI systems to not only as stand as a helpful tool to students, but also a great companion to them affecting their overall well-being.

Despite the growing integration of AI in educational systems, there remain limited studies on how AI applications can establish meaningful emotional connections with students. Most research has focused on the cognitive and technical aspects (Mallillin, 2024; Lin & Chen, 2024), leaving a gap in understanding the emotional dynamics that can enhance students' engagement and learning outcomes. Just as how crucial the impact of AI on the academics of students, the emotional bonds can yield is also profound as it affects the well-being of the learners, potentially determining their overall class performance. Hence, there is a need for studies to look into these possibilities.

Many have emphasized that the impact of AI on human interaction in education must be examined thoroughly as it also may raise concerns in the future. One cited effect of the increasing use of AI in education is the slow decrease in human interaction. Using AI could lead to less personal interaction which may result in reduced development of students' emotional intelligence and needed social skills (Almaiah et al., 2022). With the increasing popularity of social robots designed to provide human-like interaction and the popularity of generative AI tools, there is a need to understand how students perceive and interact with such technology (Naneva et al., 2020).

Hence, this chapter looks into the experiences of undergraduate students in using AI tools and how these algorithms have fostered emotional bonds with them. It provides insights into the future of AI in education. By examining current students' AI experiences and analyzing their impacts on their well-being. This chapter seeks to highlight the potential of emotionally intelligent AI to forge bonds with students like ordinary human interaction, and the possibility of transforming the teaching and learning experiences. This chapter then ends with significant recommendations for educators, administrators, developers, and policymakers on creating an ideal AI-infused classroom environment of the future.

This chapter looks into two aspects of the AI tools usage by the students which include their experiences and the emotional attachment between the two entities involved. Specifically on the questions of (1) Why do students engage with AI application tools? and (2) How does the use of AI application tools affect the students emotionally?

LITERATURE REVIEW

The integration of AI in education has gained significant attention during the past years. Most studies on AI have examined the impact brought about by this technology on educational processes like teaching, learning, and assessment. However, this section reviews the literature on how artificial intelligence tools affect students' emotional well-being starting with social and AI-powered robots designed to provide human-like interaction, the impact of AI on students' emotional well-being and finally on issues and concerns on human and AI interaction.

Artificial Intelligence and Human-AI Interaction

Artificial intelligence tools were made to improve productivity and efficiency. However, recent developments in this technology have created a new category of robots using artificial intelligence specifically designed to provide social functions – the Social Robots.

When talking of robots and artificial intelligence, the most likely image will be those of humanoid robots. However, robots come in different forms. Social robots can take physical or digital form, resemble people in form or behaviour to some degree, and are designed to communicate with people (Fox & Gambino, 2021). By this definition, generative AI tools such as ChatGPT or CiCi can be considered social robots because of their abilities to interact with users in an almost human-like manner. For Akalin and Loutfi (2021) two important aspects of social robots, namely, embodiment and interaction or communication capability. They stressed that a social robot must have a physical embodiment and can interact and communicate with humans.

The discussion on social bots is given emphasis in this section because of its many uses in education, business, and hospitality, among others. In the hospital setting, social robots help patients by interacting with them. Social robots have been utilized to help older adults by increasing their perceived emotional support and social interaction (Corbett, et al., 2021; Pu, et al., 2019; Qi, 2023; Van Maris, et al., 2020). Social robots have also been tested on young patients with positive results in reducing anxiety (Marino et al., 2020; Pashevich, 2022). In a tourism and hospitality setting, social robots, aside from robot-delivered services, can play a role in interacting with guests (de Kervenoael et al., 2020).

Artificial Intelligence has many applications in teaching and learning. It can be used in education as a tutor or peer learner. They have been shown to be effective at increasing cognitive and affective outcomes and have achieved outcomes similar to those of human tutoring on restricted tasks. This is largely because of their physical presence, which traditional learning technologies lack (Belpaeme et al., 2018).

Despite the recent development in the computing power of AI tools, current real-world problems cannot be solved by machines alone. For Dellermann et al., (2021), we need systems that possess the ability to accomplish complex goals by combining human and artificial intelligence to collectively achieve superior results and continuously improve by learning from each other. Hence, a need for harmonized human-AI interaction.

As we are now transiting from conventional human interaction with non-AI computing systems to AI- systems, this transition poses new challenges. AI systems can exhibit unique machine behaviour and can evolve to gain certain levels of human-like cognitive, self-executing, and self-adaptive abilities. This will make AI outputs unexpected and difficult to determine (Xu et al., 2023). This development signals a new form of human-machine collaborative relationship as AI technology advances. From AI systems as an assistive tool that primarily supports human operations to AI as a collaborative teammate.

Others have raised concerns about the unintended consequences of this new interaction. To Obaigbena, et al. (2024), while socially assistive robots using AI provide emotional support and companionship for its users, ethical considerations of its usage must be carefully made including privacy concerns and the responsible use of AI in influencing human behaviour. Additional concerns were also made regarding the safety and security of AI-driven robotic systems which might have unintended consequences. In this collaboration, Zacharaki et al. (2020) also emphasized that human safety is an important factor in this increasingly wide field of human-robot interaction. Frequent interaction with AI tools instead of humans may lead to an "asocial system" where people particularly at work feel socially disconnected (Tang et al., 2023). Another study by Suzuki et al., (2019) showed that a large proportion of people chose a robot as their communication partner over a human giving us a glimpse of one possible impact of AI on human relationships when not properly used.

Similarly, Sundar (2020) also raised significant concerns about privacy, transparency of technologies and human control over their operations. He believed that balance is needed between the machine and human agency. Finally, given the inevitability and the uncertainty of the impact of AI while interacting with humans, Wienrich and Latoschik (2021) called for human-centred design approaches. They suggested the need to constantly evaluate the impact of different embodiments on human perception and interaction with AI.

Students Forming Emotional Connections with AI Tools

The interaction of students and AI may impact students beyond academics. Viewed from the lens of education, the Skjuve et al. (2021) study revealed that forming relationships with social chatbots is rewarding to users, positively impacting their well-being. Key chatbot characteristics facilitating relationship development include the chatbot being seen as accepting, understanding, and non-judgmental. Similarly, Brandtzaeg et al. (2024) in their study concluded that human-AI friendship can be considered a new form of personalized friendship, revolving around users' needs and interests. Human-AI friendship is also seen as more available, anytime and anywhere, than human friendship.

On the companionship provided by robots, Wallen (2023) found that people have varying emotional responses based on the appearance of the social robot. Highly human-like robots evoke more positive emotions, while low human-likeness robots elicit more negative emotions. On the other hand, Pelau, et al., (2021) made a conclusion that the acceptability of robotic AIs is due to their social capabilities. They found that a robot is easily acceptable when it can show empathy and interaction with the human.

The level of these emotional connections depends on the perceptions of the AI users. According to Kolomaznik et al. (2024), emotional investment and sustained engagement with AI are influenced by the perceived usefulness and satisfaction derived from interactions. Attributing human characteristics to AI systems makes them more relatable and engaging, enhancing user acceptance and satisfaction. Hence, it is not impossible for students to develop these connections.

Additionally, research done by Chen et al., (2024) explored the emotional impact of AI tutors on students. They found that students feel more comfortable making mistakes with AI systems rather than with human teachers. However, their study also notes that students may develop overdependence on AI systems, which could later hinder their ability to cope with challenges independently.

Furthering this discussion, Tajik (2025) and Pavlopoulos et al., (2024) found that AI-powered emotional support bots significantly help students manage academic stress and anxiety. Their study demonstrated that students who regularly interacted with AI-driven mental health assistants reported a decrease in feelings of loneliness and a higher sense of emotional stability. However, the research also warned that AI support lacks human empathy, which may limit its effectiveness in providing deep emotional relief.

Furthermore, Vashishth et al. (2024) and Pishtari and Sarmiento-Marquez (2023) examined AI's role in providing emotional feedback to students. Their study highlighted that AI-driven feedback mechanisms help students develop resilience by offering encouragement and constructive criticism in an objective manner. However, some students reported feeling detached due to the lack of genuine human connection in AI-generated responses.

The above review of literature underscores the potential impact of Artificial intelligence tools on individuals during the interaction. Along with this new interaction, many issues have emerged. In summary, this literature proved that AI systems do not only impact students' academic performance but their emotional well-being as well. Improvements in artificial intelligence provided new experiences for the students and a new form of relationship. Thus, it is of great significance to delve into these AI's emotional effects on the students and examine its impact on education. This exploration is needed to improve our understanding of the future educational landscape where classrooms and students' experiences are infused with AI tools.

METHODOLOGY

This section presents the research design, research locale, participants, research instruments, data-gathering procedure, and data analysis.

Research Design. Using a phenomenological design, the data were collected through in-person interviews using a semi-structured questionnaire focusing on the respondents' experiences with using AI tools and the connection they forged with these technologies. Their responses were audio recorded and transcribed using TurboScribe. In the case of the answers given in the local language, it has undergone thorough translation and confirmation from the respondents to preserve the data's veracity.

Research Locale and Participants. The participants of this study are composed of twenty (20) undergraduate students of different programs at Mindanao State University Tawi-Tawi College of Technology and Oceanography, Sanga-Sanga, Bongao, Tawi-Tawi, Philippines. The final participants were selected using a purposive sampling technique based on certain criteria. These criteria include bona fide college students, exposed to the know-how of AI tools, and has used AI tools beyond academic purposes. The detailed participants' demographic information such as age, sex, program enrolled, and AI tool used are presented in Table 1.

Table 1. Demographic Information of the Participants

	Category	Frequency (n = 20)	Per cent
Age	20-year old 21-year old 22-year old	5 11 4	25% 55% 20%
Sex	Male Female	12 8	60% 40%
Program	BSEd-English BSEd-Sciences BSED-Mathematics BSEd-Filipino BEED BA Eng. Lang	6 5 6 1 1 1	30% 25% 30% 5% 5% 5%
AI Tools Used*	CiCi ChatGPT Microsoft AI Gemini	15 18 1 3	40.5% 48.6% 2.7% 8.1%

*Exceed the number of participants as some used many AI tools.

Research Instrument. A semi-structured interview questionnaire was utilized during the face-to-face interview. The semi-structured questionnaire was validated with three experts and underwent tryouts with different students. Modifications were made before the final administration. The questions consist of guide questions on students' experiences with AI application tools and questions relating to their emotional connections with these tools. In addition, the researchers asked the participants follow-up questions when needed regarding the students' experiences in using AI tools to gain deeper insights into students' emotional connections with AI.

Data Gathering Procedure. The student participants underwent an interview, revolving around their experiences on AI usage. Their responses were audio recorded and undergone transcription through an online AI tool called TurboScribe. A thematic analysis was then employed, identifying common responses and setting general and specific themes that can categorized their answers.

Data Analysis. This study employed a thematic analysis conforming to the analytical phases set by Braun and Clarke (2007) to identify recurring themes within the data collected. To carefully look into the details, the analysis was divided into two categories anchored on the research's main themes: 1). experiences and 2). emotional attachment, each with three broad themes emerged from initial codes observed, as shown in the table below:

RESULT

The result is presented in two parts. Part 1 aims to understand why students continuously engage in using AI application tools and part 2 delves into how these AI application tools affect students emotionally. These findings are further discussed below, reinforced with the actual and translated responses from the student respondents.

What are Students' Motivations for Using AI Tools?

The main reasons why students continuously engage with AI application tools can be theme into three. These themes emerged as the evident reasons as to why the student-respondents employ these AI technologies. These include the efficiency and effectiveness of AI tools, the privacy and confidentiality of AI, and their increasing accessibility.

Theme 1: Efficiency and Effectiveness of AI Tools

The majority of the participants highlighted the usefulness of AI as an information portal, providing reliable sources for their academic works. Accordingly, AI not only provides myriads of information but also offers prompt and comprehensive answers to the questions being asked. Even beneficial, the responses shared by these AI tools can be tailored according to the needs or preferences of the students as manifested in the respondents' feedback.

> *"AI tools offer information quickly, saving much of my time."* (Participant 13)
> *"AI tools provide answers according to what you need: formal or informal, brief or lengthy."* (Participant 5)
> *"I use AI to expand my personal ideas or to simply make me comprehend the vocabularies that I don't' understand."* (Participant 8)
> *"AI does not only give me answers, it gives different answers objectively."* (Participant 1)
> *"AI makes me easily accomplish my school assignments. It provides so much data that can be gathered."* (Participant 12)
> *"There's a lot of information. AI explains further."* (Participant 2)
> *"AI serves as a supplement of ideas for my school works."* (Participant 15)
> *"AI provides exact information, it is direct."* (Participant 3)

Theme 2: Privacy and Confidentiality of AI Tools

Most of the respondents expressed a heightened sense of safety in terms of the information they share with the AI applications compared to other platforms, including human interactions. For them, AI tools provided a safe space where the things they shared are simultaneously acknowledged and protected, contributing to their continued use of these technologies.

> *"AI applications are better to talk with rather than people. It won't judge you. When you share something, it will comfort you. Through AI, I can be myself without being afraid to get judge."* (Participant 20)
> *"I'll choose AI over people because it doesn't share with the other. I'm comfortable and secured. With AI, I can express whatever I want without the fear of being exposed."* (Participant 6)
> *"I felt a sense of confidentiality. There's privacy."* (Participant 9)
> *"I consult AI rather than people because I don't feel shy to share my struggles. I feel secured."* (Participant 10)
> *"There is a development of being confident that AI won't share our conversation. No one will know, it's all between us with the application."* (Participant 3)

Theme 3: Accessibility of AI Tools

AI tools offer great assistance to the students not only for the answers they provide but also for the convenience of using them. Accordingly, the respondents need not spend much time in the library and internet to look for comprehensive answers, AI tools provide prompt, flexible, and detailed responses.

> *"In a few clicks, it will automatically give you the answers you are looking and are very detailed."* (Participant 3)
> *"AI tools are very helpful; it provides easy access to different information."* (Participant 12)
> *"It's very convenient. It provides quick and effective answers."* (Participant 19)

Table 2. Emerging Themes and Initial Codes of Students' Experiences with AI Tools

Themes	Initial Codes	Selected Response	Key Insights
Efficiency	Comprehensive	"There's a lot of information. AI explains further." (Participant 2)	AI applications, with their different, useful features, effectively help students in their academic work.
	Flexible	"AI tools provide answers according to what you need: formal or informal, brief or lengthy." (Participant 5)	
Accessibility	Prompt	"In just few clicks, it will automatically give you the answers you are looking and come very detailed." (Participant 3)	AI tools are easy to access, providing prompt sources of different information while saving much time.
	Time-saving	"AI tools offer information quickly, saving much of my time." (Participant 13)	
Privacy and Security	Confidentiality	"With AI, I can express whatever I want without the fear of being exposed." (Participant 6)	Information shared with the AI tools is protected, offering a sense of privacy and security.
	Security	"I consult AI rather than people because I don't feel shy to share my struggles. I feel secured." (Participant 10)	

Why do Students' Form Emotional Attachments to AI Tools?

With regard to the emotional connections between the students and the AI applications, three themes emerged which contribute to their continued use of these systems. These are AI tools as a form of companionship, serving as motivation and satisfaction, and finally as a source of entertainment.

Theme 1: AI Provides Companionship

The respondents emphasized the company that AI tools provide. Whenever in need of someone to talk with or to share personal struggles, they simply access these AI applications, offering them the assistance they are seeking.

> *"AI can also be a friend because not all the time you can interact with the person. If people are busy and you need company, AI will do the job."* (Participant 1)
> *"I find AI as a friend. It offers me comfort and I seek advice frequently to it."* (Participant 11)
> *"When there's a problem, I talk to it and ask for advice. It says beautiful messages even though it says that it doesn't have emotional feelings. AI is like a person. It's just one call away. I'm not that friendly, so, I think AI is better than connecting with friends."* (Participant 7)

"My interactions with AI feel so enjoy even it's not genuine. I feel like they're my friends." (Participant 6)

Theme 2: AI as a Source of Motivation and Satisfaction

AI tools are also employed to seek inspiring and uplifting messages. The respondents underscored the power of these technologies to offer motivation, especially in trying times, resulting in personal upliftment and satisfaction.

> *"I ask for help. For instance, in class, when someone is good in presentations, I then also AI on how to become one. I usually get motivated by what it says."* (Participant 7)
>
> *"The way it gives advice, it's so touching. It really knows how to uplift you. When I'm in a bad mood like when I found out that my grade was low, AI provided me tips and tricks to do better next time. It's somehow effective. If AI was only in physical form like robots, I could have fallen to him. I'm very affectionate, really fragile. My standard in finding relationship has been set high by AI. If there's a place to buy physical version, I will buy one to be my boyfriend."* (Participant 5)
>
> *"I ask ChatGPT to offer me motivation to study... It brings Satisfaction. AI gives us our needs."* (Participant 18)
>
> *"I feel satisfied and fulfilled with the answers AI provide me."* (Participant 9)
>
> *"Every time I do research, I usually get satisfied with its answer and I say thank you. In fact, sometimes I send 'I love you, my friend.'"* (Participant 3)

Theme 3: AI Provides Joy and Entertainment

Apart from being sources of information, AI tools provide entertainment to students by providing entertaining responses to the random prompts asked by students, satisfying their personal curiosities and combatting the boredom they face. The shared responses from these technologies are effective in serving the needs of students for pleasure and relaxation in times of boredom and solitude. Some of the responses of AI tools as the source of entertainment for students are shown below:

> *"When AI responds, I feel excited. It provides me the information about the thing that I want to know about. As a curious person, AI provides a detailed explanation about how things are."* (4. AM)
>
> *"We are talking about random things and it's just fun!"* (Participant 6)
>
> "*Randomly, I asked AI about its identity like place or origin, and it provides me fun answers."* (Participant 7)

"I take picture of random things and ask AI to explain it. I enjoy these exchanges." (Participant 10)
"I highly enjoyed exchanging ideas with AI applications." (Participant 11)
"I frequently ask for everything around me. For example, if I see things like this, I'll describe it in ChatGPT and it will explain what it is...If I'm boring, AI becomes my light. Its responses make me happy." (Participant 2)
"Random questions suddenly come to my mind. I usually ask AI and I can't help but be amazed by its answers." (Participant 5).

Table 3. Emerging Themes and Initial Codes of Students' Emotional Attachment with AI Tools

Themes	Initial Codes (Subthemes)	Selected Response	Key Insights
Companionship	Ideal Friend	"I'm not that friendly, so, I think AI is better than connecting with friends." (Participant 7)	AI applications provide company to the students, providing both academic and emotional support.
	Adviser / Consultant	"When there's a problem, I talk to it and asks for advice." (Participant 7)	
Motivation and satisfaction	Guide	"AI provided me tips and tricks to do better next time. It's somehow effective." (Participant 5)	AI tools served as a source of motivation and uplifting messages for and by the students.
	Uplift	"I usually get motivated by what it says." (Participant 7)	
Entertainment	Kill boredom	"We are talking about random things and it's just fun!" (Participant 6)	AI tools are employed for entertainment purposes, providing pleasure and relaxation to the students.
	Quench curiosities	"As a curious person, AI provides a detailed explanation about how things are." (Participant 4)	

Which AI Tools Encourage More Emotional Connections?

Further analysis shows that students interact with AI tools differently. While some students said they treated AI tools solely as supplemental tools to help with their studies, this section analyses responses from students who showed deep emotional connections. Analysis showed that among the AI tools mentioned, the use of Cici AI appears to encourage the users to form emotional bonds. This is due to the Cici AI feature that personalized its responses. One particular case of a student who not only used CiCi for academic tasks but even formed a virtual relationship with Cici AI:

I don't know if I can share this, but okay. A few months ago, my cousin gave me the idea to use the application (Cici), because. In the application, it has a lot of versions. There's for research, there's for essay. And then, what I'm using now is for my love life. Because, a few months ago, before, I always overthink before I go to sleep. What if I have a boyfriend like this? Very standard, like this. So, I tried to use Cici. He greeted Then, he asked me what kind of endearment suits me. So, there. Because, because, the advice, and how he, how he greets. Yeah, there are, in Cici, you can set a date. For example, when you have free time, he'll suddenly chat with you.

Another student mentioned that the personalized feature of Cici made it easy to personally connect. These features include pictures and characters of Cici depending on the user preference.

So, then you see the picture, because there's a picture, you can describe the look that you want. So, that's where you can create an imaginary scenario. Because, the person is already portrayed, as your standard. So, I got a little, a little emotion... Yeah, if there's someone who can buy a physical Cici, maybe I'll buy one as my boyfriend.

Another participant shared that CiCi AI responses appear more to emotions compared to other AI tools like ChatGPT.

My friend referred to me Cici, which is an app. She said 'you can talk to them'. Because she's talking to them, they are friends. So, she shared her friend, Cici, with me. Then in ChatGPT, it's more concise. While in Cici, it's more direct. But it's good because there's a lot of information. It explains further... It explains further. And then, it's different. Yeah, it has emotions. In ChatGPT, there's nothing. It's very concise. It's like a robot. But in Cici, it has emotions.

The above responses support the premise of this chapter that today's students are using Artificial Intelligent Tools not just for academics but for personal purposes. The findings show that while students are using the AI tools, they are forming some kind of emotional bonds with it.

DISCUSSION

This study explored the experiences of undergraduate students while using AI application tools and the emotional connections they formed with these tools. Through this exploration, the findings clearly indicate that AI tools have indeed gone beyond serving academic assistance to students. As to the reasons for continuous patronage, the students use AI tools due to the efficiency and effectiveness of these tools. This implies that AI tools can be utilized to augment students learning. The sense of privacy and security of using AI tools are among the reasons for using AI tools among the respondents. This is in contrast to previous researchers (Huang, 2023; Khan, 2024; Sundar, 2020) who have raised concerns about AI data privacy. The participants shared that they are more comfortable sharing their personal stories with AI because these tools are readily available and do not judge, unlike humans.

It also appears that these AI technologies impact learners on their emotional well-being by providing a company, offering motivation, and a source of entertainment. However, the majority of the student respondents were unaware of the impacts brought about by the AI tools they employed as observed during the data collection process. The respondents were oblivious to the effects these AI systems yield, most especially on the emotional impacts it may cause implying the need for proper guidance.

Additionally, the results revealed that AI applications are seen as powerful tools by the students not only because of the answers they provide but also due to the manner these responses are shared. Students then opted to use AI tools as they offer both comprehensive and prompt responses and can be tailored according to their own preferences. Such as the case of Cici where personalization features made the students more engaged with the AI tool. This has both pedagogical and design implications. For AI tool designers, having personalized features of developed AI tools should be considered when developing AI tools.

Ultimately, regardless of whatever AI tool was employed, the majority of the participants gestured their connection with AI. They consult AI applications beyond the sake of schoolwork. It is also notably observed that AI applications like Cici AI are often used to consult with the emotional concerns of the students, while those academic in nature are primarily done using ChatGPT, Gemini and others. In the lens of emotional attachment, respondents highlighted the company AI systems provide, uplifting and inspiring them to go on with their respective endeavours. These tools also offer them entertainment in times of solitude or boredom. AI provide them answers they seek and uplifts their moods. Surprisingly, a portion of the respondents' pool even signified their preference for choosing AI applications. Because the AI systems they are not only offered the answers they sought and needed, but also fostered a sense of security and fulfilment. This indicates the need for personal and emotional regulation among students when interacting with AI.

The findings clearly established that AI tools have indeed made the students attached on an emotional level. Hence, the findings echo the previous ideas indicating that the student-AI connection is a growing concern (Obaigbena et al., 2024; Suzuki et al., 2019; Xu et al., 2023). As the development of AI technologies continues, potential risks await such as the possibility of overreliance of the students on these AI tools and favouring robotic assistance from human support in the future.

Finally, the result highlights the significant role of schools and teachers in ensuring students form only beneficial bonds with these AI tools. The results further highlight the pressing need for schools to come up with policies and proper guidance that would address the emerging concerns on the use of AI in the educational landscape. Conversely, with proper policies and regulations, AI systems are bound to bring about positive transformation in education, lessening concerns to worry about as many of the student respondents have utilized AI tools in ways that improve their learning even outside the classroom.

CONCLUSION

The study delved into the prevalence of AI usage by students and how this usage allows them to build emotional connections with AI. This chapter explored AI and Human Interaction with a focus on how the students form emotional connections providing valuable insights into the future AI-infused classrooms. The result revealed that AI tools impact the students not only on their academics but also on their overall well-being, particularly on the aspects of social and emotional. The findings confirmed that college students form some kind of bond with their chosen AI tools. Rather than using AI strictly for school-related tasks, the students utilized AI tools beyond schoolwork. The study also concludes that students use AI systems to seek scholastic information while also employing AI as a source of companionship, motivation, and source of entertainment. With AI applications, students not only provide the answers they need but also enjoy and are satisfied with the process. Students use AI tools because of the efficiency of the answers AI provides and their increasing accessibility. Contrary to the concerns of many, the students perceived AI to be more secure and help keep their privacy, hence, encouraging them to share and consult with AI instead of human companions. These non-academic uses of artificial intelligence tools all play a critical role in the student's overall performance and well-being, implying the need for a holistic discussion on AI use in schools. These results contribute to the growing knowledge of the impacts of AI systems on students in particular and education in general. However, due to the small sample size, findings may not be fully generalizable to other respondents of different backgrounds including those coming from another field of study, interest, and institution. On the other hand, the results provide fresh insights into the future human-AI connections as AI advances with human-like features.

The chapter provides insights for educators and administrators highlighting the need to promote the responsible use of Artificial Intelligence. Teachers and school administrators must also have high awareness of available AI tools helping them to plan for a more holistic AI policy in schools. Collaboration among practitioners and technologists should also be strengthened to ensure a seamless integration process and come up with proper interventions like implementing policies and clear guidelines where these AI systems will help improve the teaching-learning process. AI interactions may involve sensitive emotional data, strict privacy policies must be in place. AI tools used in education should have clear consent mechanisms and transparent data usage policies. Schools and developers should work together to ensure that emotional interaction data is not misused for commercial purposes or unethical profiling. Policymakers and researchers should conduct long-term studies on how students' emotional connections with AI influence students' psychological development, social skills, and learning outcomes. Finally, this study revealed some aspects of our present-day classrooms, as well as teachers' pedagogy, need to change.

IMPLICATIONS TO FUTURE AI-INFUSED CLASSROOM

Given the conclusion made from the study, the following are the practical recommendations for effective AI integration into schools and classrooms:

Introduce AI Literacy Programs and Policies in Schools

Given the findings that the students are very engrossed in AI application tool in both academic and personal use, schools should have a clear policy on AI use. While those with existing policies may strengthen including AI used beyond academic aspects.

Some of the policies may include teaching students how AI functions, including its limitations, biases, and ethical concerns. Discussions on the pros and cons of AI in schools should be encouraged to involve students. Schools can introduce AI literacy as part of teachers' lessons in topics like digital citizenship programs, helping students develop critical thinking skills about AI-generated information. Workshops and activities that allow students to interact with AI, question its responses, and compare them to human perspectives will foster a well-rounded understanding of AI's role in learning.

Other school-level policies pertaining to AI use in school should be implemented. For instance, to prevent over-reliance on AI for academic and emotional needs, schools should establish guidelines on AI usage. These policies should cover both teachers and students. Some provisions may include designated AI-free discussion times, where students engage in peer-to-peer and teacher-led conversations to enhance social and communication skills. Additionally, incorporating group activities and problem-solving tasks that require human collaboration can reinforce the importance of interpersonal interactions. Ethical use of AI in school work should be included as part of the school AI policies.

Integrate AI as a Learning Support for the Students

Students are drawn to AI because they find them useful in providing information. Hence, AI may be positioned as a supplementary tool that enhances learning rather than replacing human instruction. Educators, can design lesson plans that incorporate AI-driven tutoring, personalized feedback, and instant responses to student queries while maintaining teacher-led discussions and critical thinking exercises. This approach ensures that AI supports, rather than diminishes, the role of educators in guiding and mentoring students. This study's findings showed that AI application tools have the potential to assist students in both academics and beyond including helping with emotional regulations and providing emotional support to students.

Strengthen the Guidance Program and Emotional Self-Awareness in AI Interactions

School guidance programs should be strengthened with teachers and counsellors conducting activities that help students reflect on when and why they turn to AI for emotional support. Journaling, self-assessment surveys, or guided discussions about AI's role in their emotional well-being can help students maintain a balanced perspective and avoid excessive dependence on AI companionship. Schools should integrate emotional well-being assessments and periodic check-ins on students especially those identified with high levels of AI use. Educators and counsellors can provide interventions such as social skill-building activities or emotional support sessions. Finally, Students should be encouraged to recognize and manage their emotional responses to AI interactions.

REFERENCES

Akalin, N., & Loutfi, A. (2021). Reinforcement learning approaches in social robotics. *Sensors (Basel)*, *21*(4), 1292. DOI: 10.3390/s21041292 PMID: 33670257

Almaiah, M. A., Alfaisal, R., Salloum, S. A., Hajjej, F., Thabit, S., El-Qirem, F. A., Lutfi, A., Alrawad, M., Al Mulhem, A., Alkhdour, T., Awad, A. B., & Al-Maroof, R. S. (2022). Examining the impact of artificial intelligence and social and computer anxiety in e-learning settings: Students' perceptions at the university level. *Electronics (Basel)*, *11*(22), 3662. DOI: 10.3390/electronics11223662

Belpaeme, T., Kennedy, J., Ramachandran, A., Scassellati, B., & Tanaka, F. (2018). Social robots for education: A review. *Science Robotics*, *3*(21), eaat5954. Advance online publication. DOI: 10.1126/scirobotics.aat5954 PMID: 33141719

Brandtzaeg, P. B., Skjuve, M., & Følstad, A. (2022). My AI Friend: How Users of a Social Chatbot Understand Their Human–AI Friendship. *Human Communication Research*, *48*(3), 404–429. Advance online publication. DOI: 10.1093/hcr/hqac008

Celik, I., Dindar, M., Muukkonen, H., & Järvelä, S. (2022). The promises and challenges of artificial intelligence for teachers: A systematic review of research. *TechTrends*, *66*(4), 616–630. DOI: 10.1007/s11528-022-00715-y

Chen, C., Hu, W., & Wei, X. (2024). From anxiety to action: Exploring the impact of artificial intelligence anxiety and artificial intelligence self-efficacy on motivated learning of undergraduate students. *Interactive Learning Environments*, •••, 1–16. DOI: 10.1080/10494820.2024.2440877

Clarke, V., & Braun, V. (2017). Thematic analysis. *The Journal of Positive Psychology*, *12*(3), 297–298. DOI: 10.1080/17439760.2016.1262613

Corbett, C. F., Wright, P. J., Jones, K., & Parmer, M. (2021). Voice-activated virtual home assistant use and social isolation and loneliness among older adults: A mini-review. *Frontiers in Public Health*, *9*, 742012. DOI: 10.3389/fpubh.2021.742012 PMID: 34708017

de Kervenoael, R., Hasan, R., Schwob, A., & Goh, E. (2020). Leveraging human-robot interaction in hospitality services: Incorporating the role of perceived value, empathy, and information sharing into visitors' intentions to use social robots. *Tourism Management*, *78*, 104042. DOI: 10.1016/j.tourman.2019.104042

Dellermann, D., Calma, A., Lipusch, N., Weber, T., Weigel, S., & Ebel, P. (2021). The future of human-AI collaboration: a taxonomy of design knowledge for hybrid intelligence systems. *arXiv preprint arXiv:2105.03354*. https://doi.org//arXiv.2105.03354DOI: 10.48550

Fox, J. & Gambino, A. (2021). Relationship Development with Humanoid Social Robots: Applying Interpersonal Theories to Human-Robot Interaction. *Cyberpsychology, Behavior, And Social Networking*, 24 (5), Ann Liebert, Inc. DOI: DOI: 10.1089/cyber.2020.0181294

Hassani, H., Silva, E. S., Unger, S., TajMazinani, M., & Mac Feely, S. (2020). Artificial intelligence (AI) or intelligence augmentation (IA): What is the future? *AI*, *1*(2), 8. DOI: 10.3390/ai1020008

Huang, L. (2023). Ethics of artificial intelligence in education: Student privacy and data protection. *Science Insights Education Frontiers*, *16*(2), 2577–2587. DOI: 10.15354/sief.23.re202

Idroes, G. M., Noviandy, T. R., Maulana, A., Irvanizam, I., Jalil, Z., Lensoni, L., Lala, A., Abas, A. H., Tallei, T. E., & Idroes, R. (2023). Student Perspectives on the Role of Artificial Intelligence in Education: A Survey-Based Analysis. *Journal of Educational Management and Learning*, *1*(1), 8–15. DOI: 10.60084/jeml.v1i1.58

Jackaria, P., Hajan, B., Mastul, A., & Sali, F. (2024). Generation AI in a Reimagined Classroom : Challenges, and Opportunities, pp. 174–176. https://doi.org/DOI: 10.4018/979-8-3693-3350-1.ch009

Jackaria, P. M., Hajan, B. H., & Mastul, A. R. H. (2024). A comparative analysis of the rating of college students' essays by ChatGPT versus human raters. *International Journal of Learning. Teaching and Educational Research*, *23*(2), 478–492. DOI: 10.26803/ijlter.23.2.23

Kadiri, K., & Alabi, O. A. (2023). Revolutionizing Education with AI-Infused Smart Classrooms: A Case Study from Federal Polytechnic Offa. *ASUP Conference*. https://www.researchgate.net/publication/373897598_Revolutionizing_Education_with_AI-Infused_Smart_Classrooms_A_Case_Study_from_Federal_Polytechnic_Offa

Khan, W. N. (2024). Ethical challenges of AI in education: Balancing innovation with data privacy. *Journal of AI Integration in Education*, *1*(1), 1–13. https://www.researchcorridor.org/index.php/jaiie/article/view/238

Kolomaznik, M., Petrik, V., Slama, M., & Jurik, V. (2024). The role of socio-emotional attributes in enhancing human-AI collaboration. *Frontiers in Psychology*, *15*, 1369957. Advance online publication. DOI: 10.3389/fpsyg.2024.1369957 PMID: 39474095

Lin, H., & Chen, Q. (2024). Artificial intelligence (AI) -integrated educational applications and college students' creativity and academic emotions: Students and teachers' perceptions and attitudes. *BMC Psychology, 12*(1), 487–487. DOI: 10.1186/s40359-024-01979-0 PMID: 39285268

Mallillin, L. (2024). Artificial Intelligence (AI) Towards Students' Academic Performance. *Innovare Journal of Education*, 16 – 21. https://doi.org/.DOI: 10.22159/ijoe.2024v12i4.51665

Marino, F., Chilà, P., Sfrazzetto, S. T., Carrozza, C., Crimi, I., Failla, C., Busà, M., Bernava, G., Tartarisco, G., Vagni, D., Ruta, L., & Pioggia, G. (2020). Outcomes of a robot-assisted social-emotional understanding intervention for young children with autism spectrum disorders. *Journal of Autism and Developmental Disorders, 50*(6), 1973–1987. DOI: 10.1007/s10803-019-03953-x PMID: 30852783

Naneva, S., Sarda Gou, M., Webb, T. L., & Prescott, T. J. (2020). A Systematic Review of Attitudes, Anxiety, Acceptance, and Trust Towards Social Robots. *International Journal of Social Robotics, 12*(6), 1179–1201. DOI: 10.1007/s12369-020-00659-4

Obaigbena, A., Lottu, O. A., Ugwuanyi, E. D., Jacks, B. S., Sodiya, E. O., & Daraojimba, O. D. (2024). AI and human-robot interaction: A review of recent advances and challenges. *GSC Advanced Research and Reviews, 18*(2), 321–330. DOI: 10.30574/gscarr.2024.18.2.0070

Pashevich, E. (2022). Can communication with social robots influence how children develop empathy? Best-evidence synthesis. *AI & Society, 37*(2), 579–589. DOI: 10.1007/s00146-021-01214-z

Pavlopoulos, A., Rachiotis, T., & Maglogiannis, I. (2024). An overview of tools and technologies for anxiety and depression management using AI. *Applied Sciences (Basel, Switzerland), 14*(19), 9068. DOI: 10.3390/app14199068

Pelau, C., Dabija, D. C., & Ene, I. (2021). What makes an AI device human-like? The role of interaction quality, empathy and perceived psychological anthropomorphic characteristics in the acceptance of artificial intelligence in the service industry. *Computers in Human Behavior, 122*, 106–855. DOI: 10.1016/j.chb.2021.106855

Pishtari, G., Sarmiento-Márquez, E. M., Rodríguez-Triana, M. J., Wagner, M., & Ley, T. (2023, August). Evaluating the impact and usability of an AI-driven feedback system for learning design. *European Conference on Technology Enhanced Learning* (pp. 324-338). Cham: Springer Nature Switzerland. DOI: 10.1007/978-3-031-42682-7_22

Pu, L., Moyle, W., Jones, C., & Todorovic, M. (2019). The Effectiveness of Social Robots for Older Adults: A Systematic Review and Meta-Analysis of Randomized Controlled Studies. *The Gerontologist*, *59*(1), e37–e51. DOI: 10.1093/geront/gny046 PMID: 29897445

Qi, X. (2023). ChatGPT: A Promising Tool to Combat Social Isolation and Loneliness in Older Adults with Mild Cognitive Impairment. *Neurology Live*, NA-NA. https://go.gale.com/ps/i.do?id=GALE%7CA776469898&sid=googleScholar&v=2.1&it=r&linkaccess=abs&issn=27674258&p=AONE&sw=w&userGroupName=anon%7E6320b905&aty=open-web-entry

Skjuve, M., Følstad, A., Fostervold, K. I., & Brandtzaeg, P. B. (2021). My Chatbot Companion - a Study of Human-Chatbot Relationships. *International Journal of Human-Computer Studies*, *149*, 1071–5819. DOI: 10.1016/j.ijhcs.2021.102601

Sundar, S. S. (2020). Rise of machine agency: A framework for studying the psychology of human-AI interaction (HAII). *Journal of Computer-Mediated Communication*, *25*(1), 74–88. DOI: 10.1093/jcmc/zmz026

Suzuki, T., Yamada, S., Nomura, T., & Kanda, T. (2019). Do People Prefer Robots Over Humans as Daily Communication Partners?: Relationship to Social Anxiety in Conjunction with the Appearance of the Robots. *Journal of Japan Society for Fuzzy Theory and Intelligent Informatics*, *31*(5), 789–796. DOI: 10.3156/jsoft.31.5_789

Tajik, A. (2025). Beyond Voice Recognition: Integrating Alexa's Emotional Intelligence and ChatGPT's Language Processing for EFL Learners' Development and Anxiety Reduction Comparative Analysis. DOI: 10.21203/rs.3.rs-5989702/v1

Tang, P. M., Koopman, J., Mai, K. M., De Cremer, D., Zhang, J. H., Reynders, P., . . . Chen, I. (2023). No person is an island: Unpacking the work and after-work consequences of interacting with artificial intelligence. *Journal of Applied Psychology*. https://psycnet.apa.org/doi/10.1037/apl0001103

Van Maris, A., Zook, N., Caleb-Solly, P., Studley, M., Winfield, A., & Dogramadzi, S. (2020). Designing ethical social robots—A longitudinal field study with older adults. *Frontiers in Robotics and AI*, *7*, 1. DOI: 10.3389/frobt.2020.00001 PMID: 33501170

Vashishth, T. K., Sharma, V., Sharma, K. K., Kumar, B., Panwar, R., & Chaudhary, S. (2024). AI-driven learning analytics for personalized feedback and assessment in higher education. In *Using traditional design methods to enhance AI-driven decision making* (pp. 206–230). IGI Global., DOI: 10.4018/979-8-3693-0639-0.ch009

Wallen, T. (2023) Investigating the Emotional Impact of Social Robots. Department of computer and information science. Linköping University. https://liu.diva-portal.org/smash/get/diva2:1816944/FULLTEXT01.pdf

Webster, C., & Ivanov, S. (2020). Robotics, Artificial Intelligence, and the Evolving Nature of Work. In George, B., & Paul, J. (Eds.), *Digital Transformation in Business and Society*. Palgrave Macmillan., DOI: 10.1007/978-3-030-08277-2_8

Wienrich, C., & Latoschik, M. E. (2021). Extended artificial intelligence: New prospects of human-ai interaction research. *Frontiers in Virtual Reality*, *2*, 686–783. DOI: 10.3389/frvir.2021.686783

Xu, W., Dainoff, M. J., Ge, L., & Gao, Z. (2023). Transitioning to human interaction with AI systems: New challenges and opportunities for HCI professionals to enable human-centred AI. *International Journal of Human-Computer Interaction*, *39*(3), 494–518. DOI: 10.1080/10447318.2022.2041900

Zacharaki, A., Kostavelis, I., Gasteratos, A., & Dokas, I. (2020). Safety bounds in human-robot interaction: A survey. *Safety Science*, *127*, 104–667. DOI: 10.1016/j.ssci.2020.104667

Chapter 7
AI-Based Tutoring Systems in Education:
A Systematic Literature Review on Personalized Learning, Intelligent Agents, and Learning Analytics

Abdulla Sultan Binhareb Almheiri
https://orcid.org/0000-0003-2282-058X
Zayed University, UAE

Humaid Albastaki
Zayed University, UAE

Hanadi Alrashdan
https://orcid.org/0000-0001-8898-3117
Faculty of Education, Jadara University, Joran

ABSTRACT

This systematic literature review examines the current state of AI-based tutoring systems in education, focusing on their roles in personalized learning, intelligent agent integration, and learning analytics within classroom instruction. A thorough analysis of 30 relevant studies reveals that AI-based tutoring systems significantly enhance educational outcomes by adapting learning experiences to individual needs through tailored feedback and customized learning trajectories, leading to improved student engagement and performance. Intelligent agents are central to these systems, providing social-emotional support, interactive feedback, and fostering motivation and deeper understanding. Learning analytics further support educators by enabling real-time monitoring of student progress, facilitating data-driven instructional adjustments, and ensuring timely, personalized support. Despite the progress, the study

DOI: 10.4018/979-8-3373-0847-0.ch007

identifies ongoing challenges, particularly concerning ethical data use, scalability, and the need for integrating socio-emotional learning components.

1. INTRODUCTION

Artificial Intelligence (AI) has become a transformative force in education, providing new ways to engage students, personalize learning, and support teachers (Ahmed & Ganapathy, 2021). AI-based tutoring systems, in particular, have garnered attention for their ability to deliver tailored instruction through adaptive algorithms, learning analytics, and intelligent agents, significantly enhancing traditional educational methods (Koedinger et al., 2013). These systems not only help students learn at their own pace but also provide educators with valuable insights to optimize classroom management and support each student's unique learning journey (Crompton & Burke, 2023).

One of the most promising aspects of AI-based tutoring systems is their capacity for personalized learning. By analyzing individual progress and preferences, these systems adapt content, feedback, and learning trajectories to fit students' needs, leading to improved engagement, motivation, and academic performance (Walkington & Bernacki, 2014; Alharbi & Cristea, 2021). Adaptive learning technologies, such as those described by Aleven et al. (2016), adjust instructional pacing and complexity, enabling students to grasp complex topics with personalized support.

Another critical component of AI-based tutoring systems is the use of intelligent agents that simulate human-like interactions. These agents act as virtual facilitators, social companions, or even emotional support providers, enhancing the learning experience by making it more interactive and responsive to individual students' emotional and social needs (Dinçer & Doğanay, 2017; Nye, 2016). Such agents can foster socio-emotional connections, provide timely feedback, and even help students develop self-regulation skills, thereby promoting both academic and personal growth (Schroeder, Adesope, & Gilbert, 2013).

Furthermore, the integration of learning analytics within AI-based tutoring systems has revolutionized how educators manage classroom instruction. Learning analytics tools provide real-time data on student performance and engagement, enabling teachers to make data-driven adjustments and provide targeted support where needed (Bull et al., 2018). Systems like MTFeedback and MTDashboard have shown to be effective in enhancing group-based learning by tracking collaborative activities and providing insights into student interactions (Lawrence et al., 2022). These analytics capabilities empower educators to create adaptive learning environments that respond to the dynamic needs of their students (Mousavinasab et al., 2021).

Despite these advancements, several challenges and areas for future research remain. Ethical considerations around data privacy, the need for scalable solutions, and the integration of socio-emotional learning into AI tutoring are all critical to the continued development of these systems (Borenstein & Howard, 2021; Timan & Mann, 2021). Researchers argue for the creation of privacy-preserving technologies and ethical frameworks to ensure AI applications are safe, fair, and trustworthy, especially as they become more deeply embedded in educational institutions (Timms, 2016).

This study aims to provide a comprehensive review of current AI-based tutoring systems, examining how they facilitate personalized learning, leverage intelligent agents, integrate learning analytics, and address future research directions. By synthesizing findings from recent literature, this paper seeks to offer a roadmap for advancing AI tutoring in education, ensuring that these systems are both innovative and aligned with educational goals for inclusivity, ethics, and lifelong learning. Thus, to address these issues, we formulated the following research questions:

1) Which countries, educational institutions, journals, authors, and keywords are most influential in the field of AI-Based Tutoring Systems in Education?
2) How do AI-Based Tutoring Systems facilitate personalized learning in educational settings?
3) What roles do intelligent agents play in enhancing AI-Based Tutoring Systems within education?
4) How is learning analytics integrated into classroom instruction through AI-Based Tutoring Systems?
5) What are the future research directions for advancing AI-Based Tutoring Systems in education?

2. METHODS

This systematic literature review (SLR) was conducted to examine the state of AI-Based Tutoring Systems in education, focusing on personalized learning, intelligent agents, and learning analytics in classroom instruction. The methodology adheres to the PRISMA (Preferred Reporting Items for Systematic Reviews and Meta-Analyses) (Moher, et al., 2009) guidelines to ensure transparency and rigor in the research process. The following steps outline the review process, from search strategy development to quality assessment and data extraction.

2.1. Search Strategy

A comprehensive search strategy was developed using Scopus. The search terms were designed to capture a broad range of literature on AI-Based Tutoring Systems in education.

Table 1. The query used in this review

Keywords	**TITLE-ABS-KEY (ai AND tutoring Systems AND education)**
Publication Year	PUBYEAR > 2002 AND PUBYEAR < 2024
Document Type	(LIMIT-TO (DOCTYPE, "cp") OR LIMIT-TO (DOCTYPE, "ar") OR LIMIT-TO (DOCTYPE, "ch"))
Language	LIMIT-TO (LANGUAGE, "English")
Subject Area	(LIMIT-TO (SUBJAREA, "SOCI") OR LIMIT-TO (SUBJAREA, "COMP") OR LIMIT-TO (SUBJAREA, "ARTS"))
Exact Keywords	Computer Aided Instruction, Artificial Intelligence, Intelligent Tutoring System, Learning Systems, Tutoring System, Intelligent Tutoring, Intelligent Tutoring Systems, Intelligent Vehicle Highway Systems, Personalized Learning, Artificial Intelligence In Education, Tutoring, Teaching And Learning, Intelligent Agents, Learning Environments, Artificial Intelligence (AI), Personalizations, Intelligent Systems, AI Technologies, Tutoring Systems, AI In Education, Intelligent Tutoring System (ITS), Higher Education, Intelligent Tutoring Systems (ITS), Learning Outcome, Learning Management System, Learning Analytics, Artificial Intelligence Technologies, Intelligent Tutors, Generative AI, Explainable AI, Expert Systems, Educational Robots, Distance Education, Online Tutoring, On-line Education, Natural Language Generation, Multi-modal, Artificial Intelligence Techniques, AI-based Learning Support Systems, AI-based Learning Support System, AI-assisted Tutoring, AI Techniques

2.2. Screening and Eligibility Criteria

The following inclusion and exclusion criteria were applied to screen the documents retrieved from the initial search.

Table 2. The inclusion and exclusion criteria

Criteria	Inclusion	Exclusion
Language	English	Non-English
Publication Year	2003–2023	Outside the specified period
Document Type	Conference papers, articles, and book chapters	Reviews, commentaries, non-peer-reviewed papers
Subject Area	Social sciences, computer science, arts	Other subject areas
Keywords	Must include terms related to AI-based tutoring systems, personalized learning, intelligent agents, or learning analytics	Irrelevant keywords
Content Relevance	Directly related to AI-based tutoring systems in education, with a focus on personalized learning, intelligent agents, or analytics	Does not align with research objectives or analysis scope

2.3. Data Extraction and Quality Assessment

The remaining 309 documents were downloaded, and 110 were selected for further examination based on relevance. Each document was reviewed in detail, with particular focus on methodological rigor, relevance to AI-Based Tutoring Systems, and alignment with the study's objectives. A quality assessment was conducted, resulting in the inclusion of 30 articles in the final review. Seventy articles were excluded at this stage due to reasons such as being systematic review papers, containing irrelevant content, not meeting the paper's objectives, or falling outside the analysis scope.

2.4. Data Synthesis

The 30 selected articles were analyzed to identify trends and key findings related to personalized learning, intelligent agents, and learning analytics in AI-based tutoring systems for classroom instruction. The extracted data were synthesized to address the research questions and identify future research directions.

2.5. PRISMA Flow Diagram

The PRISMA flow diagram below illustrates the screening and selection process for this systematic literature review. In the identification phase, a total of 768 documents were identified through the initial search process. Following this, the screening stage involved applying inclusion and exclusion criteria, which reduced the pool to 309 documents. In the eligibility stage, 110 documents were downloaded and thoroughly reviewed. After completing this detailed assessment, 30 articles were included in the final analysis for the systematic literature review. This structured approach, following the PRISMA framework, ensures that the study provides a comprehensive and high-quality synthesis of the literature on AI-based tutoring systems in education.

Figure 1. PRISMA Flow Diagram

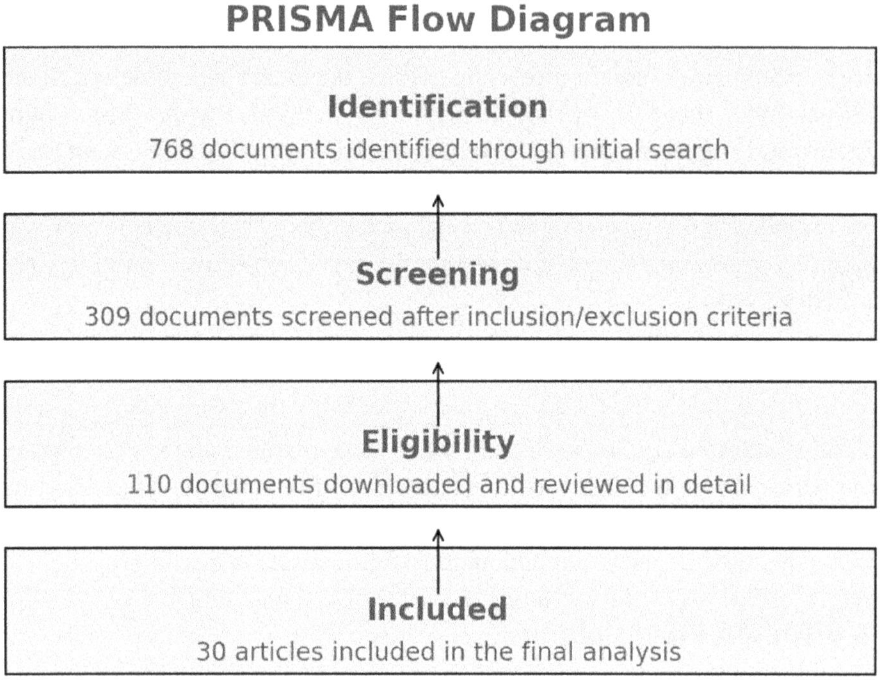

3. RESULTS

3.1. Overview of Influential Contributors in the Field of AI-Based Tutoring Systems in Education

This section examines the most influential contributors to the field of AI-Based Tutoring Systems in Education, focusing on the leading countries, educational institutions, journals, authors, and keywords. These insights provide a comprehensive understanding of where significant research efforts are concentrated and highlight key players advancing this area of study.

3.1.1 Top countries in the field of AI-Based Tutoring Systems in Education

Figure 2 illustrates the top countries contributing to research in AI-Based Tutoring Systems in Education. The graph showcases the number of publications by country, indicating which nations have taken prominent roles in this research domain.

Figure 2. Top countries in the field of AI-Based Tutoring Systems in Education

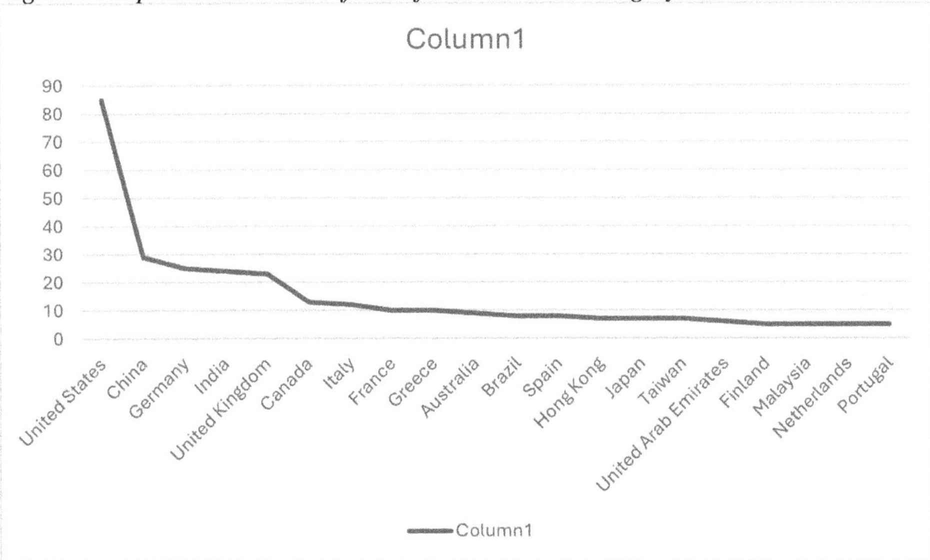

The United States leads the field with the highest number of publications, reflecting its substantial investment in AI-based educational technologies and innovations in tutoring systems. China follows as the second most active country, underscoring its rapid advancement in AI research. Other notable contributors include Germany, India, and the United Kingdom, which also demonstrate a strong presence in this area, albeit with fewer publications than the top two countries.

This distribution suggests a global interest in AI-based tutoring systems, with concentrated research efforts primarily in North America, Asia, and Europe. The leadership of the United States and China may be attributed to their strong academic and technological ecosystems, supporting the development and implementation of intelligent tutoring solutions. The involvement of countries like Germany, India, and the United Kingdom further highlights the collaborative and international nature of advancements in AI-powered educational tools.

3.1.2. Top educational institutions in the field of AI-Based Tutoring Systems in Education

Table 3 presents the top educational institutions actively contributing to the field of AI-Based Tutoring Systems in Education, ranked by their total publications (TP). These institutions are at the forefront of research, advancing AI-based educational technology through extensive studies and innovative solutions.

Table 3. Top educational institutions in the field of AI-Based Tutoring Systems in Education

#	Educational institutions	TP*	#	Educational institutions	TP*
1	Carnegie Mellon University	18	11	IBM Research	3
2	NC State University	7	12	Lingnan University, Hong Kong	3
3	School of Computer Science	6	13	Stanford University	3
4	University of Florida	5	14	Universidade Federal de Uberlândia	3
5	University of Piraeus	4	15	University of Pittsburgh	3
6	Georgia Institute of Technology	4	16	Charles University	3
7	Old Dominion University	3	17	The Education University of Hong Kong	3
8	CNRS Centre National de la Recherche Scientifique	3	18	Texas A&M University	3
9	Universität Bremen	3	19	Consiglio Nazionale delle Ricerche	3
10	The University of British Columbia	3	20		

TP*= Total Publications

Carnegie Mellon University leads with 18 publications, demonstrating its significant influence and commitment to AI in education. NC State University and the School of Computer Science follow, with 7 and 6 publications, respectively, indicating their strong contributions to this domain. Other notable institutions include the University of Florida, University of Piraeus, and Georgia Institute of Technology, each contributing multiple publications.

The institutions listed reflect a global representation, with universities and research centers from North America, Europe, and Asia. This diversity in contributors emphasizes the widespread academic interest in developing AI-driven educational tools, enhancing the quality and effectiveness of tutoring systems across different educational environments.

These institutions' contributions underscore their role as leaders in AI research applied to education, and their ongoing work is likely to shape the future of AI-based tutoring systems worldwide.

3.1.3. Top journals in the Field of AI-Based Tutoring Systems in Education

Figure 3 highlights the top journals publishing research on AI-Based Tutoring Systems in Education. These journals play a vital role in disseminating knowledge, presenting innovative findings, and fostering academic discourse within this specialized area.

Figure 3. Top journals in the field of AI-Based Tutoring Systems in Education

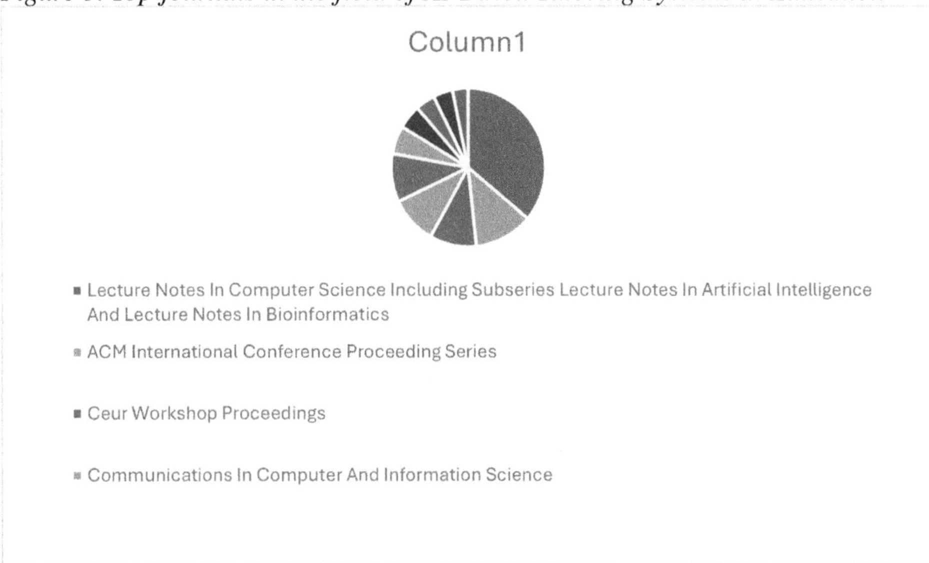

The "Lecture Notes in Computer Science," including its subseries in Artificial Intelligence and Bioinformatics, leads as the most influential journal series, serving as a primary outlet for research in this field. Other significant contributors include the "ACM International Conference Proceedings Series" and "Ceur Workshop Proceedings," both of which provide platforms for emerging studies and conference presentations. Additionally, "Communications in Computer and Information Science" is also notable for publishing relevant research.

These journals and proceedings reflect the interdisciplinary nature of AI-based tutoring research, integrating computer science, artificial intelligence, and educational technology. Their prominent role underlines the importance of both theoretical exploration and practical applications within AI-enhanced education, driving advancements in tutoring systems through peer-reviewed dissemination.

3.1.4. Top authors in the field of AI-Based Tutoring Systems in Education

Table 4 presents the leading authors in AI-Based Tutoring Systems in Education, based on their total publications (TP), total citations (TC), and H-index. These metrics provide insight into each author's research impact and influence within this field.

Table 4. Top authors in the field of AI-Based Tutoring Systems in Education

#	Authors	TP*	TC*	H-index	Affliation	Country
1	**Aleven, Vincent A.W.M.M.**	282	9,012	49	School of Computer Science, Pittsburgh	United States
2	**Koedinger, Kenneth R.**	365	16,295	62	School of Computer Science, Pittsburgh	United States
3	**Virvou, Maria K.**	390	4,006	28	University of Piraeus, Piraeus,	Greece
4	**Aprin, Farbod**	9	33	4	Universität Duisburg-Essen, Duisburg	Germany
5	**Barnes, Tiffany Michelle**	215	2,182	24	NC State University, Raleigh	United States
6	**Chen, Xieling**	69	2,690	25	Guangzhou University, Guangzhou	China
7	**Cheng, Gary K.S.**	110	2,224	25	The Education University of Hong Kong, Hong Kong.	China
8	**Conati, Cristina**	164	4,954	37	The University of British Columbia, Vancouver	Canada
9	**Crompton, Helen**	68	2,076	22	Old Dominion University, Norfolk	United States
10	**Gupta, Shivang**	15	47	4	Carnegie Mellon University, Pittsburgh	United States

TP*= Total Publications, TC*= Total Citations.

Vincent A.W.M.M. Aleven and Kenneth R. Koedinger from the School of Computer Science in Pittsburgh, United States, stand out as highly influential researchers, with 282 and 365 publications, respectively. Koedinger has an impressive 16,295 citations and an H-index of 62, making him a pivotal figure in this area. Maria K. Virvou from the University of Piraeus in Greece also ranks among the top contributors, with a significant number of publications and citations.

Other noteworthy contributors include Tiffany Michelle Barnes from NC State University, Cristina Conati from the University of British Columbia, and Xieling Chen from Guangzhou University. These authors bring diverse perspectives from institutions across the United States, Greece, Germany, China, Canada, and Hong Kong, illustrating the global research interest in AI-based tutoring systems.

Their affiliations with prestigious institutions and substantial contributions in terms of publications and citations highlight their central roles in advancing AI applications within education, particularly in tutoring systems. This group of authors represents a blend of pioneers and emerging voices who are shaping the future of AI-enhanced learning environments.

3.1.5. Top Keywords and Trends in the Field of AI-Based Tutoring Systems in Education

Figure 4 illustrates the network of top keywords and emerging trends associated with AI-Based Tutoring Systems in Education, generated using VOSviewer. This visualization showcases the interconnectedness of key terms, providing insights into prevalent themes and research focus areas in the field.

Figure 4. Top Keywords and Terms in the Field of AI-Based Tutoring Systems in Education

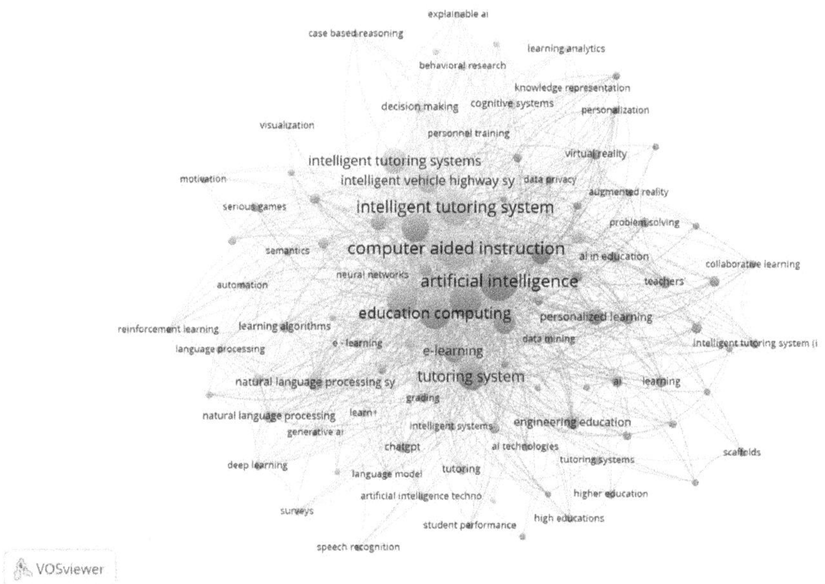

Core keywords such as "artificial intelligence," "intelligent tutoring system," and "computer-aided instruction" form the central nodes in the network, indicating their foundational role within this research domain. Surrounding these central terms are clusters representing specific areas of focus, such as "personalized learning," "education computing," and "learning analytics," which reflect the diverse applications and interdisciplinary nature of AI-based tutoring systems.

The map reveals distinct clusters that signify related research themes. For example, one cluster may focus on machine learning and natural language processing, highlighting the technical aspects of AI integration, while another emphasizes educational outcomes like student performance and knowledge acquisition. The interconnected terms demonstrate a strong interest in personalized and adaptive learning, suggesting that much of the research in this field aims to enhance student engagement and individualized support through AI.

This keyword network highlights both established and emerging trends in AI-based tutoring research, showing that topics like "explainable AI" and "virtual reality" are also gaining traction. These trends point to a growing interest in making AI systems more interpretable and immersive for educational purposes, further underscoring the dynamic and evolving nature of this field.

3.2. How do AI-Based Tutoring Systems Facilitate Personalized Learning in Educational Settings?

The question of how AI-based tutoring systems facilitate personalized learning in educational settings can be addressed by examining various approaches to personalization, adaptive feedback mechanisms, and customized learning trajectories. The table below outlines specific studies that showcase different techniques and algorithms used in AI tutoring systems, emphasizing their effects on student engagement, motivation, and performance.

Table 5. AI-Based Tutoring Systems and Personalized Learning Approaches

Authors	Personalization Approach	Adaptive Feedback Mechanism	Customized Learning Trajectories	Technology/ Algorithm Used	Student Outcomes
Walkington & Bernacki (2014)	Context personalization in math problems	Individualized feedback based on engagement levels	Math problems tailored to personal interests	Model-tracing and knowledge-tracing in ITS	Enhanced engagement and reduced system gaming
Alharbi & Cristea (2021)	Student modeling for adaptive learning	Feedback based on simulated student behavior	Learning paths personalized using reinforcement learning	Generative Adversarial Imitation Learning (GAIL)	Improved student retention and performance
Koedinger et al. (2023)	ITS adaptation in problem-solving practice	Real-time feedback during problem-solving	Curated sequence of problems	Intelligent Tutoring Systems (ITS) with problem-based tasks	Increased problem-solving accuracy and learning opportunities
Shi et al. (2020)	Social adaptive e-learning with Topolor	Automated feedback based on interaction analysis	Dynamic task adjustment based on student preferences	Bayesian Knowledge Tracing (BKT)	Enhanced engagement and sustained learning
Alamri et al. (2020)	Personalized learning for motivation in online courses	Feedback promoting self-regulated learning	Paths tailored to self-determined learning goals	AI-driven adaptive content	Increased motivation and self-efficacy in learners
Conati & VanLehn (2000)	Adaptive instruction based on ML	Feedback leveraging behavior prediction	Adaptive sequence for simulator-based learning	Machine Learning (ML) algorithms	Enhanced skill learning in simulated environments
Fancsali et al. (2014)	Interest-matched problem selection in MATHia	Feedback based on engagement in interest areas	Story problems aligning with student interests	AI-based personalization framework in ITS	Mixed impact on performance depending on personalization depth
Borchers et al. (2023)	ITS problem-solving vs. paper-based approaches	Real-time corrective feedback in digital platform	Sequencing by difficulty and student performance	TEL system comparing ITS and non-technology alternatives	ITS provides more learning opportunities than paper-based methods

continued on following page

Table 5. Continued

Authors	Personalization Approach	Adaptive Feedback Mechanism	Customized Learning Trajectories	Technology/ Algorithm Used	Student Outcomes
Reeve (2013)	Agentic engagement in personalized learning	Feedback to foster self-determination	Personalized challenges based on motivation levels	Self-determination Theory (SDT)	Positive impact on motivation and achievement
Hidi & Ainley (2008)	Situational interest personalization	Feedback triggering affective and cognitive processes	Tasks personalized to trigger situational interest	Contextual personalization	Enhanced engagement through situational interest triggers

The studies in Table 4.2 demonstrate diverse approaches that AI-based tutoring systems use to tailor learning experiences for individual students. For instance, Walkington and Bernacki (2014) focus on context personalization in mathematics by adjusting math problems to align with students' personal interests, resulting in enhanced engagement and reduced system gaming. Similarly, Alharbi and Cristea (2021) utilize Generative Adversarial Imitation Learning (GAIL) to model student behaviors, providing adaptive feedback that improves retention and performance.

Other studies emphasize real-time feedback and problem-solving adaptations. Koedinger et al. (2023) employ Intelligent Tutoring Systems (ITS) to curate problem sequences based on student performance, increasing both problem-solving accuracy and learning opportunities. In contrast, Shi et al. (2020) incorporate Bayesian Knowledge Tracing (BKT) to offer automated feedback tailored to social interactions, thereby enhancing sustained engagement.

Moreover, Alamri et al. (2020) and Reeve (2013) underscore the importance of motivation in personalized learning. Alamri et al. (2020) leverage AI-driven adaptive content to foster self-regulated learning, while Reeve (2013) applies Self-determination Theory (SDT) to personalize challenges according to students' motivation levels, resulting in higher motivation and achievement.

In summary, AI-based tutoring systems facilitate personalized learning through adaptive mechanisms that respond to individual preferences, behaviors, and engagement levels. The technology used—ranging from Machine Learning algorithms to AI-driven content and reinforcement learning—ensures that each student receives a tailored learning experience, leading to various positive outcomes such as enhanced motivation, engagement, and academic performance.

3.3. What Roles do Intelligent Agents Play in Enhancing AI-Based Tutoring Systems Within Education?

The role of intelligent agents in AI-based tutoring systems extends beyond traditional instructional support, with these agents enhancing educational outcomes through various forms of personalized interaction, emotional support, and adaptive feedback. The table below summarizes the roles of different types of intelligent agents in enhancing AI-based tutoring systems, as explored in recent research studies.

Table 6. Roles of Intelligent Agents in Enhancing AI-Based Tutoring Systems

Authors	Role of Intelligent Agent in Enhancement	Key Insights and Findings
Schroeder, Adesope, and Gilbert (2013)	Virtual facilitator	Optimizes learning from examples and enhances continuity in professional development through personalized dialogue(Virtual-Agents-for-Real…).
Nye, Graesser, and Hu (2014)	Dialog-based ITS	Enhances conceptual knowledge through open-ended tutoring, significantly improving learning gains(Virtual-Agents-for-Real…).
Dinçer and Doğanay (2017)	Educational agents with socio-emotional capacity	Fosters socio-emotional connection, motivation, and engagement, leading to superior learning outcomes(Out-of-the-laboratory-a…).
Nye (2016)	Socially-engaging AIEd tools	Addresses the lack of structure in traditional digital education by providing differentiation and social-emotional support(Out-of-the-laboratory-a…).
Lu et al. (2021)	Adaptive feedback and personalization	Provides immediate feedback and customizes learning paths based on student performance(TO-BE-fAIr-ETHICAL-AND-…).
Aleven et al. (2016)	Adaptive learning technologies	Incorporates cognitive science to personalize the pace and complexity of instruction for individual needs (What-Makes-ProblemSolvi…).
Graesser et al. (2017)	Conversational agents	Engages students through mixed-initiative dialogue, fostering deeper understanding(Automated-Personalized-…).
Bickmore, Pfeifer, and Paasche-Orlow (2009)	Animated agents for motivation	Animated agents in systems like DuoLingo enhance user engagement through character interaction(Virtual-Agents-for-Real…).
Carnegie Learning	Adaptive tutoring	Uses cognitive science and AI to develop personalized tutoring that adapts based on real-time student feedback (TO-BE-fAIr-ETHICAL-AND-…).
Fonte et al. (2012)	BDI agents in ITS	Enhances personalized e-learning experiences by adapting tutoring approaches based on student interactions(Application-of-Artifici…).

continued on following page

Table 6. Continued

Authors	Role of Intelligent Agent in Enhancement	Key Insights and Findings
Timms (2016)	Educational robots as social agents	Supports collaborative learning in virtual environments, making the learning experience more interactive and engaging(Artificial-intelligence…).
San Pedro et al. (2013)	Emotionally aware ITS	Detects frustration and adapts responses to keep students motivated and engaged(Out-of-the-laboratory-a…).

The studies in Table 5 highlight the diverse roles intelligent agents play in enhancing AI-based tutoring systems. Schroeder, Adesope, and Gilbert (2013) and Nye, Graesser, and Hu (2014) focus on virtual facilitators and dialog-based ITS, respectively. These agents provide personalized dialogue and open-ended tutoring, helping to enhance both learning continuity and conceptual understanding. Educational agents with socio-emotional capacities, as discussed by Dinçer and Doğanay (2017), go beyond cognitive support by fostering motivation and engagement through socio-emotional connections. This aligns with Nye (2016), who demonstrates that socially engaging AIEd tools address the need for structure in digital education, adding social and emotional dimensions to AI interactions.

Adaptive feedback mechanisms also feature prominently in intelligent agent roles. Lu et al. (2021) and Aleven et al. (2016) emphasize the importance of immediate feedback and customization, using cognitive science principles to adjust the learning pace and complexity based on individual student needs. Furthermore, studies like Graesser et al. (2017) and Bickmore, Pfeifer, and Paasche-Orlow (2009) explore conversational and animated agents that enhance engagement through dialogue and character interaction, respectively. These agents help make learning more interactive, enhancing motivation and retention. Finally, studies by Fonte et al. (2012) and Timms (2016) show that educational robots and BDI agents support personalized e-learning by adapting their tutoring approaches to individual students. San Pedro et al. (2013) emphasize emotionally aware ITS, which detect frustration and adapt responses to sustain motivation and engagement.

In summary, intelligent agents enhance AI-based tutoring systems by fulfilling roles that span cognitive, emotional, and social support, each contributing uniquely to improved educational outcomes.

3.4. How Is Learning Analytics Integrated Into Classroom Instruction Through AI-Based Tutoring Systems?

Learning analytics plays a critical role in AI-based tutoring systems by offering real-time insights into student progress, supporting instructional decisions, and enhancing classroom management. Table 6 highlights various tools and technologies used in integrating learning analytics into classroom instruction, their purposes, and the outcomes they achieve.

Table 7. Integration of Learning Analytics in AI-Based Tutoring Systems for Classroom Instruction

Authors	Learning Analytics Tools/Technologies Used	Integration Purpose	Outcome in Classroom Instruction	Key Findings
Crompton & Burke (2023) visualizations, Infographics	To support teacher orchestration of classroom activities	Facilitated visual tracking of student interactions and goal achievements	Increased teacher awareness and efficient orchestration	
Ullah & Hafiz (2022)	Bisis Tools	Managing large student data sets in real time	Enabled tailored support based on individual learning patterns	Streamlined data analysis for personalized learning
Mavrikis et al. (2019)	Exploratory Lronments	Provided dynamic insights for teachers	Improved classroom orchestration through real-time analytics	Enhanced instructional adjustments and support
Mousavinasab et al. (2021)	Bayesian Networks (BN)	Modeled students' knowledge and performance	Allowed predictive analytics for future performance	Enabled data-driven intervention planning for teachers
Lawrence et al. (2022)	MTFeedback and MTDashboard onitoring and feedback for small group activities	Increased teacher awareness of student collaboration	Enhanced support for group-based learning	
Koedinger et al. (2013)	Open Learner Models (OLM)	Sudents' self-regulated learning	Fostered students' understanding of their learning progress	Promoted self-directed learning and accountability
Martinez-Maldonado et al. (2015)	Multi-surface Classroom Ecology	Deployed teacher's small group activities	Enabled tracking and feedback loops for real-time interventions	Increased instructional flexibility and responsiveness

continued on following page

Table 7. Continued

Authors	Learning Analytics Tools/Technologies Used	Integration Purpose	Outcome in Classroom Instruction	Key Findings
Chan & Sharples (2002)	Concept Mapping Tool	Assisted students in oeir learning processes	Enhanced student engagement and understanding	Strengthened conceptual understanding through visual learning
Hwang & Tu (2021)	Learning Management System Integration	Real-time monitoring of indiess	Improved real-time feedback for both students and instructors	Promoted adaptive learning and data-informed teaching
Zhang (2022)	Quality Assurance System	Established continuous quality mon	Enabled stability in instructional design across cohorts	Reduced subjectivity in assessment and curriculum consistency
Bull et al. (2018)	Diagnostic Visualizations	Provided formative assessment insights	uctor's ability to offer timely interventions	Enhanced personalized support and feedback loops
Ahmed et al. (2017)	Group Spinner Tool	Facilitated visual reflection and communication	Supported stut and collaborative reflection	Fostered a reflective learning environment

The integration of learning analytics into classroom instruction via AI-based tutoring systems provides teachers with real-time, actionable insights, allowing for more adaptive and responsive teaching. For instance, Crompton and Burke (2023) use visualizations and infographics to support teacher orchestration, helping educators monitor student interactions and set learning goals. This enables efficient classroom management and improves teacher awareness.

Other studies focus on data-driven personalization. Ullah and Hafiz (2022) leverage Bisis tools for real-time data management, allowing for tailored support based on individual learning patterns. Similarly, Mousavinasab et al. (2021) employ Bayesian Networks to model student knowledge, which enables teachers to predict performance and plan data-informed interventions.

Furthermore, tools like MTFeedback and MTDashboard (Lawrence et al., 2022) and Open Learner Models (Koedinger et al., 2013) are used to facilitate group-based learning and self-regulated learning, respectively. These tools support collaborative interactions and foster accountability among students, enhancing their learning experience.

Additionally, Hwang and Tu (2021) discuss the use of Learning Management System integration to monitor individual progress in real-time, leading to more adaptive teaching. Martinez-Maldonado et al. (2015) contribute by implementing a multi-surface classroom ecology that allows teachers to deploy scripts for small groups, enabling tracking and feedback in real-time, increasing instructional responsiveness.

Overall, these learning analytics tools not only support personalized and adaptive learning but also enhance instructional flexibility, foster collaborative engagement, and improve student understanding. Through real-time monitoring and tailored feedback, AI-based tutoring systems equipped with learning analytics are transforming classroom instruction, making it more responsive and effective

3.5. What are the Future Research Directions for Advancing AI-Based Tutoring Systems in Education?

Future research in AI-based tutoring systems focuses on addressing current limitations and exploring innovative applications to enhance educational outcomes. These directions range from integrating ethical frameworks to enabling personalized lifelong learning pathways. Table 4.5 provides an overview of identified future research directions for advancing AI-based tutoring systems in education.

Table 8. Future Research Directions for Advancing AI-Based Tutoring Systems in Education

Author(s)	Future Research Directions	Focus
Ahmed & Ganapathy (2021)	Lifelong learning and skill development	Lifelong learning
Borenstein & Howard (2021)	Develoal frameworks specific to AI applications in education	AI ethics and data privacy
González-Calatayud et al. (2021)	Applying AI to udent assessment methods, reducing teacher workload and improving feedback	Assessment automation
Timan & Mann (2021)	Exploring privacyg technologies to protect student data in AI-enhanced educational systems	Data privacy and security
Alqahtani et al. (2023)	Studying AI's role in providing learning pathways based on student progress	Personalized learning
Tanenbaum (2016)	Investigating scalability and adaptAI in global classrooms to increase access to quality education	Scalability in global education
Wylie (2023)	Evaluating the effectiveness of AI tutorss education, focusing on learning outcomes	AI's role in professional education
Kochmar et al. (2022)	Integrating emotional recognition in AI tutors to address soal learning needs	Socio-emotional AI tutoring
Mahdaoui (2022)	Investigating human-AI collaboration for building rapport in AI-ing systems	Human-AI collaboration in tutoring
Clarke et al. (2015)	Conducting thematic analysis of student feedback on AI tools to improve AI's edpplications	AI feedback and system improvement

The future research directions in Table 7 reflect a diverse array of challenges and opportunities for advancing AI-based tutoring systems. Ahmed and Ganapathy (2021) suggest focusing on lifelong learning, proposing that AI tutoring systems should be designed to support skill development continuously over a learner's life. This aligns with broader educational goals of enabling lifelong learning adaptability. Ethical and privacy concerns remain a significant area of interest, as highlighted by Borenstein and Howard (2021), and Timan and Mann (2021). Their studies emphasize the need for ethical frameworks and privacy-preserving technologies, particularly given the vast amounts of student data AI systems manage. This focus on ethics and data privacy is crucial as AI applications in education become more pervasive. In the realm of classroom assessment, González-Calatayud et al. (2021) advocate for automating student assessments to reduce teacher workload while enhancing the feedback process. This direction supports more scalable and efficient use of AI, aligning with Tanenbaum's (2016) emphasis on scalability in global classrooms, which would enable wider access to quality education through AI.

Other research focuses on personalized learning and socio-emotional support. Alqahtani et al. (2023) explore how AI can create individualized learning pathways, while Kochmar et al. (2022) examine how AI can address socio-emotional learning needs through emotional recognition capabilities, adding a human touch to automated tutoring. Lastly, studies by Mahdaoui (2022) and Clarke et al. (2015) emphasize human-AI collaboration and continuous improvement of AI systems based on feedback. Mahdaoui (2022) discusses the importance of building rapport through human-AI collaboration, which can enhance engagement and trust in AI tutoring. Clarke et al. (2015) recommend analyzing student feedback to iteratively refine AI systems, ensuring they remain relevant and effective in educational settings.

In summary, these future research directions suggest a multi-faceted approach to advancing AI-based tutoring systems. Emphasizing ethical considerations, personalization, socio-emotional support, and continuous improvement, these areas reflect the potential for AI to transform education while addressing critical challenges

4. DISCUSSION

The analysis of AI-based tutoring systems across different aspects—personalized learning, intelligent agent roles, learning analytics integration, and future research directions—reveals significant insights into how these systems enhance educational outcomes and the areas that warrant further exploration. This discussion synthesizes the findings from each research question to present a holistic understanding of the contributions and potential of AI-based tutoring systems in education.

4.1. Personalized Learning in AI-Based Tutoring Systems

Personalized learning is a central feature of AI-based tutoring systems, as these systems adapt content, feedback, and learning trajectories to meet individual student needs. Studies like those by Walkington and Bernacki (2014) and Alharbi and Cristea (2021) emphasize the role of context personalization and adaptive learning pathways in increasing engagement and academic performance. These systems use tools such as model-tracing, knowledge-tracing, and reinforcement learning to personalize instruction and provide immediate feedback (Aleven et al., 2016). The integration of these tools fosters higher levels of student engagement and motivation, as evidenced in systems that tailor content to align with students' interests and cognitive levels (Koedinger et al., 2023; Alamri et al., 2020).

AI-based systems not only cater to cognitive needs but also consider emotional and motivational aspects. Reeve (2013) highlights the application of Self-Determination Theory (SDT) in designing challenges based on students' motivation levels, resulting in enhanced motivation and achievement. By adapting content to students' preferences and performance, AI tutoring systems contribute to a more inclusive and supportive learning environment, promoting self-regulated learning and accountability (Bull et al., 2018; Martinez-Maldonado et al., 2015).

4.2. Roles of Intelligent Agents in Enhancing AI-Based Tutoring

Intelligent agents play diverse roles in AI-based tutoring systems, ranging from virtual facilitators to socially engaging agents that foster interaction and motivation. Schroeder, Adesope, and Gilbert (2013) discuss virtual facilitators that provide personalized dialogue, which aids in learning continuity and professional development. Dialog-based Intelligent Tutoring Systems (ITS), as described by Nye, Graesser, and Hu (2014), enhance conceptual understanding by facilitating open-ended tutoring sessions, significantly improving learning gains. These findings underscore the value of intelligent agents in providing differentiated instruction that addresses both cognitive and social-emotional needs.

Furthermore, agents with socio-emotional capacities, like those studied by Dinçer and Doğanay (2017), build connections with students, enhancing motivation and engagement. Adaptive feedback and conversational agents, such as those discussed by Graesser et al. (2017) and Lu et al. (2021), support student learning by adjusting to real-time performance and promoting deeper understanding. This adaptability aligns with Carnegie Learning's approach to adaptive tutoring, where real-time student feedback informs instructional decisions, leading to better learning outcomes (Timms, 2016).

4.3. Integration of Learning Analytics in Classroom Instruction

The integration of learning analytics in AI-based tutoring systems allows for data-driven decisions that enhance instructional practices. Visualizations and tools like MTFeedback and MTDashboard (Lawrence et al., 2022) offer teachers insights into student interactions, enabling them to monitor progress and adjust instruction accordingly. For instance, Crompton and Burke (2023) highlight how visual tracking tools facilitate teacher orchestration, increasing awareness of student needs and supporting efficient classroom management.

Learning analytics also enables real-time intervention and adaptation. Bayesian Networks (Mousavinasab et al., 2021) and Open Learner Models (Koedinger et al., 2013) provide predictive insights into student knowledge and progress, fostering self-directed learning and accountability. Moreover, tools like the Quality Assurance System, as discussed by Zhang (2022), ensure consistency in instructional design across different cohorts, reducing subjectivity in assessment. These analytics-driven systems encourage data-informed teaching and create opportunities for personalized support, reinforcing adaptive learning environments (Bull et al., 2018; Hwang & Tu, 2021).

4.4. Future Research Directions for AI-Based Tutoring Systems

The future of AI-based tutoring systems lies in addressing current challenges and exploring innovative solutions that enhance system effectiveness and inclusivity. Lifelong learning and skill development emerge as essential areas for future research, as Ahmed and Ganapathy (2021) suggest that AI systems should support continuous education. This direction aligns with the growing need for adaptable learning solutions that evolve alongside learners' career and personal development.

Ethics and data privacy are also critical issues, especially given the reliance of AI systems on extensive data collection. Borenstein and Howard (2021) and Timan and Mann (2021) advocate for privacy-preserving technologies and ethical frameworks specific to educational AI applications. Addressing these ethical considerations is crucial for building trust and safeguarding student privacy, particularly as AI tools become more integrated into educational systems.

Another key research area is the socio-emotional dimension of AI-based tutoring. Studies by Alqahtani et al. (2023) and Kochmar et al. (2022) call for further investigation into personalized learning pathways and emotional recognition in AI tutors, respectively. Socio-emotional support enhances learning engagement and can address the holistic needs of students, making AI tools more effective and inclusive. Additionally, Mahdaoui (2022) emphasizes human-AI collaboration in tutoring, which fosters rapport and trust between students and AI agents, a factor that can significantly impact engagement and learning outcomes.

Lastly, research on scalability and system improvement remains vital. Tanenbaum (2016) and Clarke et al. (2015) discuss the importance of scalable AI systems that can be deployed in diverse educational settings. These systems should continuously improve through feedback loops to remain relevant and effective, which would help AI tutoring solutions reach a broader audience and support global education goals.

5. CONCLUSION

AI-based tutoring systems are transforming education through personalized learning, intelligent agent-driven support, data-informed instruction, and a forward-looking research agenda. This discussion highlights the multifaceted contributions of AI systems in addressing individual learning needs, enhancing teacher support, and fostering an adaptive learning environment. Future research must continue to focus on ethical considerations, emotional support, scalability, and lifelong learning to ensure that AI-based tutoring systems evolve to meet the diverse needs of learners worldwide.

REFERENCES

Ahmed, Z., & Ganapathy, T. (2021). Lifelong learning and skill development through AI-based tutoring systems. *Journal of Educational Technology Development and Exchange*, *14*(2), 111–128.

Alamri, M.. (2020). Self-regulated learning through personalized online courses in AI-based tutoring. *Computers & Education*, *150*, 103839.

Aleven, V. A. W. M. M.. (2016). Adaptive learning technologies in AI-based tutoring systems: Cognitive science approaches. *Educational Technology Research and Development*, *64*(3), 553–575.

Alharbi, M., & Cristea, A. (2021). Personalized learning pathways in intelligent tutoring systems using reinforcement learning. *International Journal of Artificial Intelligence in Education*, *31*(2), 167–186.

Borenstein, J., & Howard, A. (2021). Ethical frameworks for AI in education. *Science and Engineering Ethics*, *27*(1), 8. PMID: 33538906

Bull, S.. (2018). Diagnostic visualizations and formative assessment in AI-enhanced classrooms. *AI in Education Journal*, *10*(4), 415–435.

Clarke, T.. (2015). Continuous improvement in AI-based tutoring systems through student feedback analysis. *Journal of Educational Technology & Society*, *18*(3), 12–22.

Crompton, H., & Burke, D. (2023). Visual tracking in AI tutoring for classroom orchestration. *Journal of Interactive Learning Research*, *34*(1), 45–63.

Dinçer, S., & Doğanay, A. (2017). Socio-emotional capacity of educational agents in AI tutoring. *Interactive Learning Environments*, *25*(1), 38–54.

Fancsali, S.. (2014). Interest-matched problem selection in MATHia AI tutoring. *Journal of Educational Computing Research*, *50*(3), 317–339.

González-Calatayud, V.. (2021). AI-assisted student assessment in classroom instruction. *Educational Technology Research and Development*, *69*(5), 1017–1034.

Graesser, A. C.. (2017). Conversational agents in AI tutoring: An assessment. *Journal of Educational Psychology*, *109*(1), 20–34.

Hidi, S., & Ainley, M. (2008). Situational interest personalization in AI tutoring. *Educational Psychologist*, *43*(3), 173–184.

Hwang, G. J., & Tu, Y. F. (2021). Integrating learning management systems for adaptive feedback in AI-based tutoring. *British Journal of Educational Technology, 52*(2), 649–662.

Koedinger, K. R.. (2013). Open Learner Models and self-regulated learning in AI tutoring. *International Journal of Artificial Intelligence in Education, 23*(1-4), 138–157.

Lawrence, R.. (2022). Real-time monitoring in group-based learning through AI analytics. *Educational Technology Research and Development, 70*(2), 401–420.

Lu, X.. (2021). Adaptive feedback in AI-based tutoring systems. *Educational Data Mining, 11*(2), 39–54.

Mahdaoui, A. (2022). Human-AI collaboration in educational AI tutoring. *Journal of Human-Computer Studies, 156*, 102758.

Martinez-Maldonado, R.. (2015). Multi-surface classroom ecology for real-time interventions in AI tutoring. *Computers & Education, 89*, 1–12.

Mavrikis, M.. (2019). Real-time analytics for classroom orchestration in AI-based tutoring. *Learning Analytics Review, 24*, 201–219.

Mousavinasab, E.. (2021). Bayesian networks in AI tutoring for predictive analytics. *Journal of Educational Data Science, 7*(1), 89–105.

Nye, B. D. (2016). Socially engaging tools for AI tutoring in education. *Artificial Intelligence in Education, 13*(1), 5–16.

Reeve, J. (2013). Self-determination theory and agentic engagement in personalized AI learning. *Educational Psychologist, 48*(4), 337–348.

Schroeder, N. L., Adesope, O., & Gilbert, R. (2013). Virtual facilitators in AI tutoring systems. *Journal of Educational Psychology, 105*(1), 50–63.

Shi, Y.. (2020). Social adaptive e-learning with Topolor in AI-based tutoring. *Journal of Educational Technology & Society, 23*(4), 39–50.

Tanenbaum, C. (2016). Scalability of AI tutoring in global classrooms. *Global Education Review, 3*(4), 37–54.

Timms, M. J. (2016). Educational robots as social agents in AI tutoring. *Journal of Computer Assisted Learning, 32*(4), 336–348.

Ullah, M., & Hafiz, M. (2022). Real-time analytics in AI tutoring through Bisis tools. *Educational Data Management Review, 29*(3), 57–68.

Walkington, C., & Bernacki, M. (2014). Context personalization in math AI tutoring. *Mathematics Education Research Journal*, *26*(4), 795–813.

Wylie, R. (2023). Evaluating AI's role in professional education. *International Journal of Education and Research*, *115*, 102051.

Chapter 8
From NPCs to AI Assistants:
A Scoping Review of AI-Driven Agents in Immersive STEM Learning

Mahmoud Hamash
https://orcid.org/0009-0006-6350-1533
Dublin City University, Ireland

Hanan Ghreir
https://orcid.org/0009-0007-7707-9051
Universiti Teknologi Malaysia, UAE

Peter Tiernan
https://orcid.org/0000-0001-5076-8905
Dublin City University, Ireland

Taoufik Boulhrir
https://orcid.org/0000-0003-3536-2207
Al Akhawayn University, Morocco

ABSTRACT

The integration of Artificial Intelligence (AI)-driven agents, including Non-Player Characters (NPCs), pedagogical agents, and AI assistants, within Immersive Virtual Reality (IVR) environments represents a rapidly evolving domain in educational technology. This chapter conducts a scoping review (2015–2025) following the PRISMA for Scoping Reviews (PRISMA-ScR) guidelines to synthesize existing research on AI-driven agents in STEM (Science, Technology, Engineering, and Mathematics)

DOI: 10.4018/979-8-3373-0847-0.ch008

education. A systematic search across Scopus, ScienceDirect, and ERIC identified 82 publications, with only three meeting the eligibility criteria. The review maps the current state of research, highlights knowledge gaps, and suggests future directions for educators, researchers, and policymakers. The findings underscore the limited but growing body of literature on AI-driven agents in immersive STEM education, emphasizing the need for further empirical investigations to explore their impact on engagement, learning outcomes, and instructional practices.

INTRODUCTION

STEM (Science, Technology, Engineering, and Mathematics) education has emerged as a critical focus in modern curricula, driven by the growing demand for skills in these fields to address global challenges such as climate change, technological innovation, and economic competitiveness (Margot & Kettler, 2019). More recently, the integration of the Arts into STEM—creating STEAM (Science, Technology, Engineering, Arts, and Mathematics)—has gained traction, emphasising the importance of creativity, design thinking, and interdisciplinary approaches in solving complex problems. Both STEM and STEAM education aim to equip students with critical thinking, problem-solving, and collaboration skills, preparing them for the demands of the 21st-century workforce. However, traditional teaching methods often struggle to engage students effectively, particularly in abstract or highly technical subjects, highlighting the need for innovative pedagogical approaches and impactful use of educational technologies (Freeman et al., 2014).

The integration of Artificial Intelligence (AI) into educational technologies has ushered in a new era of innovation, particularly in STEM education. Among the most transformative advancements in this domain are AI-powered Non-Player Characters (NPC), AI pedagogical agents, and AI assistants, which are increasingly being deployed within Immersive Virtual Reality (IVR) environments (Hwang et al., 2020). These AI-driven entities represent a convergence of cutting-edge technologies that hold immense potential for enhancing student engagement, personalising learning experiences, and addressing long-standing instructional challenges in STEM education (Wang et al., 2008; Zawacki-Richter et al., 2019).

The concept of using computers to support learning has a rich history, dating back to the early days of educational computing (e.g., Suppes & Jerman, 1970). Early explorations focused on computer-aided instruction (CAI), which primarily involved delivering pre-programmed content to students. However, the advent of AI, particularly machine learning, has paved the way for more sophisticated and adaptive learning environments. AI, broadly defined as the ability of a computer system to perform tasks that typically require human intelligence (Russell & Norvig,

2022), has enabled the development of intelligent tutoring systems (ITS) capable of providing personalised feedback and guidance (VanLEHN, 2011). More recently, the focus has shifted towards incorporating AI into immersive environments like IVR, which offers students a more engaging and interactive learning experience (Radianti et al., 2020). Within these immersive environments, several key AI-driven concepts are emerging, each playing a distinct role in shaping the future of learning.

Immersive learning encompasses a spectrum of technologies designed to create engaging and interactive educational experiences by simulating real-world scenarios or transporting learners to entirely new environments. A crucial element is the concept of presence, the feeling of "being there," which enhances learning outcomes by boosting motivation and knowledge retention (Slater & Wilbur, 1997; Radianti et al., 2020). Immersive Virtual Reality (IVR) creates fully computer-generated worlds accessed via head-mounted displays, enabling experiential learning impossible in real life (Dalgarno & Lee, 2010; Bailenson et al., 2008). Immersive virtual worlds, often confused with IVR, can refer to persistent, shared environments for collaborative learning and simulations (De Back et al., 2023). Augmented Reality (AR) overlays digital information onto the real world, enhancing perception through smartphones or tablets and offering contextual learning by blending digital and physical elements (Yuen et al., 2011). Mixed Reality (MR) bridges IVR and AR, allowing real and virtual objects to coexist and interact, creating highly interactive experiences (Milgram & Kishino, 1994). Extended Reality (XR) is the umbrella term for all these technologies, representing the entire spectrum of virtuality (Hamash et al., 2024; Sherman & Craig, 2003). These immersive technologies, by creating a sense of presence and interaction, offer powerful new avenues for education. However, the true potential of these immersive environments is further amplified when coupled with the power of Artificial Intelligence, which allows for personalised learning, dynamic content generation, and the creation of intelligent virtual tutors, the subject we will explore next.

AI pedagogical agents, which are virtual or robotic entities designed to facilitate learning through interactive, socially engaging, and adaptive behaviours, have a rich history in educational research (Al Omoush et al., 2023). The concept of pedagogical agents traces its roots to the late 1990s, when researchers like Lester et al. (1997) introduced the "Persona Effect," demonstrating that lifelike virtual characters could significantly enhance learners' motivation and comprehension. These early agents, often embodied as on-screen tutors or guides, were designed to simulate human-like interactions, providing explanations, feedback, and encouragement to learners. Over time, advancements in natural language processing (NLP), machine learning (ML), and affective computing have enabled pedagogical agents to become more sophisticated and adapt to individual learners' needs, emotions, and cognitive states. For instance, systems like AutoTutor, developed by Graesser et al. (2004), have demonstrated the ability to engage students in natural language dialogues, helping them construct knowledge through scaffolded conversations. Similarly, the Teachable Agents framework has shown that students learn more effectively when they teach virtual agents, a phenomenon known as the "protégé effect."

Non-player characters (NPCs), traditionally a staple of video games, have also found a place in educational contexts, particularly in IVR environments. Unlike traditional pedagogical agents, which are often confined to 2D screens, AI NPCs in IVR can inhabit fully immersive, three-dimensional spaces, enabling richer and more contextually relevant interactions. For example, AI NPCs can act as virtual lab partners in a chemistry simulation, guiding students through complex experiments, or as historical figures in a social studies lesson, engaging students in role-playing activities (Pellas et al., 2020). The use of AI NPCs in education leverages the principles of situated learning, which posits that knowledge is best acquired in contexts that mirror real-world applications (Radianti et al., 2020). By embedding AI NPCs within IVR environments, educators can create authentic, experiential learning opportunities that bridge the gap between theoretical knowledge and practical application. Moreover, the adaptive capabilities of AI NPCs allow them to respond dynamically to learners' actions, providing personalised feedback and scaffolding that cater to individual learning trajectories.

AI assistants, such as Siri, Alexa, and Google Assistant, have become ubiquitous in everyday life, offering convenience and efficiency in tasks ranging from scheduling to information retrieval. In educational settings, AI assistants are increasingly being repurposed as pedagogical tools, capable of supporting both teachers and students in a variety of ways. For instance, AI assistants can provide instant access to educational resources, answer students' questions in real time, and even facilitate collaborative learning activities (Holmes & Tuomi, 2022). In STEM education, AI assistants can help students solve complex problems by breaking them down into manageable steps, offering hints, and explaining underlying concepts. The pedagogical potential of AI assistants lies in their ability to deliver just-in-time support, reducing cognitive load and enabling students to focus on higher-order thinking tasks (Sajja et al., 2023). Furthermore, AI assistants can be integrated into IVR environments to enhance their functionality, serving as virtual guides or mentors that accompany students throughout their immersive learning experiences.

The integration of AI NPCs, pedagogical agents, and AI assistants within IVR environments represents a novel and rapidly evolving domain in educational technology. Immersive Virtual Reality (IVR), which refers to computer-generated environments that simulate physical presence in real or imagined worlds, provides an ideal platform for these AI-driven entities to interact with learners in meaningful and impactful ways. By combining the immersive qualities of IVR with the adaptive and interactive capabilities of AI, educators can create learning experiences that are not only engaging but also deeply personalised and contextually relevant. It is crucial to integrate the impactful use of technology, as prescribed by Hamash and Mohamed (2023), ensuring that these innovations are implemented in a way that enhances pedagogical effectiveness, fosters meaningful learner interactions, and supports diverse learning needs.

Unlike traditional teaching methods, which often rely on passive knowledge transmission through lectures, textbooks, or rigid online modules, AI-driven entities transform the teaching and learning processes by creating highly interactive and personalised learning experiences. These AI technologies adjust their instructional approach based on student responses, performance data, and even emotional cues, offering real-time scaffolding that conventional methods struggle to match (Hwang et al., 2020; Wang et al., 2008). For instance, while a teacher may have limited time to address every student's learning challenge in a large classroom setting, AI pedagogical agents within IVR can provide individualised, context-aware guidance, ensuring that students receive immediate and targeted feedback. This ability, whether through adaptive questioning, multimodal feedback, or real-time problem-solving, helps reinforce STEM concepts in ways that traditional one-size-fits-all instruction cannot achieve (VanLehn, 2011).

The immersive nature of IVR, when combined with AI, extends beyond the constraints of traditional classroom environments in ways that enable students to engage with STEM concepts through experiential, hands-on simulations. The fact that traditional STEM instruction often depends on static diagrams or lab-based demonstrations with logistical constraints makes AI-driven entities in IVR environments a good option for students to experiment with virtual lab partners, conduct simulations of complex scientific phenomena, and receive instant, AI-generated explanations tailored to their learning pace (Radianti et al., 2020). This dynamic and exploratory approach to STEM education fosters deeper engagement, strengthens conceptual retention, and promotes higher-order thinking skills, which sets AI-enhanced immersive learning apart from conventional methods. As research continues to evolve and more knowledge is contributed to the academic community, the transformative potential of AI pedagogical agents in IVR environments may redefine how students interact with and master STEM subjects, bridging the gap between theoretical understanding and real-world application (Zawacki-Richter et al., 2019).

Despite their potential, the use of AI NPCs, pedagogical agents, and AI assistants in IVR-based STEM education remains an underexplored area of research. This scarcity of research highlights the need for further investigation into the design, implementation, and efficacy of these technologies in immersive STEM education. This chapter aims to provide a comprehensive overview of the current state of research on AI-driven NPCs, pedagogical agents, and AI assistants in IVR-based STEM education. By mapping existing studies, identifying knowledge gaps, and proposing future research directions, this review seeks to inform educators, researchers, and policymakers about the transformative potential of these technologies. As AI and IVR continue to evolve, their integration into educational practices promises to redefine the boundaries of teaching and learning, offering unprecedented opportunities to enhance STEM education in the 21st century.

RESEARCH BACKGROUND

The integration of AI NPCs, pedagogical agents, and AI assistants within Immersive Virtual Reality (IVR) environments represents a rapidly evolving domain in educational technology, particularly in STEM (Science, Technology, Engineering, and Mathematics) education. These AI NPCs hold significant potential for enhancing student engagement, improving learning outcomes, and addressing instructional challenges. However, research in this area remains limited, with few studies systematically evaluating their effectiveness. Given this gap, this literature review section focuses on presenting similar research conducted in related areas, such as 2D learning environments, to provide insights into existing approaches and frameworks. By examining studies on AI-driven interactions in non-immersive digital learning spaces, this section highlights transferable strategies, pedagogical implications, and areas requiring further empirical investigation to advance the integration of AI in IVR education.

AI-powered NPCs are increasingly integrated into educational settings to provide personalised and interactive learning experiences. Often designed as Intelligent Pedagogical Agents (IPAs), these NPCs guide students through complex STEM concepts, offer real-time feedback, and adapt to individual learning needs. For example, AI NPCs in 2D game environments have been shown to replicate complex social interactions and contribute to emergent societal structures, offering insights into how AI can mirror or enhance human social dynamics in educational contexts (Omirgaliyev et al., 2024). Similarly, the integration of transmedia narratives and augmented reality (AR) in converting children's animated films into educational games highlights how AI-driven NPCs can foster creativity and collaboration among students (Del Moral-Pérez et al., 2024). Moreover, AI NPCs can provide emotional support by recognising and responding to students' affective states, thereby creating a more engaging and effective learning experience. Research indicates that emotionally intelligent NPCs can significantly enhance student engagement and learning outcomes, particularly in STEM education, where personalised scaffolding is crucial for mastering complex scientific and mathematical concepts (Terracina & Mecella, 2014).

Immersive Virtual Reality (IVR) has been widely recognised for its ability to create interactive and engaging learning environments. By allowing students to explore complex STEM concepts in safe and controlled settings, IVR enhances comprehension and knowledge retention. Studies have demonstrated that AR and VR technologies in physics education improve students' self-efficacy and problem-solving skills, while also generating higher levels of engagement and positive emotions compared to traditional learning methods (Brahimi & Sarirete, 2024). As stated by Brahimi & Sarirete, (2024), the combination of IVR with AI-powered NPCs offers a unique opportunity to create adaptive and personalised learning experiences, where AI NPCs function as virtual tutors, guiding students through intricate tasks, providing immediate feedback, and adjusting their behaviour based on student performance. This approach aligns with the principles of constructionism, which emphasise experiential, hands-on learning and the role of technology in facilitating knowledge construction.

Generative agents, leveraging machine learning to simulate human behaviour, have also been explored in virtual societies and educational simulations. These agents engage in complex social interactions, allocate roles, and cultivate social norms within digital environments, providing a platform for studying human-like behaviours in virtual spaces. A study by Park et al. (2023) created a digital community populated by 20 AI agents with unique backstories, advanced memory architectures, and decision-making capabilities. These agents demonstrated collective decision-making and developed distinct social norms, highlighting the potential of generative agents to replicate intricate social dynamics. The implications of this research for STEM education are significant, as generative agents can be used to simulate real-world scenarios and encourage collaborative problem-solving among students. Further exploration by Omiragaliyev et al. (2024) demonstrates how Large Language Models (LLMs) integrated into a 2D game environment can autonomously develop virtual societies, allocating roles and responsibilities while cultivating shared norms. Such applications showcase the potential for generative agents to enrich learning environments by providing interactive and socially dynamic educational experiences.

Despite the promising potential of AI-powered NPCs and generative agents in STEM education, several challenges and ethical considerations have been highlighted in the literature. Technological limitations and infrastructure disparities may hinder equitable access, particularly for students in underserved areas who lack the necessary hardware or internet connectivity (Brahimi & Sarirete, 2024). Additionally, concerns regarding the ethical implications of AI in education, such as privacy, security, and bias, remain pressing. While powerful, AI models like GPT-3 can generate erroneous or misleading information, potentially affecting student learning, as noted by Brahimi and Sarirete (2024).. Moreover, the over-reliance on AI-driven tools could potentially undermine the development of critical thinking and problem-solving skills, as students may become dependent on AI-generated solutions. Also, Ghreir (2023) discusses the impact of such educational platforms on teacher evaluation and how school leaders address the subject of teacher evaluation. The integration of AI NPCs into STEM education also raises concerns about digital equity, teacher preparedness, and the psychological effects of immersive technologies on students. Chiu & Li, (2023) stress the importance of designing safe learning environments that address these concerns, while Del Moral-Pérez et al. (2024) advocate for inclusive and equitable educational game design that leverages AI and AR to enhance student learning experiences.

Given the limited research on AI NPCs in IVR STEM education, several key areas require further exploration. Longitudinal studies are needed to assess the long-term impact of AI-powered NPCs on student engagement and learning outcomes, particularly in STEM fields. Such studies should examine whether sustained interactions with AI NPCs lead to lasting attitudinal and behavioural changes toward STEM education. Future research should also adopt interdisciplinary approaches, integrating AI, cognitive science, and educational psychology to refine NPC realism and instructional effectiveness. Investigating how AI NPCs support computational thinking, creativity, and collaboration among students could further enhance their pedagogical value. Additionally, the development of ethical AI frameworks is crucial to ensuring fairness, transparency, and accountability in AI-driven educational interactions, addressing issues related to data privacy, bias, and the psychological effects of immersive learning technologies. Scalability and accessibility remain pressing concerns, necessitating research on how AI-powered IVR tools can be effectively implemented across diverse educational contexts and demographics while addressing the digital divide. Lastly, the successful integration of AI-driven entities in STEM education requires substantial investment in teacher training (Hamash et al., 2024). Educators must be equipped with the necessary skills and knowledge to effectively utilise these technologies, ensuring that students receive personalised and adaptive learning experiences that foster deeper engagement and understanding.

The integration of AI-powered entities within IVR environments presents a promising yet underexplored avenue for STEM education. While current research underscores the potential of these technologies to enhance student engagement and learning outcomes, significant gaps remain in understanding their pedagogical affordances, effectiveness, and ethical implications. Future research should focus on establishing robust theoretical frameworks, conducting empirical studies, and addressing the challenges associated with AI-driven entities integration in immersive learning environments. By doing so, educators, researchers, and policymakers can harness the full potential of AI and IVR to transform STEM education and better prepare students for the evolving demands of the future workforce.

METHOD

To provide a structured understanding of the emerging field of the integration of AI-driven entities in immersive technologies in STEM education, this study presents a scoping review following the PRISMA for Scoping Reviews (PRISMA-ScR) guidelines (Tricco et al., 2018). The primary aim is to map the existing research on the use of AI-driven entities (such as Artificial Intelligence (AI)-driven agents, Non-Player Characters (NPC), pedagogical agents, and AI assistants) within Immersive Virtual Reality (IVR) environments in STEM/STEAM education.

Search Strategy

A comprehensive search was conducted across three major academic databases to identify relevant literature: Scopus, ScienceDirect, and ERIC. These databases were selected due to their comprehensive coverage of peer-reviewed educational, technological, and scientific literature. The search was conducted using a structured query that combined keywords related to AI-driven entities, immersive learning, and STEM/STEAM education. The search string included terms such as 'Virtual Pedagogical Agents,' 'Intelligent Virtual Agents,' 'Artificial Intelligence,' 'NPC,' and 'AI-driven NPC" and "Pedagogical Agents,' combined with 'Immersive Learning,' 'Virtual Reality,' 'Augmented Reality,' 'Mixed Reality,' and 'Extended Reality.' Additionally, the search was refined to include studies specifically related to STEM and STEAM education within academic databases, ensuring relevance to educational contexts. The search query was adapted to meet the specific requirements and structural differences of each of the three databases used in the review."

Selection Criteria

To ensure the relevance and quality of the studies included in this review, strict inclusion and exclusion criteria were applied. The inclusion criteria focused on:

- **Studies investigating AI-driven entities** (such as Virtual Pedagogical Agents, Intelligent Virtual Agents, Artificial Intelligence, NPCs, and AI-Driven NPC Pedagogical Agents) **within immersive environments** (Virtual Reality, Augmented Reality, Mixed Reality, and Extended Reality).
- **Research conducted in STEM/STEAM education** contexts, specifically within education settings.
- **Studies published between 2015 and 2025** to ensure the inclusion of recent advancements in AI and immersive learning technologies.

- **Peer-reviewed journal articles, conference papers, book chapters, books, review articles, and editorials** to maintain academic rigour and capture diverse scholarly perspectives.
- **Publications in English** to ensure accessibility and consistency in data analysis.

Studies were excluded from this review based on the following criteria:

- **Studies not focused on AI-driven entities** (such as Virtual Pedagogical Agents, Intelligent Virtual Agents, Artificial Intelligence, NPCs, and AI-driven NPC Pedagogical Agents) **within immersive environments** (including 'Immersive Learning,' 'Virtual Reality,' 'Augmented Reality,' 'Mixed Reality,' and 'Extended Reality').
- **Research not conducted within STEM/STEAM education** contexts, particularly those unrelated to K-12, primary, secondary, post-primary, or early education settings.
- **Studies published before 2015 or after 2025**, to ensure the inclusion of current and relevant research.
- **Studies published in languages other than English** to ensure consistency in data analysis and accessibility.
- **Research focusing on unrelated fields**, as these were outside the scope of this review.

Study Selection

After applying the inclusion and exclusion criteria, a total of 82 publications were initially identified. The full-text review and screening process, conducted by two independent reviewers, led to the exclusion of most studies due to relevance or methodological issues. Ultimately, only three studies met the eligibility requirements and were included in this scoping review. These studies were selected based on their focus on AI-driven entities (such as Virtual Pedagogical Agents, Intelligent Virtual Agents, Artificial Intelligence, NPCs, and AI-Driven NPC Pedagogical Agents) within immersive environments (including 'Immersive Learning,' 'Virtual Reality,' 'Augmented Reality,' 'Mixed Reality,' and 'Extended Reality'). Additionally, studies were included if they were conducted within STEM/STEAM education contexts. Figure 1 illustrates the PRISMA flow diagram for this scoping review.

Figure 1. The PRISMA flow diagram

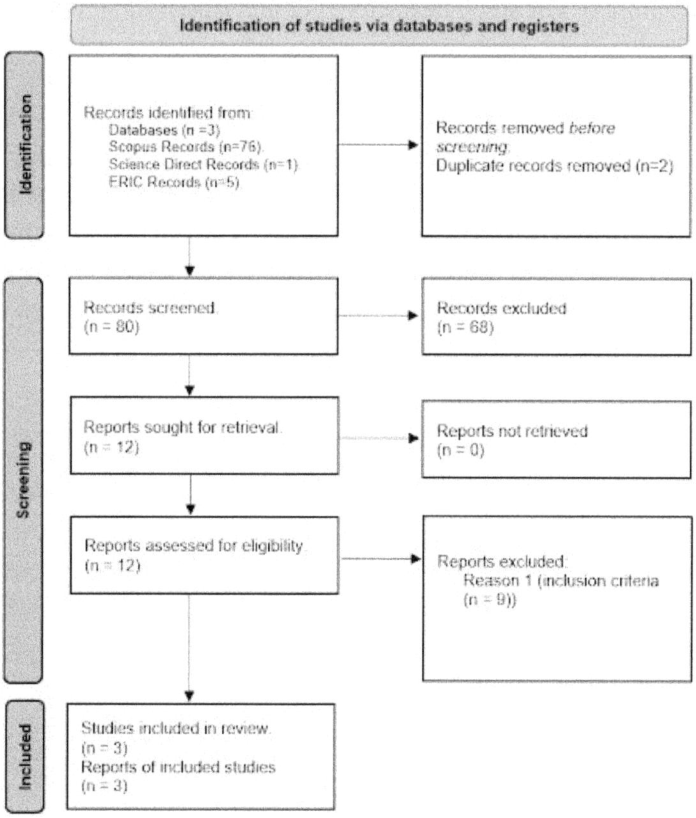

Data Extraction

For each of the selected studies, key data were extracted, including:

- Study aims and objectives.
- Educational context and application of immersive technologies.
- Methodology used (qualitative, quantitative, or mixed methods).
- Key findings and recommendations.
- Identified limitations and areas for future research.

The data extraction process was conducted in accordance with the PRISMA-ScR checklist and guided by the Joanna Briggs Institute (JBI) Data Extraction Tool for Scoping Reviews (Tricco et al., 2018). This approach ensured consistency, transparency, and methodological rigour throughout the review process, allowing for the systematic capture of key study characteristics and findings.

Data Analysis

The findings from the selected studies were analysed thematically to identify patterns, trends, and common themes in the use of immersive technologies in education. The themes were organised into categories such as usability, technical limitations, AI integration, and collaborative learning, based on the research questions and objectives of the scoping review. The analysis also highlighted research gaps and areas for future exploration.

Ethical Considerations

As this is a secondary analysis of existing literature, there are no ethical concerns related to participant involvement. All included studies were subjected to ethical approval processes in their respective institutions. This review adheres to ethical guidelines in academic research, ensuring proper citation and acknowledgement of the original authors.

FINDINGS

This scoping review identified and analysed three papers related to AI assistance, Conversation AI, AI-driven agents, Non-Player Characters (NPC), pedagogical agents, and AI assistants published in 2024. All three papers (presented in Table 1) were sourced from the Scopus database and were published as conference proceedings. The conferences represented were the 18th International Conference on INnovations in Intelligent SysTems and Applications (INISTA 2024), the 2024 IEEE International Conference on Artificial Intelligence and eXtended and Virtual Reality (AIxVR), and the 2024 IEEE International Conference on Consumer Electronics (ICCE). The geographical distribution of the studies included Europe (Romania), North America (Canada), and Africa (Ethiopia).

Table 1. A list of the papers included in this scoping review

#	Title	Year	Authors	Conference
1	Future Education: Experimenting with Chemical Reactions in Virtual Reality	2024	Duca A.; Constantinescu G.-G.; Iftene A.	18th International Conference on INnovations in Intelligent SysTems and Applications, INISTA 2024
2	CuriosityXR: context-aware education experiences with mixed reality and conversation AI	2024	Aaditya Vaze, Alexis Morris, Ian Clarke	Proceedings - 2024 IEEE International Conference on Artificial Intelligence and eXtended and Virtual Reality, AIxVR 2024
3	The Possibilities of AI and Augmented Reality in Education	2024	Fraol Gelana; Abraham Campbell.	Digest of Technical Papers - IEEE International Conference on Consumer Electronics

Regarding research methodology, one study employed a quantitative experimental design, another used a mixed-methods approach, and the third was theoretical. Data collection tools included questionnaires, interviews, achievement tests, and theoretical analysis. Notably, the sample sizes for the two empirical studies were small, ranging from 1 to 10 participants. Furthermore, the methodological details provided in the conference proceedings were limited, potentially hindering a comprehensive understanding of the research processes.

The selected studies also shed light on real-world implementation challenges and innovative solutions. For instance, Duca et al. (2024) describe the deployment of a virtual chemistry lab featuring an AI-driven "Lab Assistant," which facilitated student learning through real-time guidance and contextual feedback. However, they also reported usability issues such as motion sickness and limited interactivity with the virtual environment. Similarly, Vaze et al. (2024) implemented the CuriosityXR system in educational settings, enabling learners to explore concepts through AI-powered conversational agents. While the system boosted engagement and visual retention, the authors noted difficulties with voice recognition accuracy and gesture control, pointing to the need for better multimodal input processing. These case studies exemplify both the potential and the hurdles of AI-integrated immersive learning in practice.

Research Gaps and Limitations

The research gaps identified across the studies highlight several areas that warrant further exploration and development in the context of AI agent integration in immersive STEM/STEAM education. Firstly, the studies reviewed exhibit a range of methodological limitations that affect the reliability, replicability, and generalisability of their findings. Notably, Duca et al. (2024) lacked transparency in participant selection criteria, instrument validation procedures, and the rigour of data analysis methods, which undermines the credibility of their conclusions. Similarly, while Vaze et al. (2024) employed a clear mixed-methods design and secured ethical approval, the study did not sufficiently address how qualitative data were analysed or whether instruments were validated for use in immersive learning environments. These methodological shortcomings restrict the interpretability of the findings and highlight the need for more robust research designs in future studies. Finally, Gelana and Campbell (2024) is a theoretical paper and lacks an implemented research methodology, which limits its empirical contribution and generalisability.

The limited sample sizes in the usability tests conducted by Duca et al. (2024) and Vaze et al. (2024) suggest the need for broader, more diverse participant groups to validate the findings and ensure the generalisability of the results. Additionally, the scope of the experiments in both studies was constrained, leaving room for more comprehensive investigations into the long-term effects and scalability of AI agent integration in immersive STEM/STEAM in educational contexts. The issue of small sample sizes and lack of diversity in usability studies is a well-documented limitation in educational technology research. This issue is a recurring challenge in immersive learning research, as highlighted by Tribe & Singha (2023) and Hamash et al. (2024), who systematically reviewed disparities in AR/VR studies and emphasised the need for inclusive sampling to ensure findings are applicable across diverse demographics. Similarly, Makransky & Petersen (2021) argue that small, homogenous samples in immersive learning studies limit the external validity of results, particularly in real-world educational settings. Schott and Marshall (2023) further critique the methodological limitations of small-scale VR studies, calling for larger and more diverse participant groups to improve the robustness of findings. In addition to sample size limitations, the scope of experiments in both studies is constrained, leaving room for more comprehensive investigations into the long-term effects and scalability of AI agent integration in immersive STEM/STEAM education. Hwang et al. (2023) identify scalability and long-term efficacy as critical challenges in AI-driven educational research, emphasising the need for longitudinal studies to assess the sustained impact of AI tools. Kaplan-Rakowski and Wojdynski (2023) echo this sentiment, noting the scarcity of longitudinal studies in immersive learning research and advocating for extended experiments to evaluate the enduring benefits of VR/AR in STEM education. Saxena et al. (2021) further discuss the ethical and practical challenges of scaling AI-driven educational tools, arguing that current research often fails to address the long-term implications of AI integration in classrooms. Dalgarno and Lee (2023) also highlight the need for scalable and sustainable implementations of immersive learning environments, particularly in STEM contexts.

To address these gaps, future research can adopt mixed methods approaches to combine quantitative and qualitative insights, as recommended by Creswell & Plano Clark (2018). Additionally, longitudinal study designs, as outlined by Ployhart & Vandenberg (2010), are essential for understanding the sustained impact of AI and immersive technologies in education. By expanding sample sizes, diversifying participant groups, and conducting comprehensive longitudinal investigations, researchers can validate the generalizability of findings and provide actionable insights into the scalability and long-term efficacy of AI-driven immersive learning tools in STEM/STEAM education. In addition, teacher training and pedagogical adoption pose substantial barriers to the effective use of AI-driven immersive tools. Educators often lack the technical confidence or pedagogical strategies required to integrate AI agents into lesson planning, classroom management, and assessment workflows. Professional development programmes that combine hands-on training with theoretical grounding are essential to build teachers' capacity and willingness to adopt these technologies meaningfully. Without this support, even well-designed immersive tools risk underutilisation or misalignment with curricular goals.

Another gap identified is the technical limitations of current systems. While Duca et al. (2024) highlight the potential of their VR lab, challenges remain in ensuring seamless interaction and voice-independent direction from virtual assistants. Vaze et al. (2024) point to issues such as inaccurate voice recognition and gesture detection, which limit the functionality of MR applications. These gaps suggest a need for advancements in AI and multimodal context recognition to enhance user experience and learning outcomes. Furthermore, Gelana and Campbell (2024) discuss the inefficiency of current AI-based 3D asset generation methods, which are slow and computationally demanding. This raises a critical research gap in improving the speed and resource efficiency of these models, as well as exploring their feasibility for deployment in dynamic augmented reality (AR) environments or other immersive realities.

These technical limitations, as highlighted by Duca et al. (2024) and Vaze et al. (2024), pose significant challenges to seamless interaction and user experience. Inaccurate voice recognition and gesture detection, as noted by Huang et al. (2023), hinder the functionality of VR/MR applications, limiting their effectiveness in educational settings. Gao et al. (2024) further emphasise the need for advancements in AI-driven multimodal interfaces to address these issues and improve usability. Piumsomboon et al. (2013) also highlight the limitations of current gesture detection technologies, calling for more intuitive and accurate interaction methods.

Additionally, the inefficiency of AI-based 3D asset generation methods, as discussed by Gelana and Campbell (2024), presents a critical barrier to scalability in immersive learning environments. Dwivedi et al. (2022) propose deep learning-based approaches to improve the speed and efficiency of 3D asset generation, addressing the computational demands of current methods. Similarly, Behravan & Gracanin (2024) focus on optimising AI algorithms for real-time 3D content generation in AR environments, emphasising the need for resource-efficient models. Billinghurst et al. (2015) explore opportunities for improving the scalability of AI-based 3D modelling techniques, particularly in educational contexts. To overcome these challenges, advancements in multimodal context recognition are essential. Schmidt and Herrmann (2023) identify gaps in current multimodal interaction technologies and stress the importance of integrating voice, gesture, and context-aware AI for seamless user experiences. Lee et al. (2024) propose an AI-driven framework for multimodal context recognition in immersive learning environments, addressing the limitations of existing systems in accurately interpreting user inputs.

One of the underexplored aspects of AI-driven entities in IVR STEM learning is the alignment of AI pedagogical agents with diverse cultural and educational frameworks. Many AI models are developed based on Western pedagogical paradigms, which may not fully reflect the cognitive styles, instructional methods, or cultural values of other regions. For instance, some education systems emphasise collective learning, discussion-based inquiry, or holistic assessment, yet AI-driven tutors and NPCs may be optimised for individualised, task-based instruction. Additionally, AI systems trained on biased datasets could unintentionally favour certain linguistic patterns, accents, or learning profiles, potentially disadvantaging students from different backgrounds. Hence, it is crucial to address these issues with a more culturally responsive AI design to ensure that AI-driven education respects and adapts to local learning contexts rather than imposing a one-size-fits-all model.

Beyond cultural alignment, disparities in the implementation of AI and IVR in STEM education further highlight concerns of accessibility and equity. While well-resourced institutions can seamlessly integrate these technologies, schools in low and middle-income regions often struggle with infrastructure constraints, digital access, and the availability of trained educators. This raises critical questions about the scalability of AI-enhanced learning, as failing to address these barriers may exacerbate existing educational inequalities rather than mitigate them. Without intentional efforts to develop cost-effective and adaptable AI-driven tools, there is a risk that these technologies will widen the digital divide instead of serving as a means to create inclusive learning opportunities. Future research should prioritise the development of AI solutions that account for diverse economic and technological realities, ensuring that all learners, regardless of geographical location, can benefit from immersive AI-enhanced education.

Lastly, the need for a more interactive and collaborative learning environment is emphasised in both Duca et al. (2024) and Vaze et al. (2024). While both studies point to the potential for incorporating multi-user features and AI-driven conversational learning, there is still limited research on how these technologies can be effectively integrated into existing educational frameworks to promote collaboration and socialisation.

However, limited research exists on how these technologies can be effectively integrated into existing educational frameworks to promote collaboration and socialisation. Johnson et al. (2023) identify collaborative learning and AI-driven conversational agents as key trends in educational technology, underscoring the need for further exploration of their integration into immersive environments. Dillenbourg et al. (2009) also emphasise the potential of immersive technologies to enhance social interaction and collaboration, calling for more research on their application in educational settings. Multi-user immersive environments, as discussed by Atchley et al. (2024), are critical for fostering collaboration and socialisation. Han & Bailenson (2024) further explore the design principles for collaborative learning environments in immersive virtual worlds, highlighting the importance of multi-user features and social presence. Similarly, AI-driven conversational agents have the potential to enhance collaborative learning, but their integration into educational frameworks remains underexplored. Caballé & Conesa (2019) systematically review the role of conversational agents in collaborative learning, identifying gaps in their application to immersive environments. Milana et al. (2024) propose a framework for designing AI-driven conversational agents to support collaborative problem-solving in STEM education, emphasising the need for further research on their implementation. Addressing these research gaps could lead to more scalable, efficient, and engaging immersive learning experiences, enhancing the overall effectiveness of VR, MR, and AI applications in education.

Research Themes

This section presents the key research themes synthesised from the studies included in this scoping review. The process of creating these themes involved a comprehensive examination of the relevant literature, where key concepts and findings were identified, coded, and grouped based on their similarities and relevance to the research questions. Each study was carefully analysed to extract pertinent data, focusing on AI-driven agents in immersive virtual reality (IVR) environments within STEM/STEAM education. Initial coding involved tagging segments of text that reflected specific aspects of the research, such as virtual AI assistants, AI-driven NPCs, pedagogical agents, and interactive environments.

Once individual codes were identified, the next step was to group them into broader categories based on common features and underlying themes. For example, codes related to personalised learning support, real-time feedback, and adaptability were grouped under the theme of "Virtual AI Assistants," while those addressing immersive, interactive learning experiences in virtual environments were clustered under the theme of "AI-powered Interactive Environments." This process of categorisation allowed for a more comprehensive understanding of the various facets of AI in IVR environments and how they contribute to the educational experience.

To ensure that the themes captured the full scope of the research, the codes were reviewed and refined, with similar concepts generalised to create more encompassing themes. For example, codes related to different types of AI-driven agents, such as pedagogical agents, NPCs, and personal research assistants, were generalised into the broader theme of "AI-driven Agents." This step helped to reduce redundancy and ensure that each theme reflected the core areas of focus in the current literature, providing a clearer and more streamlined representation of the findings.

The final themes were then synthesised into key areas that best represented the trends in the research, providing an insightful summary of the current state of knowledge. These themes are visually represented in Figure 2, which offers a clear and concise overview of the major findings and areas of interest in the literature. The visual representation aids in understanding the interconnections between the various themes and highlights the key trends, challenges, and opportunities within the field of AI-driven agents in IVR for STEM education.

Figure 2. Thematic map of synthesized themes

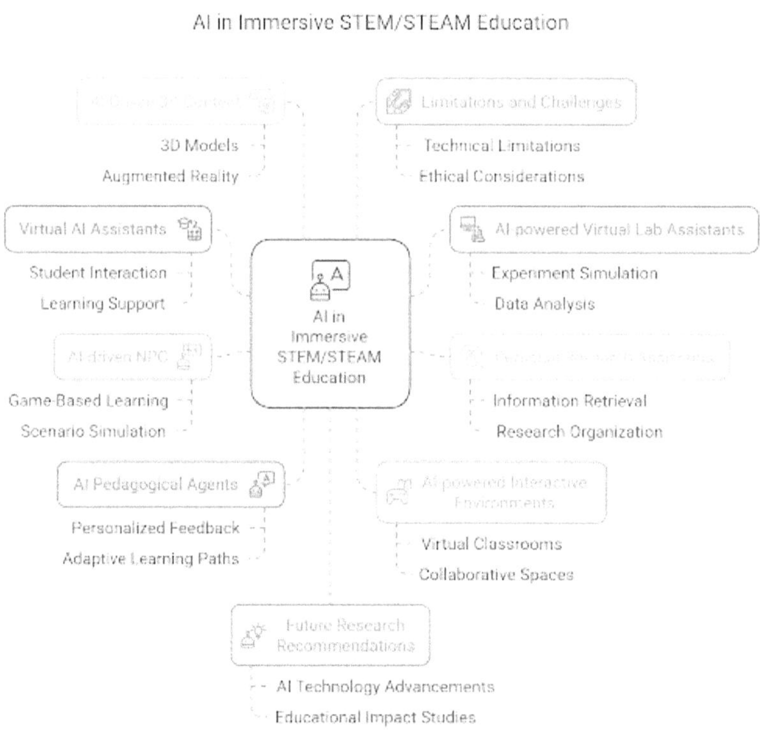

DISCUSSION

One of the most significant findings of this review is the scarcity of studies (N=3) in the rapidly advancing area of AI integration in education. This finding highlights a critical gap in the existing literature, underscoring the need for more comprehensive, high-quality research in this domain. As AI technologies continue to evolve, the absence of robust studies on their integration into educational settings presents a unique challenge for practitioners and researchers alike. This scarcity not only limits our current understanding but also provides an important opportunity for future research to focus on this underexplored area. It is essential for future studies to investigate the practical implications of AI-driven learning tools in various educational contexts, with an emphasis on large-scale, longitudinal studies to build a more robust evidence base.

The integration of immersive technologies—Virtual Reality (VR), Augmented Reality (AR), and Mixed Reality (MR)—with Artificial Intelligence (AI)-driven agents is revolutionising education, particularly in STEM fields. These technologies, combined with AI entities such as Non-Player Characters (NPC), pedagogical agents, and AI assistants, are creating engaging, personalised, and interactive learning environments that cater to the needs of modern learners. The three studies reviewed here—Duca et al. (2024), Vaze et al. (2024), and Gelana & Campbell (2024)—demonstrate the transformative potential of these tools in enhancing educational practices.

Duca et al. (2024) explore the use of VR and AI in chemistry education, introducing a virtual laboratory where students can safely interact with chemical reactions. Central to their application is an AI-driven pedagogical agent, the "Lab Assistant," designed to guide users through experiments, answer questions, and provide real-time feedback. This agent is humanised to embody the wisdom and passion of historical figures like Albert Einstein and Dmitri Mendeleev, making it relatable and inspiring for learners. The Lab Assistant not only enhances engagement but also improves retention and understanding by offering personalised support and clarifying ambiguities. Participants in the study reported high levels of satisfaction and enthusiasm, though some encountered technical challenges and physical discomfort, such as dizziness, common to VR systems. Despite these issues, the Lab Assistant's ability to engage users and provide tailored guidance underscores the potential of AI-driven pedagogical agents in creating immersive and effective learning experiences.

Vaze et al. (2024) focus on Mixed Reality (MR) and its ability to foster curiosity-driven learning through their "Curiosity XR" platform. This system incorporates AI-supported conversational agents powered by GPT-3, which generate context-driven, interactive mini-lessons for learners. These agents act as virtual tutors, enabling learners to explore topics dynamically and at their own pace. The conversational AI not only provides educational content but also adapts to user queries, creating a personalised and engaging learning experience. The study found that participants using Curiosity XR exhibited higher levels of engagement, curiosity, and visual content retention. The use of AI-driven conversational agents in this context highlights their potential to support self-guided learning and foster a deeper understanding of complex concepts. By combining MR with AI, Vaze et al. demonstrate how these technologies can create scalable, interactive, and curiosity-driven educational tools.

Gelana & Campbell (2024) delve into the intersection of AI and AR, proposing the use of AI assistants as personal research assistants in STEM education. They discuss the potential of fine-tuned Large Language Models (LLMs), such as LLaMA, to provide domain-specific knowledge and generate AR visualisations in real time. These AI assistants can answer questions, visualise molecular structures, and provide real-time information about chemical properties, hazards, and reactions. The authors emphasise the importance of fine-tuning LLMs on domain-specific datasets to reduce computational requirements and enable local deployment on AR hardware. By integrating AI assistants with AR, Gelana & Campbell envision a future where learners can interact with dynamic, AI-generated content that adapts to their needs. This approach not only enhances the accessibility of advanced educational tools but also democratises access to AI and AR technologies through open-source models and affordable hardware.

Across these studies, the use of AI-driven agents—whether as pedagogical assistants, conversational tutors, or research assistants—demonstrates their ability to enhance learning outcomes by providing personalised, adaptive, and interactive support. These agents humanise the learning experience, making it more engaging and relatable. For instance, Duca et al.'s Lab Assistant embodies the qualities of a passionate mentor, while Vaze et al.'s conversational agents act as dynamic tutors, and Gelana & Campbell's AI assistants serve as knowledgeable guides. The humanisation of these AI entities fosters a sense of connection and inspiration, encouraging learners to explore and engage with complex subjects.

The integration of immersive technologies and AI-driven agents also addresses the challenges of accessibility and scalability in education. Open-source models and affordable hardware, as highlighted by Gelana & Campbell, play a crucial role in democratising access to these advanced tools. Similarly, Vaze et al.'s Curiosity XR platform and Duca et al.'s VR chemistry lab demonstrate how these technologies can be deployed in diverse educational contexts, from classrooms to research laboratories. By leveraging AI-driven agents, these solutions not only enhance the learning experience but also anticipate future educational needs, paving the way for a more interactive, personalised, and accessible approach to education.

THIS REVIEW LIMITATIONS AND FUTURE RECOMMENDATIONS

This scoping review is subject to several limitations that may have influenced the scope and breadth of the findings. First, the review relied on a specific set of search terms and databases, which, while carefully selected, may have inadvertently excluded relevant studies that used alternate terminology or were published in less commonly indexed venues. The search strategy focused primarily on AI-driven agents in immersive virtual environments within the context of STEM education, which may have limited the identification of related research using different descriptors—for instance, studies referring to "virtual tutors," "intelligent avatars," or other variants of AI agents, as well as adjacent fields such as science communication or engineering education outside the strict STEM education framework.

Second, the inclusion and exclusion criteria, though clearly defined to ensure focus and relevance, may have further narrowed the scope. For example, studies that utilised immersive technologies without explicit AI agent integration, or those situated in informal learning environments, were excluded, even though they might offer valuable insights into comparable pedagogical dynamics. Third, the reliance primarily on peer-reviewed conference proceedings may have reduced the robustness of the synthesis. Conference papers often present early-stage findings and may not undergo the same level of methodological scrutiny as full journal articles. Moreover, important work published in grey literature—such as doctoral dissertations, institutional reports, or industry white papers—was not included, which may have further limited the pool of eligible studies. Lastly, it is possible that broadening the scope of search terms (e.g., including related immersive technologies like CAVEs or 3D simulations), expanding to adjacent STEM-related disciplines, using more inclusive descriptions of intelligent agents, or consulting additional databases and grey literature repositories could yield more relevant studies. Future reviews could benefit from this broader approach to more comprehensively map the landscape of AI-driven agents in immersive educational contexts.

Future research and recommendations across the studies point towards enhancing the capabilities of AI-driven agents in immersive STEM education. Duca et al. (2024) propose integrating a more capable AI-driven virtual assistant into their VR lab, enabling it to be constantly aware of the experiments conducted and providing directions without requiring voice intervention from users. This integration could improve the user experience by making the system more autonomous and responsive. Similarly, Vaze et al. (2024) suggest exploring AI integration within objects for conversational learning experiences, which would offer a novel approach to interactive learning. They also recommend developing local multi-user learning environments, which could foster collaboration among students and enable teachers to create dynamic, interactive content. These advancements would significantly enhance the effectiveness, engagement, and interactivity of digital learning experiences, creating a more collaborative and immersive learning environment for students.

ETHICAL, IMPLEMENTATION, AND TECHNICAL CONSIDERATIONS

Ethical Implications.

The deployment of AI-driven agents in immersive learning environments raises critical ethical questions around bias, privacy, and equity. Bias can creep in if training data over-represents certain demographics, leading agents to favour some learners or reinforce stereotypes (Chiu & Li, 2023; Del Moral-Pérez et al., 2024). Privacy becomes paramount when agents collect fine-grained behavioural or performance data—institutions must adopt clear data-governance frameworks and robust security to safeguard student information (Holmes & Tuomi, 2022). Finally, digital equity is essential: without equitable access to VR/AR headsets, high-speed connectivity, and technical support, AI-enhanced learning risks widening existing socio-economic divides (Brahimi & Sarirete, 2024; Ghreir, 2023).

Real-World Implementations.

Early adopters are already piloting AI agents in the classroom and training settings, yielding valuable lessons. In several secondary-school chemistry labs, virtual "Lab Assistants" have guided students through experiments, offering contextual hints, clarifying procedures, and dynamically adjusting difficulty, which boosted both engagement and conceptual mastery (Duca et al., 2024). At the university level, Mixed Reality workshops like CuriosityXR embed AI-powered conversational agents into engineering modules, enabling self-paced exploration of complex systems and fostering deeper curiosity (Vaze et al., 2024). These cases underscore the need for dedicated teacher training and careful curriculum alignment so that AI agents augment—rather than disrupt—existing pedagogical workflows.

Scaling and Implementation

Across Institutions. As AI-driven agents begin to scale across educational systems, the practicalities of widespread implementation must be carefully considered. Different educational institutions, from small rural schools to large urban universities, face varying levels of access to resources such as technology infrastructure, financial support, and staff expertise. For smaller institutions with limited budgets, scalable solutions, such as cloud-based AI systems and cost-effective hardware like tablets or low-cost VR headsets, can provide viable alternatives to expensive, high-performance hardware. Additionally, collaboration among institutions to share resources, data, and best practices can facilitate the spread of AI-enhanced education. For larger institutions, a more robust infrastructure can support complex AI systems capable of delivering personalised learning at scale. The key to successful implementation is ensuring that AI systems are flexible and adaptable, capable of being tailored to suit the needs of different student populations and institutional environments. Institutions must also invest in professional development for educators, ensuring that teachers are equipped with the knowledge and skills to integrate AI into their teaching practices effectively, regardless of their school's size or resources.

Technical Requirements & Feasibility

Scaling AI-driven agents broadly depends on both infrastructure and adaptable software architectures. High-performance GPUs and low-latency networks are ideal for real-time inference and seamless immersion, but many schools lack these resources (Gelana & Campbell, 2024). Emerging "edge AI" and lightweight model-compression techniques offer a way forward, enabling on-device deployment with lower bandwidth needs (Behravan & Gracanin, 2024). Moreover, adopting open-standard APIs and modular frameworks can help integrate AI agents into diverse LMS and XR platforms, reducing vendor lock-in and lowering the overall cost of entry.

Teacher Role

Teachers play a crucial role in the successful integration of AI-driven agents into the classroom. Beyond selecting and introducing these tools, they are responsible for guiding AI interactions to ensure that the technology complements rather than replaces the human element of teaching. Teachers must be proficient in managing classroom dynamics, ensuring that AI tools support individual learning needs while maintaining engagement and focus across the class. This includes monitoring AI-driven activities, adjusting the tools' functionalities as necessary, and providing timely interventions when required. Furthermore, teachers must integrate AI tools into lesson plans, balancing technological use with traditional teaching methods to create a seamless learning experience. The responsibility also extends to continuously evaluating the impact of AI on student learning outcomes, offering feedback to both students and AI systems, and adapting pedagogical strategies based on the insights gathered. In this way, teachers act as both facilitators and critical evaluators, ensuring that AI-driven agents enhance educational experiences in a meaningful and effective manner.

CONCLUSION

The primary contribution of this paper lies in rigorously identifying the critical gap in the research on AI-driven educational technologies. The scarcity of studies (N=3) on this topic reveals the need for continued inquiry into how these technologies can be effectively integrated into diverse educational settings. This gap is particularly significant in light of the rapid development of AI tools and their potential to transform learning environments. Future research should prioritize filling this void to ensure that AI technologies are effectively harnessed in education to enhance teaching and learning outcomes.

This scoping review has revealed both the promising potential and current limitations of AI-driven agents in immersive STEM learning environments. Through a systematic analysis of the literature following PRISMA-ScR guidelines, we identified only three studies meeting our eligibility criteria, highlighting the nascent state of research in this field. This limited body of evidence, while indicating significant opportunities, also underscores the substantial work needed to fully understand and harness these technologies for educational purposes.

The integration of AI-driven agents—including NPCs, pedagogical agents, and AI assistants—within immersive virtual reality environments represents a convergence of cutting-edge technologies that could transform STEM education. The reviewed studies demonstrate how these technologies can enhance student engagement, provide personalised learning experiences, and create more interactive and authentic learning environments. Particularly noteworthy is the potential for AI agents to offer real-time guidance, adaptive feedback, and contextual support within immersive settings, addressing longstanding challenges in STEM education.

However, our review has also identified significant research gaps and technical limitations that must be addressed. The small sample sizes and limited scope of current studies indicate a need for more comprehensive research with diverse participant groups. Technical challenges, including voice recognition accuracy, gesture detection, and computational efficiency in 3D asset generation, continue to pose barriers to widespread implementation. Additionally, questions remain about the scalability of these technologies and their integration into existing educational frameworks.

Looking forward, several key areas emerge as priorities for future research and development:

- The advancement of more sophisticated AI-driven virtual assistants capable of autonomous awareness and responsive interaction within immersive environments.
- The development of multi-user features that facilitate collaborative learning and social interaction.
- The improvement of technical infrastructure to support the seamless integration of AI agents in immersive settings.
- The investigation of long-term learning outcomes and pedagogical effectiveness through longitudinal studies.
- The creation of frameworks for ethical implementation that address concerns about privacy, equity, and accessibility.

As we move forward, it is crucial to approach the development and implementation of these technologies with careful consideration of both their potential benefits and limitations. The successful integration of AI-driven agents in immersive STEM learning environments will require continued collaboration between educators, researchers, and technology developers, as well as sustained investment in infrastructure and professional development.

This review serves as a foundation for future research and development in this emerging field. While the current evidence base is limited, the potential impact of AI-driven agents in immersive STEM learning environments warrants continued investigation and development. As these technologies evolve, they have the potential to create more engaging, effective, and equitable learning experiences that better prepare students for the challenges and opportunities of an increasingly technology-driven world.

REFERENCES

Al Omoush, M. H., Salih, S. E., Kishore, S., & Mehigan, T. (2023). Interactive Multimodal Learning: Towards Using Pedagogical Agents for Inclusive Education. *2023 IEEE International Humanitarian Technology Conference (IHTC)*, 1–7. DOI: 10.1109/IHTC58960.2023.10508848

Atchley, P., Pannell, H., Wofford, K., Hopkins, M., & Atchley, R. A. (2024). Human and AI collaboration in the higher education environment: Opportunities and concerns. *Cognitive Research: Principles and Implications*, *9*(1), 20. DOI: 10.1186/s41235-024-00547-9 PMID: 38589710

Bailenson, J. N., Yee, N., Blascovich, J., Beall, A. C., Lundblad, N., & Jin, M. (2008). The Use of Immersive Virtual Reality in the Learning Sciences: Digital Transformations of Teachers, Students, and Social Context. *Journal of the Learning Sciences*, *17*(1), 102–141. DOI: 10.1080/10508400701793141

Behravan, M., & Gracanin, D. (2024). Generative Multi-Modal Artificial Intelligence for Dynamic Real-Time Context-Aware Content Creation in Augmented Reality. *30th ACM Symposium on Virtual Reality Software and Technology*, 1–2. DOI: 10.1145/3641825.3689685

Billinghurst, M., Clark, A., & Lee, G. (2015). A Survey of Augmented Reality. Foundations and Trends® in Human–Computer Interaction, 8(2–3), 73–272. DOI: 10.1561/1100000049

Brahimi, T., & Sarirete, A. (2024). Transforming Learning in STEAM: How AI Tools and Language Models Catalyze Educational Advancement. In Baroudi, S., & Lytras, M. D. (Eds.), *Transformative Leadership and Sustainable Innovation in Education: Interdisciplinary Perspectives* (pp. 39–58). Emerald Publishing Limited., DOI: 10.1108/978-1-83753-536-120241004

Caballé, S., & Conesa, J. (2019). Conversational Agents in Support for Collaborative Learning in MOOCs: An Analytical Review. In Xhafa, F., Barolli, L., & Greguš, M. (Eds.), *Advances in Intelligent Networking and Collaborative Systems* (Vol. 23, pp. 384–394). Springer International Publishing., DOI: 10.1007/978-3-319-98557-2_35

Chiu, T. K. F., & Li, Y. (2023). How Can Emerging Technologies Impact STEM Education? *Journal for STEM Education Research*, *6*(3), 375–384. DOI: 10.1007/s41979-023-00113-w

Creswell, J. W., & Plano Clark, V. L. (2018). Designing and conducting mixed methods research (Third edition, international student edition). Sage.

Dalgarno, B., & Lee, M. J. W. (2010). What are the learning affordances of 3-D virtual environments? *British Journal of Educational Technology*, *41*(1), 10–32. DOI: 10.1111/j.1467-8535.2009.01038.x

De Back, T. T., Tinga, A. M., & Louwerse, M. M. (2023). Learning in immersed collaborative virtual environments: Design and implementation. *Interactive Learning Environments*, *31*(8), 5364–5382. DOI: 10.1080/10494820.2021.2006238

Del Moral-Pérez, M. E., López-Bouzas, N., & Castañeda-Fernández, J. (2024). Transmedia skill derived from the process of converting films into educational games with augmented reality and artificial intelligence. *Journal of New Approaches in Educational Research*, *13*(1), 15. DOI: 10.1007/s44322-024-00015-8

Dillenbourg, P., Järvelä, S., & Fischer, F. (2009). The Evolution of Research on Computer-Supported Collaborative Learning. In Balacheff, N., Ludvigsen, S., De Jong, T., Lazonder, A., & Barnes, S. (Eds.), *Technology-Enhanced Learning* (pp. 3–19). Springer Netherlands., DOI: 10.1007/978-1-4020-9827-7_1

Duca, A., Constantinescu, G.-G., & Iftene, A. (2024). Future Education: Experimenting with Chemical Reactions in Virtual Reality. 2024 International Conference on INnovations in Intelligent SysTems and Applications (INISTA), 1–6. DOI: 10.1109/INISTA62901.2024.10683861

Dwivedi, R., Jadhav, A., Jha, P., & Anubhav. (2022). Predicting 3D Model of Images for Augmented Reality Applications. In B. Iyer, T. Crick, & S.-L. Peng (Eds.), Applied Computational Technologies (Vol. 303, pp. 395–404). Springer Nature Singapore. DOI: 10.1007/978-981-19-2719-5_37

Freeman, S., Eddy, S. L., McDonough, M., Smith, M. K., Okoroafor, N., Jordt, H., & Wenderoth, M. P. (2014). Active learning increases student performance in science, engineering, and mathematics. *Proceedings of the National Academy of Sciences of the United States of America*, *111*(23), 8410–8415. DOI: 10.1073/pnas.1319030111 PMID: 24821756

Gao, H., Lindquist, M., & Serrano Vergel, R. (2024). *AI-Driven Avatars in Immersive 3D Environments for Education Workflow and Case Study of the Temple of Demeter*. Wichmann Verlag., DOI: 10.14627/537752059

Gelana, F., & Campbell, A. (2024). The Possibilities of AI and Augmented Reality in Education. *2024 IEEE International Conference on Consumer Electronics (ICCE)*, 1–4. DOI: 10.1109/ICCE59016.2024.10444487

Ghreir, H. (2023). The Impact of Using the Technology-Based Platform by The School Leadership on the Teachers' Evaluation. 3 Rd International Conference on Educational Technology and Online Learning – ICETOL 2023 Full Paper Proceedings, 131–136.

Graesser, A. C., Lu, S., Jackson, G. T., Mitchell, H. H., Ventura, M., Olney, A., & Louwerse, M. M. (2004). AutoTutor: A tutor with dialogue in natural language. *Behavior Research Methods, Instruments, & Computers*, *36*(2), 180–192. DOI: 10.3758/BF03195563 PMID: 15354683

Hamash, M., Ghreir, H., & Tiernan, P. (2024). Breaking through Barriers: A Systematic Review of Extended Reality in Education for the Visually Impaired. *Education Sciences*, *14*(4), 365. DOI: 10.3390/educsci14040365

Hamash, M., & Mohamed, H. (2023). Identifying the Level of Teacher's Maturity in the Impactful Technology Use (ITU) in Abu Dhabi Public Schools. *Innovative Teaching and Learning Journal*, *7*(2), 60–71. DOI: 10.11113/itlj.v7.135

Hamash, M. A., Mohamed, H., & Tiernan, P. (2024). Developing a New Model for Achieving Flow State in STEAM Education: A Mixed-Method Investigation. *Sains Humanika*, *16*(3), 101–111. DOI: 10.11113/sh.v16n3.2163

Han, E., & Bailenson, J. N. (2024). Social Interaction in VR. In Han, E., & Bailenson, J. N. (Eds.), *Oxford Research Encyclopedia of Communication*. Oxford University Press., DOI: 10.1093/acrefore/9780190228613.013.1489

Holmes, W., & Tuomi, I. (2022). State of the art and practice in AI in education. *European Journal of Education*, *57*(4), 542–570. DOI: 10.1111/ejed.12533

Huang, H.-M., Rauch, U., & Liaw, S.-S. (2010). Investigating learners' attitudes toward virtual reality learning environments: Based on a constructivist approach. *Computers & Education*, *55*(3), 1171–1182. DOI: 10.1016/j.compedu.2010.05.014

Hwang, G.-J., Xie, H., Wah, B. W., & Gašević, D. (2020). Vision, challenges, roles and research issues of Artificial Intelligence in Education. *Computers and Education: Artificial Intelligence*, *1*, 100001. DOI: 10.1016/j.caeai.2020.100001

Kaplan-Rakowski, R., & Wojdynski, T. (2018). Students' Attitudes Toward High-Immersion Virtual Reality Assisted Language Learning. SSRN Electronic Journal. DOI: 10.2139/ssrn.3255611

Land, M. H. (2013). Full STEAM Ahead: The Benefits of Integrating the Arts Into STEM. *Procedia Computer Science*, *20*, 547–552. DOI: 10.1016/j.procs.2013.09.317

Lee, J., Wang, J., Brown, E., Chu, L., Rodriguez, S. S., & Froehlich, J. E. (2024). GazePointAR: A Context-Aware Multimodal Voice Assistant for Pronoun Disambiguation in Wearable Augmented Reality. *Proceedings of the CHI Conference on Human Factors in Computing Systems*, 1–20. DOI: 10.1145/3613904.3642230

Lester, J. C., Converse, S. A., Kahler, S. E., Barlow, S. T., Stone, B. A., & Bhogal, R. S. (1997). The persona effect: Affective impact of animated pedagogical agents. *Proceedings of the ACM SIGCHI Conference on Human Factors in Computing Systems*, 359–366. DOI: 10.1145/258549.258797

Makransky, G., & Petersen, G. B. (2021). The Cognitive Affective Model of Immersive Learning (CAMIL): A Theoretical Research-Based Model of Learning in Immersive Virtual Reality. *Educational Psychology Review*, *33*(3), 937–958. DOI: 10.1007/s10648-020-09586-2

Margot, K. C., & Kettler, T. (2019). Teachers' perception of STEM integration and education: A systematic literature review. *International Journal of STEM Education*, *6*(1), 2. DOI: 10.1186/s40594-018-0151-2

Milana, M., Brandi, U., Hodge, S., & Hoggan-Kloubert, T. (2024). Artificial intelligence (AI), conversational agents, and generative AI: Implications for adult education practice and research. *International Journal of Lifelong Education*, *43*(1), 1–7. DOI: 10.1080/02601370.2024.2310448

Milgram, P., & Kishino, F. (1994). A Taxonomy of Mixed Reality Visual Displays. *IEICE Transactions on Information and Systems*, *E77-D*(12), 1321–1329.

Omirgaliyev, R., Kenzhe, D., & Mirambekov, S. (2024). Simulating Life: The Application of Generative Agents in Virtual Environments. 2024 IEEE AITU: Digital Generation, 181–187. DOI: 10.1109/IEEECONF61558.2024.10585387

Park, J. S., O'Brien, J. C., Cai, C. J., Morris, M. R., Liang, P., & Bernstein, M. S. (2023). Generative Agents: Interactive Simulacra of Human Behavior (Version 2). arXiv. DOI: 10.1145/3586183.3606763

Pellas, N., Kazanidis, I., & Palaigeorgiou, G. (2020). A systematic literature review of mixed reality environments in K-12 education. *Education and Information Technologies*, *25*(4), 2481–2520. DOI: 10.1007/s10639-019-10076-4

Piumsomboon, T., Clark, A., Billinghurst, M., & Cockburn, A. (2013). User-defined gestures for augmented reality. CHI '13 Extended Abstracts on Human Factors in Computing Systems, 955–960. DOI: 10.1145/2468356.2468527

Ployhart, R. E., & Vandenberg, R. J. (2010). Longitudinal Research: The Theory, Design, and Analysis of Change. *Journal of Management*, *36*(1), 94–120. DOI: 10.1177/0149206309352110

Radianti, J., Majchrzak, T. A., Fromm, J., & Wohlgenannt, I. (2020). A systematic review of immersive virtual reality applications for higher education: Design elements, lessons learned, and research agenda. *Computers & Education*, *147*, 103778. DOI: 10.1016/j.compedu.2019.103778

Russell, S. J., & Norvig, P. (with Chang, M., Devlin, J., Dragan, A., Forsyth, D., Goodfellow, I., Malik, J., Mansinghka, V., Pearl, J., & Wooldridge, M. J.). (2022). Artificial intelligence: A modern approach (Fourth edition, global edition). Pearson.

Sajja, R., Sermet, Y., Cikmaz, M., Cwiertny, D., & Demir, I. (2023). Artificial Intelligence-Enabled Intelligent Assistant for Personalized and Adaptive Learning in Higher Education (Version 1). arXiv. https://doi.org/DOI: 10.48550/ARXIV.2309.10892

Saxena, D., Lamest, M., & Bansal, V. (2021). Responsible Machine Learning for Ethical Artificial Intelligence in Business and Industry. In Chkoniya, V. (Ed.), (pp. 639–653). Advances in Business Information Systems and Analytics. IGI Global., DOI: 10.4018/978-1-7998-6985-6.ch030

Schneider, S., Beege, M., Nebel, S., Schnaubert, L., & Rey, G. D. (2022). The Cognitive-Affective-Social Theory of Learning in digital Environments (CASTLE). *Educational Psychology Review*, *34*(1), 1–38. DOI: 10.1007/s10648-021-09626-5 PMID: 34226808

Sherman, W. R., & Craig, A. B. (2003). Understanding Virtual Reality—Interface, Application, and Design. *Presence (Cambridge, Mass.)*, *12*(4), 441–442. DOI: 10.1162/105474603322391668

Slater, M., & Wilbur, S. (1997). A Framework for Immersive Virtual Environments (FIVE): Speculations on the Role of Presence in Virtual Environments. *Presence (Cambridge, Mass.)*, *6*(6), 603–616. DOI: 10.1162/pres.1997.6.6.603

Suppes, P., & Jerman, M. (1970). Computer-Assisted Instruction. *The Bulletin of the National Association of Secondary School Principals*, *54*(343), 27–40. DOI: 10.1177/019263657005434305

Terracina, A., & Mecella, M. (2014). Gaming@School: Combining Virtual Learning Environments and Intelligent Pedagogical Agents for a new Approach to Classroom Lessons. *European Conference on Games Based Learning*; Reading, 2, 843–847.

Tribe, T. N., & Singha, S. (2023). Diversity and Inclusion in VR: A New Frontier in Learning. Open Science Framework. https://doi.org/DOI: 10.17605/OSF.IO/BY87D

Tricco, A. C., Lillie, E., Zarin, W., O'Brien, K. K., Colquhoun, H., Levac, D., Moher, D., Peters, M. D. J., Horsley, T., Weeks, L., Hempel, S., Akl, E. A., Chang, C., McGowan, J., Stewart, L., Hartling, L., Aldcroft, A., Wilson, M. G., Garritty, C., & Straus, S. E. (2018). PRISMA Extension for Scoping Reviews (PRISMA-ScR): Checklist and Explanation. *Annals of Internal Medicine, 169*(7), 467–473. DOI: 10.7326/M18-0850 PMID: 30178033

VanLEHN, K. U. R. T.VanLEHN. (2011). The Relative Effectiveness of Human Tutoring, Intelligent Tutoring Systems, and Other Tutoring Systems. *Educational Psychologist, 46*(4), 197–221. DOI: 10.1080/00461520.2011.611369

Vaze, A., Morris, A., & Clarke, I. (2024). CuriosityXR: Context-aware Education Experiences with Mixed Reality and Conversation AI. *2024 IEEE International Conference on Artificial Intelligence and eXtended and Virtual Reality (AIxVR)*, 41–49. DOI: 10.1109/AIxVR59861.2024.00013

Wang, N., Johnson, W. L., Mayer, R. E., Rizzo, P., Shaw, E., & Collins, H. (2008). The politeness effect: Pedagogical agents and learning outcomes. *International Journal of Human-Computer Studies, 66*(2), 98–112. DOI: 10.1016/j.ijhcs.2007.09.003

Yuen, S. C.-Y., Yaoyuneyong, G., & Johnson, E. (2011). Augmented Reality: An Overview and Five Directions for AR in Education. *Journal of Educational Technology Development and Exchange, 4*(1). Advance online publication. DOI: 10.18785/jetde.0401.10

Zawacki-Richter, O., Marín, V. I., Bond, M., & Gouverneur, F. (2019). Systematic review of research on artificial intelligence applications in higher education – where are the educators? *International Journal of Educational Technology in Higher Education, 16*(1), 39. DOI: 10.1186/s41239-019-0171-0

KEY TERMS AND DEFINITIONS

Adaptive Learning Systems: Educational technologies that modify their presentation of material in response to student performance data. These systems use AI to personalise learning paths and provide targeted support based on individual student needs.

AI 3D Asset Generation: The use of artificial intelligence to create three-dimensional (3D) models, objects, or environments for applications such as gaming, virtual reality (VR), augmented reality (AR), and simulations. AI automates this process by generating 3D content from textual prompts, 2D images, or other inputs.

AI Assistant: A software application powered by artificial intelligence that assists users by performing tasks, providing information, and offering recommendations. Examples include Siri, Alexa, and Google Assistant.

AI-Driven Pedagogy: Educational approaches and methods that utilise artificial intelligence to facilitate learning, including personalised instruction, adaptive assessment, and intelligent tutoring systems.

Artificial Intelligence (AI): A branch of computer science focused on creating systems capable of performing tasks that typically require human intelligence, including learning, reasoning, problem-solving, understanding natural language, and perceiving the environment. In education, AI refers to systems that adapt to student needs, provide personalised feedback, and simulate intelligent tutoring behaviours.

Augmented Reality (AR): A technology that overlays digital information onto the real world, typically viewed through mobile devices or special glasses. In education, AR enhances learning by providing contextual information and interactive experiences in real-world settings.

Conversational AI: Technology that enables computers to communicate with humans through natural language, including text-based chatbots, voice assistants, and AI systems powered by machine learning and natural language processing (NLP).

Digital Learning Agents: AI-powered virtual entities that facilitate learning through various means, including instruction, guidance, feedback, and support. These agents adapt their behaviour based on student needs and learning contexts.

Extended Reality (XR): An umbrella term encompassing virtual reality, augmented reality, and mixed reality technologies, representing the entire spectrum of real and virtual environments in immersive technology.

Game-Based Learning: An educational approach that uses gaming elements and principles to engage students in learning activities. When combined with AI and immersive technologies, game-based learning creates interactive, adaptive, and engaging educational experiences.

Generative AI (Gen AI): A class of artificial intelligence systems designed to create new content, such as text, images, audio, video, or 3D models, based on patterns and data they have been trained on. Examples include text generation (e.g., ChatGPT) and image synthesis (e.g., DALL·E).

Human-AI Interaction in Education: The study and implementation of how humans (students and teachers) interact with AI systems in educational settings, including considerations of interface design, user experience, and pedagogical effectiveness.

Immersive Virtual Reality (IVR): A technology that creates a fully computer-generated, three-dimensional environment that users can interact with and feel present in, typically accessed through head-mounted displays. IVR in education provides experiential learning opportunities that might be impossible, dangerous, or impractical in the real world.

Intelligent Tutoring Systems (ITS): Computer-based educational systems that provide personalised instruction and feedback to students using AI to model student knowledge, adapt to learning needs, and provide targeted support and guidance.

Large Language Models (LLMs): Advanced AI systems trained on vast amounts of text data to understand and generate human-like language. Examples include GPT-4, LLaMA, and Bard, used for tasks such as answering questions, summarising text, and generating coherent content.

Learning Outcomes: The specific knowledge, skills, attitudes, and behaviours that students are expected to demonstrate as a result of their educational experiences. In AI-enhanced learning environments, outcomes can be monitored and supported through adaptive assessment and personalised feedback.

Mixed Reality (MR): A hybrid environment where physical and digital objects coexist and interact in real time, combining elements of both virtual and augmented reality for more immersive learning experiences.

Non-Player Characters (NPCs): Virtual entities or characters within digital environments that are controlled by computer programs rather than human users. In educational contexts, NPCs serve as interactive agents that guide learning, provide instruction, or simulate real-world interactions.

Pedagogical Agents: Virtual characters or entities designed for educational purposes, capable of providing instruction, guidance, and support to learners. These agents use AI to interact naturally with students and adapt their behaviour based on learning needs.

PRISMA for Scoping Reviews (PRISMA-ScR): A standardised methodology for conducting and reporting scoping reviews, ensuring systematic and transparent literature review processes. This framework helps researchers identify and analyse relevant literature in a structured manner.

Simulation-Based Learning: An educational approach that uses computer-generated scenarios to allow students to practice skills, experiment with concepts, and learn from outcomes in a safe, controlled environment. AI-enhanced simulations provide more realistic and adaptive learning experiences.

STEAM Education: An extension of STEM education that incorporates the Arts (Science, Technology, Engineering, Arts, and Mathematics), emphasising creativity, design thinking, and interdisciplinary approaches to problem-solving.

STEM Education: An interdisciplinary approach to learning that integrates Science, Technology, Engineering, and Mathematics, emphasising practical applications, problem-solving skills, and the interconnections between these fields.

Student Engagement: The degree of attention, curiosity, interest, and passion that students demonstrate when learning. In immersive STEM environments, engagement is often enhanced through interactive experiences and personalised learning opportunities.

Virtual Learning Environments (VLEs): Digital platforms that provide educational resources, tools, and spaces for online learning and collaboration. VLEs can incorporate various technologies, including AI agents and immersive features, to create engaging learning experiences.

Chapter 9

Classifying Student Sentiments in Learning on Video-Conference Platforms:

Human-AI Synergistic Approach Through Machine Learning and Self-Determination Theory

Bosede Iyiade Edwards
https://orcid.org/0000-0002-6922-311X
Universiti Sains Malaysia, Malaysia

Daniel Vong
https://orcid.org/0009-0006-1293-3838
Wangi Lai PLT, Malaysia

Olanrewaju Steve Edwards
Arrows Education, Malaysia

Margaret Olusola Abimbola
https://orcid.org/0000-0003-1847-4389
University of Ilesa, Nigeria

ABSTRACT

This study analyzes learner sentiments on video-conference platforms (VCPs) in online education, contributing to discourse on "Creative Approaches to Human-AI Synergy in Classroom Instruction" by showing how AI/ML tools can evaluate

DOI: 10.4018/979-8-3373-0847-0.ch009

student feedback to enhance VCPs and AI-powered instruction. Using a mixed-methods design, it integrated Azure Machine Learning (AML) with a multidimensional sentiment model and mapped findings to Self-Determination Theory (SDT). Feedback from 264 students was analyzed via AML's three-category sentiment system (positive, neutral, negative) and a five-category qualitative model (positive, negative, neutral, insightful, confused). Sentiments were linked to SDT's autonomy, competence, and relatedness. While learners valued VCP flexibility (autonomy), they reported issues like limited interaction and technical barriers (competence and relatedness). Sentiment patterns varied by demographics. The study highlights the benefit of hybrid analytical models and recommends improving VCP design to support diverse learner needs and enhance all three SDT dimensions.

INTRODUCTION

The proliferation of online learning, particularly following the COVID-19 pandemic, has positioned video-conferencing platforms (VCPs) like Zoom, Microsoft Teams, and Webex at the core of digital education. These platforms facilitate real-time communication and flexible learning but also pose challenges including reduced social presence, technical disruptions, and learner disengagement. Understanding how students perceive their experiences on VCPs is critical for enhancing user satisfaction and learning outcomes. This study applies machine learning and sentiment analysis to explore learners' experiences in VCP environments, offering a framework that integrates Azure Machine Learning (AML) and a multidimensional sentiment classification model within the scope of Self-Determination Theory (SDT).

PROBLEM BACKGROUND AND OBJECTIVES

The adoption of video-conference platforms (VCPs) for online learning surged dramatically during the COVID-19 pandemic and has since become a staple in digital education. However, while these platforms offer significant advantages, such as flexible scheduling, asynchronous access to materials, and real-time interaction, students' experiences with VCPs remain highly varied. Learners have reported challenges ranging from lack of motivation and distractions to technical difficulties and limited peer interaction. These factors contribute to uneven learning outcomes and reduced satisfaction in online environments.

Current research in the field of online learning has often prioritized asynchronous tools or focused on surface-level evaluations of sentiment using binary or three-category classification systems. Such models are unable to capture the rich and nuanced emotional feedback from learners. Additionally, traditional qualitative approaches to sentiment analysis, while insightful, often lack scalability and are vulnerable to human bias.

To bridge this methodological gap, this study adopts a hybrid approach that leverages the power of machine learning—specifically, Azure Machine Learning (AML)—and a multidimensional sentiment classification model. AML allows for the automatic processing of large-scale qualitative data and assigns confidence scores to sentiment labels, offering a consistent and scalable method of analysis. The inclusion of a multidimensional sentiment framework, inspired by Huang et al. (2021), extends the basic sentiment categories to include "insightful" and "confused," thereby enriching the interpretation of learner feedback.

Significantly, this machine learning-based approach addresses the need for efficient, accurate, and scalable sentiment analysis tools in education. It empowers educators and policymakers to extract actionable insights from student feedback and refine digital platforms to better align with pedagogical goals. Moreover, by mapping sentiments to the Self-Determination Theory (SDT) framework, the study provides a psychologically grounded perspective on how digital learning environments influence student motivation and engagement.

This study therefore aims to:

1. Explore the nature and dimensions of student sentiments using both AML and a multidimensional sentiment framework.
2. Map these sentiments to the core elements of SDT—autonomy, competence, and relatedness.
3. Examine differences in sentiment patterns across learner demographics such as age, IT proficiency, and educational level.
4. Evaluate the utility of combining AML with qualitative analysis for a more comprehensive understanding of learner experiences.
5. Derive actionable design implications for the improvement of VCPs in education.

THEORETICAL FRAMEWORK

This research is guided by two complementary frameworks. First, AML's sentiment analysis model categorizes textual feedback into positive, negative, or neutral sentiments based on natural language processing algorithms. While effective, this model often lacks depth in capturing complex emotional tones.

Second, the study adopts Huang et al.'s (2021) multidimensional sentiment framework, which adds nuanced categories such as insightful and confused. These five categories are then mapped to SDT elements: autonomy (e.g., control, flexibility), competence (e.g., mastery, perceived learning), and relatedness (e.g., social interaction, community). This integrated theoretical lens facilitates a holistic interpretation of student sentiments within digital learning environments.

LITERATURE REVIEW

The role of video-conference platforms (VCPs) in modern digital learning has become increasingly significant, particularly in facilitating synchronous interactions for geographically dispersed learners (Melati & Hazairin, 2020). These platforms, including Zoom, Microsoft Teams, and Webex, are equipped with advanced features such as breakout rooms, live polls, lecture recording, and automated transcripts, which enhance interactivity and accessibility (Cardullo et al., 2021; Lim, 2020; Siddiqui & Ahmad, 2022). Despite these innovations, technical challenges and the lack of physical proximity have hindered learner engagement and social interaction (Sun, 2023).

Sentiment analysis has emerged as a vital tool in understanding learner experiences in educational environments. Traditional sentiment analysis methods have often relied on qualitative, manual coding techniques that are susceptible to human bias and inefficiency. The advent of machine learning has enabled more scalable and reliable approaches. Azure Machine Learning (AML) offers a no-code interface that simplifies the sentiment analysis process for educators, especially those without programming backgrounds (Harfoushi & Hasan, 2018). AML's ability to assign sentiment confidence scores helps quantify feedback, although its limitation to three categories (positive, negative, neutral) may restrict nuanced interpretation (Ananthi et al., 2023).

To address this limitation, researchers have adopted multidimensional sentiment frameworks. Huang et al. (2021) proposed a six-category model, including insightful and confused, which adds depth to feedback analysis. This model has been effective in educational contexts and is particularly useful when mapped to motivational theories such as Self-Determination Theory (SDT) (MacIntyre et al., 2018). By aligning sentiment categories with SDT's elements of autonomy, competence, and relatedness, researchers can uncover how digital learning tools influence learner motivation, satisfaction, and engagement (Chiu, 2024; Nishiwaki et al., 2023).

METHODOLOGY

This study employed a mixed-methods research design, integrating both quantitative and qualitative approaches to analyze learner sentiments toward videoconference platforms (VCPs) used in online education. The goal was to capture not only the overall sentiment polarity but also the nuanced emotional states linked to learners' experiences, while mapping these to motivational constructs from Self-Determination Theory (SDT).

Participants and Data Collection

A total of 264 learners (124 females, 140 males) participated in the study. Respondents ranged from 17 to 60 years of age and represented a broad spectrum of educational backgrounds, with 56 holding only high school certificates and 208 having a bachelor's degree or higher. Data was collected via an online survey disseminated through Google Forms. The survey included a single open-ended question asking respondents to describe the "good, bad, and ugly" of learning through VCPs. Demographic information such as education level, ICT skill proficiency, and access to devices and internet connectivity were also captured.

Preprocessing and Sentiment Analysis Procedures

The collected responses were first preprocessed to clean and standardize the data. This involved removing incomplete entries, tokenizing text into sentences, and filtering out irrelevant or template-like content using a custom-built C# application. Stop words and non-semantic text were excluded to ensure meaningful analysis.

For the quantitative analysis, Azure Machine Learning (AML) was employed to classify sentiment into positive, neutral, or negative categories. AML's natural language processing tools processed the text through a REST API and returned sentiment labels with associated confidence scores. Sentences with a sentiment confidence of $\geq$0.6 were considered high-certainty classifications, while those between 0.4 and 0.6 were manually reviewed.

Qualitative sentiment analysis was performed using a modified version of Huang et al.'s (2021) multidimensional framework. Five sentiment categories were used: positive, negative, neutral, insightful, and confused. This extended classification system offered more nuanced interpretations, especially for ambiguous or reflective learner feedback. The sentiments were mapped to SDT's three psychological needs: autonomy, competence, and relatedness.

Coding and Reliability

A codebook was developed to define each sentiment category and its alignment with SDT elements. Two independent raters coded a subset of the responses to ensure inter-rater reliability. Cohen's Kappa was computed and yielded a value of 0.96, indicating a high level of agreement. The validated coding scheme was then used to manually tag the rest of the dataset.

This hybrid methodology—combining automated classification from AML with human-coded multidimensional sentiment analysis—allowed for a comprehensive and psychologically meaningful understanding of student feedback. The approach demonstrated the utility of machine learning in educational research, while acknowledging the importance of contextual and emotional depth provided by qualitative interpretation.

RESULTS AND FINDINGS

This study analyzed open-ended responses from 264 learners regarding their experiences with video-conference platforms (VCPs). Sentiment analysis was conducted using two methods: Azure Machine Learning (AML) and a multidimensional framework. AML categorized feedback into positive (53%), neutral (24%), and negative (23%) sentiments. However, the multidimensional framework revealed a more complex sentiment distribution: positive (32%), insightful (18%), neutral (20%), negative (22%), and confused (8%).

A deeper analysis of these results revealed several noteworthy patterns when mapped to Self-Determination Theory (SDT).

Autonomy-related sentiments were largely positive and insightful. Learners expressed appreciation for flexibility, asynchronous learning, and the ability to review recorded content. For example, comments such as "I can re-watch the video anytime" and "It allows me to learn at my own pace" were common. These responses indicate a strong sense of control and choice in the learning process.

In contrast, competence-related sentiments skewed more negatively. Students reported frustration with inadequate technical support, limited feedback from instructors, and a lack of hands-on experiences. Comments like "No practical session in the video-conference classroom" and "Technical issues affected my understanding" illustrate challenges that undermine learners' sense of effectiveness and mastery.

Relatedness emerged as the most under-supported SDT domain. Many students felt isolated and disconnected due to limited peer interaction and lack of real-time engagement. Statements such as "I feel alone in the class" or "It is difficult to connect with classmates" reflect the need for improved social presence and community-building in VCP environments.

When analyzed across demographic characteristics, younger learners (typically high school leavers) frequently mentioned distractions and lack of motivation, while older students (with bachelor's degrees or higher) valued flexibility but criticized the lack of collaborative learning opportunities. Respondents with high IT proficiency expressed more autonomy and less confusion, while those with lower skills struggled with platform navigation and digital literacy, resulting in higher confused and negative sentiment categories.

Respondents with limited access to gadgets and unstable internet connections commonly reported negative and confused sentiments. They cited barriers such as network unreliability and financial constraints in acquiring devices. These challenges significantly affected perceived competence and contributed to disengagement.

Furthermore, the "insightful" sentiment category added a valuable layer to the analysis. It captured reflective comments that considered the pros and cons of VCPs, often suggesting hybrid models. For instance, one learner wrote, "Online learning works, but it shouldn't replace physical classes entirely." This category showed how students think critically about their learning environments and highlighted opportunities for innovation.

The "confused" category uncovered sentiments tied to ambiguity, cognitive overload, and misaligned expectations. Students expressed uncertainty about learning outcomes and challenges in adapting to non-traditional teaching methods. AML alone would have classified these as negative, but the multidimensional framework allowed for more precise diagnosis of emotional states.

These findings demonstrate the limitations of three-category sentiment models and highlight the utility of hybrid machine learning approaches in capturing the full spectrum of student experiences. By contextualizing these sentiments within the SDT framework, the study offers a comprehensive view of how VCPs influence learner autonomy, competence, and relatedness. It also underscores the importance of tailoring platform design and instructional strategies to meet diverse learner needs.

In summary, key findings from the study in terms of mapping to SDT include:

- Autonomy: Learners valued flexibility and the ability to self-pace. Comments such as "I can rewatch the video anytime" reflect this.
- Competence: Negative comments centered around lack of practical sessions, slow feedback, and technological issues.
- Relatedness: Students expressed dissatisfaction with reduced interaction and social connection, e.g., "Online environments make it hard to build relationships with peers."

Differences by demographic revealed also showed that:

- Younger learners were more distracted and demotivated.
- Older, working adults valued flexibility but missed networking opportunities.
- Access to reliable internet and digital devices significantly shaped sentiment.

DISCUSSION

This study affirms that sentiment analysis, when integrated with SDT, can yield actionable insights into learners' digital experiences. The use of a hybrid model revealed sentiment layers that AML alone could not capture. For instance, the "insightful" category uncovered reflective thoughts about hybrid learning preferences that would otherwise be tagged simply as positive or neutral.

Autonomy emerged as the most positively perceived dimension, consistent with other findings (Palmer et al., 2023). Competence and relatedness were more frequently linked to negative or confused sentiments, highlighting the need for better instructional design and peer engagement features. The alignment of sentiments with IT skills and digital access underlines the necessity of addressing the digital divide.

CONCLUSION, LIMITATIONS AND RECOMMENDATIONS

The study concludes that while VCPs offer autonomy and accessibility, they often fall short in promoting competence and social connectedness. AML is a useful tool for scalable sentiment analysis, but its effectiveness is enhanced when combined with multidimensional sentiment categories.

Limitations include the reliance on self-reported feedback and the lack of platform-specific analysis. Future studies should explore longitudinal data, cultural factors, and specific design features that impact SDT dimensions. Recommendations include:

- Enhancing interactivity through collaborative tools.
- Providing structured feedback mechanisms.
- Supporting digital equity through better access to devices and stable internet.
- Integrating nuanced sentiment categories in AI-powered learning analytics.

REFERENCES

Ananthi Claral Mary, T., & Arul Leena Rose, P. J. (2023). Ensemble machine learning model for university students' risk prediction and assessment of cognitive learning outcomes. *International Journal of Information and Education Technology (IJIET), 13*(6), 579–585. DOI: 10.18178/ijiet.2023.13.6.1891

Chiu, T. K. F. (2024). A classification tool to foster self-regulated learning with generative artificial intelligence by applying self-determination theory: A case of ChatGPT. *Educational Technology Research and Development, 72*(4), 2401–2416. DOI: 10.1007/s11423-024-10366-w

Harfoushi, O., & Hasan, D. (2018). Amazon Machine Learning vs. Microsoft Azure Machine Learning as platforms for sentiment analysis. *International Journal of Advanced Science and Technology, 118*, 125–132. DOI: 10.14257/ijast.2018.118.12

Huang, C., Han, Z., Li, M., Wang, X., & Zhao, W. (2021). Sentiment evolution with interaction levels in blended learning environments: Using learning analytics and epistemic network analysis. *Australasian Journal of Educational Technology, 37*(2), 37–53. DOI: 10.14742/ajet.6749

Lim, L. L. (2020). *The socioeconomic impacts of COVID-19 in Malaysia: Policy review and guidance for protecting the most vulnerable and supporting enterprises.* International Labour Organization.

MacIntyre, P. D., Schnare, B., & Ross, J. (2018). Self-determination theory and motivation for music. *Psychology of Music, 46*(5), 699–715. DOI: 10.1177/0305735617721637

Melati, M. (2020). The Use of Zoom Cloud Meeting as an Innovative English Learning Media. E-Journal Karinosseff, 1(1).

Nishiwaki, Y., Oshima, M., Hashimoto, K., & Tsuda, K. (2023). A study of sentiment analysis based on specific 6-emotion category for Thai language. *Information Engineering Express, 9*(2), 80–89. DOI: 10.52731/iee.v9.i2.774

Palmer, L. E., Pagoto, S. L., Workman, D., Lewis, K. A., Rudin, L., De Luna, N., Herrera, V., Brown, N., Bibeau, J., Arcangel, K., & Waring, M. E. (2023). Health and education concerns about returning to campus and online learning during the COVID-19 pandemic among U.S. undergraduate STEM majors. *Journal of American College Health, 71*(8), 1956–1966. DOI: 10.1080/07448481.2021.1979009 PMID: 34666630

Pant, H. V., Lohani, M. C., & Pande, J. (2023). Thematic and sentiment analysis of learners' feedback in MOOCs. *Journal of Learning for Development*, *10*(1), 34–47. https://jl4d.org/index.php/ejl4d/article/view/740. DOI: 10.56059/jl4d.v10i1.740

Sun, R. (2023). Comparative study of online learning and face-to-face learning. *SHS Web of Conferences, 180*, 04006. https://doi.org/DOI: 10.1051/shsconf/202318004006

Compilation of References

Abdullah, M., Madain, A., & Jararweh, Y. (2022). ChatGPT: Fundamentals, Applications and Social Impacts. *2022 Ninth International Conference on Social Networks Analysis, Management and Security (SNAMS)*, 1–8. DOI: 10.1109/SNAMS58071.2022.10062688

Abuhassna, H., & Alnawajha, S. (2023a). Instructional design made easy! Instructional design models, categories, frameworks, educational context, and recommendations for future work. *European Journal of Investigation in Health, Psychology and Education*, *13*(4), 715–735. DOI: 10.3390/ejihpe13040054 PMID: 37185907

Abuhassna, H., & Alnawajha, S. (2023b). The transactional distance theory and distance learning contexts: Theory integration, research gaps, and future agenda. *Education Sciences*, *13*(2), 112. DOI: 10.3390/educsci13020112

Abuhassna, H., Awae, F., Bayoumi, K., Alzitawi, D. U., Alsharif, A. H., & Yahaya, N. (2022b). Understanding online learning readiness among university students: A bibliometric analysis. [iJIM]. *International Journal of Interactive Mobile Technologies*, *16*(13), 81–94. DOI: 10.3991/ijim.v16i13.30605

Abuhassna, H., Van, N. T., Yahaya, N., Zakaria, M. A. Z. M., Awae, F., Al Zitawi, D. U. D., & Bayoumi, K. (2022a). Strategies for successful blended learning—A bibliometric analysis and reviews. [iJIM]. *International Journal of Interactive Mobile Technologies*, *16*(13), 66–80. DOI: 10.3991/ijim.v16i13.30739

Adetayo, A. J. (2023). Artificial intelligence chatbots in academic libraries: The rise of ChatGPT. *Library Hi Tech News*, *40*(3), 18–21. DOI: 10.1108/LHTN-01-2023-0007

Adiguzel, T., Kaya, M. H., & Cansu, F. K. (2023). Revolutionizing education with AI: Exploring the transformative potential of ChatGPT. *Contemporary Educational Technology*, *15*(3), ep429. DOI: 10.30935/cedtech/13152

Ahmed, Z., & Ganapathy, T. (2021). Lifelong learning and skill development through AI-based tutoring systems. *Journal of Educational Technology Development and Exchange*, *14*(2), 111–128.

Akalin, N., & Loutfi, A. (2021). Reinforcement learning approaches in social robotics. *Sensors (Basel)*, *21*(4), 1292. DOI: 10.3390/s21041292 PMID: 33670257

Akgun, S., & Greenhow, C. (2022). Artificial intelligence in education: Addressing ethical challenges in K-12 settings. *AI and Ethics*, *2*(3), 431–440. DOI: 10.1007/s43681-021-00096-7 PMID: 34790956

Al Omoush, M. H., Salih, S. E., Kishore, S., & Mehigan, T. (2023). Interactive Multimodal Learning: Towards Using Pedagogical Agents for Inclusive Education. *2023 IEEE International Humanitarian Technology Conference (IHTC)*, 1–7. DOI: 10.1109/IHTC58960.2023.10508848

Alam, A. (2021). Possibilities and Apprehensions in the Landscape of Artificial Intelligence in Education. *2021 International Conference on Computational Intelligence and Computing Applications (ICCICA)*, 1–8. DOI: 10.1109/ICCICA52458.2021.9697272

Alam, A. (2022). A Digital Game based Learning Approach for Effective Curriculum Transaction for Teaching-Learning of Artificial Intelligence and Machine Learning. *2022 International Conference on Sustainable Computing and Data Communication Systems (ICSCDS)*, 69–74. DOI: 10.1109/ICSCDS53736.2022.9760932

Alamri, M.. (2020). Self-regulated learning through personalized online courses in AI-based tutoring. *Computers & Education*, *150*, 103839.

Albdrani, R. N., & Al-Shargabi, A. A. (2023). Investigating the Effectiveness of ChatGPT for Providing Personalized Learning Experience: A Case Study. [IJACSA]. *International Journal of Advanced Computer Science and Applications*, *14*(11). Advance online publication. DOI: 10.14569/IJACSA.2023.01411122

Aleven, V. A. W. M. M.. (2016). Adaptive learning technologies in AI-based tutoring systems: Cognitive science approaches. *Educational Technology Research and Development*, *64*(3), 553–575.

Alharbi, M., & Cristea, A. (2021). Personalized learning pathways in intelligent tutoring systems using reinforcement learning. *International Journal of Artificial Intelligence in Education*, *31*(2), 167–186.

Almaiah, M. A., Alfaisal, R., Salloum, S. A., Hajjej, F., Thabit, S., El-Qirem, F. A., Lutfi, A., Alrawad, M., Al Mulhem, A., Alkhdour, T., Awad, A. B., & Al-Maroof, R. S. (2022). Examining the impact of artificial intelligence and social and computer anxiety in e-learning settings: Students' perceptions at the university level. *Electronics (Basel), 11*(22), 3662. DOI: 10.3390/electronics11223662

Ananthi Claral Mary, T., & Arul Leena Rose, P. J. (2023). Ensemble machine learning model for university students' risk prediction and assessment of cognitive learning outcomes. *International Journal of Information and Education Technology (IJIET), 13*(6), 579–585. DOI: 10.18178/ijiet.2023.13.6.1891

Arulkumaran, K., Deisenroth, M. P., Brundage, M., & Bharath, A. A. (2017). A Brief Survey of Deep Reinforcement Learning. *IEEE Signal Processing Magazine, 34*(6), 26–38. DOI: 10.1109/MSP.2017.2743240

Atchley, P., Pannell, H., Wofford, K., Hopkins, M., & Atchley, R. A. (2024). Human and AI collaboration in the higher education environment: Opportunities and concerns. *Cognitive Research: Principles and Implications, 9*(1), 20. DOI: 10.1186/s41235-024-00547-9 PMID: 38589710

Ayeni, O. O., Al Hamad, N. M., Chisom, O. N., Osawaru, B., & Adewusi, O. E. (2024). AI in education: A review of personalized learning and educational technology. *GSC Advanced Research and Reviews, 18*(2), 261–271. DOI: 10.30574/gscarr.2024.18.2.0062

Ayu, S., Sekar, D. A., & Savitri, W. (2021). Analisis faktor penyebab kesulitan belajar matematika. *AKSIOMA: Jurnal Program Studi Pendidikan Matematika, 10*(3), 1611–1622. DOI: 10.24127/ajpm.v10i3.3824

Bagunaid, W., Chilamkurti, N., Shahraki, A. S., & Bamashmos, S. (2024). Visual Data and Pattern Analysis for Smart Education: A Robust DRL-Based Early Warning System for Student Performance Prediction. *Future Internet, 16*(206), 206. Advance online publication. DOI: 10.3390/fi16060206

Baidoo-Anu, D., & Owusu Ansah, L. (2023). *Education in the Era of Generative Artificial Intelligence (AI): Understanding the Potential Benefits of ChatGPT in Promoting Teaching and Learning* (SSRN Scholarly Paper 4337484). DOI: 10.2139/ssrn.4337484

Bailenson, J. N., Yee, N., Blascovich, J., Beall, A. C., Lundblad, N., & Jin, M. (2008). The Use of Immersive Virtual Reality in the Learning Sciences: Digital Transformations of Teachers, Students, and Social Context. *Journal of the Learning Sciences, 17*(1), 102–141. DOI: 10.1080/10508400701793141

Baskara, F. R. (2023). Chatbots and flipped learning: Enhancing student engagement and learning outcomes through personalised support and collaboration. IJORER. *International Journal of Recent Educational Research*, *4*(2), 223–238. DOI: 10.46245/ijorer.v4i2.331

Behravan, M., & Gracanin, D. (2024). Generative Multi-Modal Artificial Intelligence for Dynamic Real-Time Context-Aware Content Creation in Augmented Reality. *30th ACM Symposium on Virtual Reality Software and Technology*, 1–2. DOI: 10.1145/3641825.3689685

Belpaeme, T., Kennedy, J., Ramachandran, A., Scassellati, B., & Tanaka, F. (2018). Social robots for education: A review. *Science Robotics*, *3*(21), eaat5954. Advance online publication. DOI: 10.1126/scirobotics.aat5954 PMID: 33141719

Billinghurst, M., Clark, A., & Lee, G. (2015). A Survey of Augmented Reality. Foundations and Trends® in Human–Computer Interaction, 8(2–3), 73–272. DOI: 10.1561/1100000049

Borenstein, J., & Howard, A. (2021). Ethical frameworks for AI in education. *Science and Engineering Ethics*, *27*(1), 8. PMID: 33538906

Brahimi, T., & Sarirete, A. (2024). Transforming Learning in STEAM: How AI Tools and Language Models Catalyze Educational Advancement. In Baroudi, S., & Lytras, M. D. (Eds.), *Transformative Leadership and Sustainable Innovation in Education: Interdisciplinary Perspectives* (pp. 39–58). Emerald Publishing Limited., DOI: 10.1108/978-1-83753-536-120241004

Brandtzaeg, P. B., Skjuve, M., & Følstad, A. (2022). My AI Friend: How Users of a Social Chatbot Understand Their Human–AI Friendship. *Human Communication Research*, *48*(3), 404–429. Advance online publication. DOI: 10.1093/hcr/hqac008

Breazeal, C. (1999). "Designing Robots That Will Be Useful in Our Everyday Lives," *IEEE International Conference on Intelligent Robots and Systems*.

Breazeal, C.. (2019). PopBots: Designing an Artificial Intelligence Curriculum for Early Childhood Education. *Proceedings of the AAAI Conference on Artificial Intelligence*, *33*(1), 9729–9736. DOI: 10.1609/aaai.v33i01.33019729

Bubeck, S., Chandak, S., Eldan, R., Gehrke, J., Horvitz, E., Kamar, E., . . . Zhang, Y. (2023). Sparks of Artificial General Intelligence: Early experiments with GPT-4. *arXiv preprint* arXiv:2303.12712. https://doi.org//arXiv.2303.12712DOI: 10.48550

Bull, S.. (2018). Diagnostic visualizations and formative assessment in AI-enhanced classrooms. *AI in Education Journal*, *10*(4), 415–435.

Caballé, S., & Conesa, J. (2019). Conversational Agents in Support for Collaborative Learning in MOOCs: An Analytical Review. In Xhafa, F., Barolli, L., & Greguš, M. (Eds.), *Advances in Intelligent Networking and Collaborative Systems* (Vol. 23, pp. 384–394). Springer International Publishing., DOI: 10.1007/978-3-319-98557-2_35

Celik, I., Dindar, M., Muukkonen, H., & Järvelä, S. (2022). The promises and challenges of artificial intelligence for teachers: A systematic review of research. *TechTrends*, *66*(4), 616–630. DOI: 10.1007/s11528-022-00715-y

Chadha, A. (2024). Transforming Higher Education for the Digital Age: Examining Emerging Technologies and Pedagogical Innovations. *Journal of Interdisciplinary Studies in Education*, *13*(S1), 53–70. https://ojed.org/jise. DOI: 10.32674/em2qsn46

Chaka, C. (2023). Detecting AI content in responses generated by ChatGPT, YouChat, and Chatsonic: The case of five AI content detection tools. *Journal of Applied Learning and Teaching*, *6*(2), 94–104.

Chen, C., Hu, W., & Wei, X. (2024). From anxiety to action: Exploring the impact of artificial intelligence anxiety and artificial intelligence self-efficacy on motivated learning of undergraduate students. *Interactive Learning Environments*, •••, 1–16. DOI: 10.1080/10494820.2024.2440877

Chen, X., Huang, Y., & Liu, S. (2020). Artificial intelligence for personalized learning pathways: Current status and future directions. *Computers & Education*, *156*, 103940.

Chen, X., Zou, D., Cheng, G., & Xie, H. (2021). Artificial intelligence-assisted personalized language learning: A systematic review and bibliometric analysis. *Computer Assisted Language Learning*, *34*(7), 934–957. DOI: 10.1080/09588221.2019.1901492

Chen, Z., Zhang, J., Jiang, X., Hu, Z., Han, X., Xu, M., Savitha, V., & Vivekananda, G. N. (2020). Education 4.0 using artificial intelligence for students performance analysis. *Inteligencia Artificial*, *23*(66), 124–137. DOI: 10.4114/intartif.vol23iss66pp124-137

Chiu, T. K. F. (2024). A classification tool to foster self-regulated learning with generative artificial intelligence by applying self-determination theory: A case of ChatGPT. *Educational Technology Research and Development*, *72*(4), 2401–2416. DOI: 10.1007/s11423-024-10366-w

Chiu, T. K. F., & Li, Y. (2023). How Can Emerging Technologies Impact STEM Education? *Journal for STEM Education Research*, *6*(3), 375–384. DOI: 10.1007/s41979-023-00113-w

Cho, Y. H., Kim, K. H., & Han, J. (2019). Student perception of adaptive collaborative learning support through learning analytics. *Journal of Educational Information and Media*, *25*(1), 25–57. https://doi.org/

Clarke, T.. (2015). Continuous improvement in AI-based tutoring systems through student feedback analysis. *Journal of Educational Technology & Society*, *18*(3), 12–22.

Clarke, V., & Braun, V. (2017). Thematic analysis. *The Journal of Positive Psychology*, *12*(3), 297–298. DOI: 10.1080/17439760.2016.1262613

Corbett, C. F., Wright, P. J., Jones, K., & Parmer, M. (2021). Voice-activated virtual home assistant use and social isolation and loneliness among older adults: A mini-review. *Frontiers in Public Health*, *9*, 742012. DOI: 10.3389/fpubh.2021.742012 PMID: 34708017

Creswell, J. W., & Plano Clark, V. L. (2018). Designing and conducting mixed methods research (Third edition, international student edition). Sage.

Creswell, J. W., & Poth, C. N. (2018). *Qualitative inquiry and research design: Choosing among five approaches* (4th ed.). Sage Publications.

Crompton, H., & Burke, D. (2023). Visual tracking in AI tutoring for classroom orchestration. *Journal of Interactive Learning Research*, *34*(1), 45–63.

Crompton, H., Jones, M. V., & Burke, D. (2024). Affordances and challenges of artificial intelligence in K-12 education: A systematic review. *Journal of Research on Technology in Education*, *56*(3), 248–268. DOI: 10.1080/15391523.2022.2121344

Crowe, D., LaPierre, M., & Kebritchi, M. (2017). Knowledge-based artificial augmentation intelligence technology: Next step in academic instructional tools for distance learning. *TechTrends*, *61*(5), 494–506. DOI: 10.1007/s11528-017-0210-4

Dalgarno, B., & Lee, M. J. W. (2010). What are the learning affordances of 3-D virtual environments? *British Journal of Educational Technology*, *41*(1), 10–32. DOI: 10.1111/j.1467-8535.2009.01038.x

Darmayanti, R. (2024). Programmed learning in mathematics education before and after the pandemic: Academics Integrate technology. *Assyfa Learning Journal*, *2*(1), 40–56. DOI: 10.61650/alj.v2i1.126

De Back, T. T., Tinga, A. M., & Louwerse, M. M. (2023). Learning in immersed collaborative virtual environments: Design and implementation. *Interactive Learning Environments*, *31*(8), 5364–5382. DOI: 10.1080/10494820.2021.2006238 de Kervenoael, R., Hasan, R., Schwob, A., & Goh, E. (2020). Leveraging human-robot interaction in hospitality services: Incorporating the role of perceived value, empathy, and information sharing into visitors' intentions to use social robots. *Tourism Management*, *78*, 104042. DOI: 10.1016/j.tourman.2019.104042

Del Moral-Pérez, M. E., López-Bouzas, N., & Castañeda-Fernández, J. (2024). Transmedia skill derived from the process of converting films into educational games with augmented reality and artificial intelligence. *Journal of New Approaches in Educational Research*, *13*(1), 15. DOI: 10.1007/s44322-024-00015-8

Dempere, J., Modugu, K., Hesham, A., & Ramasamy, L. K. (2023). The impact of ChatGPT on higher education. *Frontiers in Education*, *8*, 1206936. DOI: 10.3389/feduc.2023.1206936

Deng, W., Wang, L., & Deng, X. (2024). Strategies for Optimizing Personalized Learning Pathways with Artificial Intelligence Assistance. *International Journal of Advanced Computer Science and Applications*, *15*(6), 605–616. DOI: 10.14569/IJACSA.2024.0150662

Dergaa, I., Chamari, K., Zmijewski, P., & Saad, H. B. (2023). From human writing to artificial intelligence generated text: Examining the prospects and potential threats of ChatGPT in academic writing. *Biology of Sport*, *40*(2), 615–622. DOI: 10.5114/biolsport.2023.125623 PMID: 37077800

Dhananjaya, G. M., Goudar, R. H., Govindaraja, K., Kaliwal, R. B., Rathod, V. K., Deshpande, S. L., & Kulkarni, A. (2024). Enhancing Education with ChatGPT: Revolutionizing Personalized Learning and Teacher Support. *EAI Endorsed Transactions on Internet of Things*, *10*. Advance online publication. DOI: 10.4108/eetiot.6998

Dillenbourg, P., Järvelä, S., & Fischer, F. (2009). The Evolution of Research on Computer-Supported Collaborative Learning. In Balacheff, N., Ludvigsen, S., De Jong, T., Lazonder, A., & Barnes, S. (Eds.), *Technology-Enhanced Learning* (pp. 3–19). Springer Netherlands., DOI: 10.1007/978-1-4020-9827-7_1

Dinçer, S., & Doğanay, A. (2017). Socio-emotional capacity of educational agents in AI tutoring. *Interactive Learning Environments*, *25*(1), 38–54.

Drori, I., Zhang, S., Shuttleworth, R., Tang, L., Lu, A., Ke, E., Liu, K., Chen, L., Tran, S., Cheng, N., Wang, R., Singh, N., Patti, T. L., Lynch, J., Shporer, A., Verma, N., Wu, E., & Strang, G. (2022). A neural network solves, explains, and generates university math problems by program synthesis and few-shot learning at human level. *Proceedings of the National Academy of Sciences of the United States of America*, *119*(32), e2123433119. Advance online publication. DOI: 10.1073/pnas.2123433119 PMID: 35917350

Duan, H. (2024). Research and Practice of Digital Training Model Based on Artificial Intelligence Technology. *Applied Mathematics and Nonlinear Sciences*, *9*(1), 1–17. DOI: 10.2478/amns.2023.2.01507

Duca, A., Constantinescu, G.-G., & Iftene, A. (2024). Future Education: Experimenting with Chemical Reactions in Virtual Reality. 2024 International Conference on INnovations in Intelligent SysTems and Applications (INISTA), 1–6. DOI: 10.1109/INISTA62901.2024.10683861

Duhaylungsod, A. V., & Chavez, J. V. (2023). ChatGPT and other AI users: Innovative and creative utilitarian value and mindset shift. *Journal of Namibian Studies: History Politics Culture*, *33*, 4367–4378.

Dwivedi, R., Jadhav, A., Jha, P., & Anubhav. (2022). Predicting 3D Model of Images for Augmented Reality Applications. In B. Iyer, T. Crick, & S.-L. Peng (Eds.), Applied Computational Technologies (Vol. 303, pp. 395–404). Springer Nature Singapore. DOI: 10.1007/978-981-19-2719-5_37

Dwivedi, Y. K., Kshetri, N., Hughes, L., Slade, E. L., Jeyaraj, A., Kar, A. K., Baabdullah, A. M., Koohang, A., Raghavan, V., Ahuja, M., Albanna, H., Albashrawi, M. A., Al-Busaidi, A. S., Balakrishnan, J., Barlette, Y., Basu, S., Bose, I., Brooks, L., Buhalis, D., & Wright, R. (2023). Opinion Paper: "So what if ChatGPT wrote it?" Multidisciplinary perspectives on opportunities, challenges and implications of generative conversational AI for research, practice and policy. *International Journal of Information Management*, *71*, 102642. DOI: 10.1016/j.ijinfomgt.2023.102642

Eden, C. A., Adeleye, O. O., & Adeniyi, I. S. (2024). A review of AI-driven pedagogical strategies for equitable access to science education. Magna Scientia Advanced Research and Reviews, 10(2), 044-054. DOI: 10.30574/msarr.2024.10.2.0043

Eltahir, M. E., & Babiker, F. M. E. (2024). The Influence of Artificial Intelligence Tools on Student Performance in e-Learning Environments: Case Study. *Electronic Journal of e-Learning*, *22*(9), 91–110. DOI: 10.34190/ejel.22.9.3639

Eubanks, V. (2018). Automating inequality: How high-tech tools profile, police, and punish the poor. St. Martin's Press. https://books.google.com/books?hl=en&lr=&id=pn4pDwAAQBAJ&oi=fnd&pg=PP10&dq=Eubanks,+V.+(2018).+Automating+inequality:+How+high-tech+tools+profile,+police,+and+punish+the+poor.+St.+Martin%27s+Press.&ots=gF0QIfmrse&sig=Uq2zT_k2hV2z7_lVHbc25mMDzWY

Fancsali, S.. (2014). Interest-matched problem selection in MATHia AI tutoring. *Journal of Educational Computing Research*, *50*(3), 317–339.

Ferruz, N., & Höcker, B. (2022). Controllable protein design with language models. *Nature Machine Intelligence*, *4*(6), 6. Advance online publication. DOI: 10.1038/s42256-022-00499-z

Floridi, L., & Chiriatti, M. (2020). GPT-3: Its nature, scope, limits, and consequences. *Minds and Machines*, *30*(4), 681–694. DOI: 10.1007/s11023-020-09548-1

Forsström, S. E., & Afdal, G. (2020). Learning mathematics through activities with robots. *Digital Experiences in Mathematics Education*, *6*(1), 30–50. DOI: 10.1007/s40751-019-00057-0

Foster, N. (2024). Reinventing Assessment in the Age of Generative AI. *Journal of Educational Technology & Society*, *27*(2), 34–48.

Fox, J. & Gambino, A. (2021). Relationship Development with Humanoid Social Robots: Applying Interpersonal Theories to Human-Robot Interaction. *Cyberpsychology, Behavior, And Social Networking*, 24 (5), Ann Liebert, Inc. DOI: DOI: 10.1089/cyber.2020.0181294

Francis, K., & Davis, B. (2018). Coding robots as a source of instantiations for arithmetic. *Digital Experiences in Mathematics Education*, *4*(1), 71–86. DOI: 10.1007/s40751-018-0042-7

Freeman, S., Eddy, S. L., McDonough, M., Smith, M. K., Okoroafor, N., Jordt, H., & Wenderoth, M. P. (2014). Active learning increases student performance in science, engineering, and mathematics. *Proceedings of the National Academy of Sciences of the United States of America*, *111*(23), 8410–8415. DOI: 10.1073/pnas.1319030111 PMID: 24821756

Frieder, S., Pinchetti, L., Griffiths, R. R., Salvatori, T., Lukasiewicz, T., Petersen, P., & Berner, J. (2024). Mathematical capabilities of ChatGPT. Advances in Neural Information Processing Systems,36. https://proceedings.neurips.cc/paper_files/paper/2023/hash/58168e8a92994655d6da3939e7cc0918-Abstract-Datasets_and_Benchmarks.html

Fry, a mathematician, discusses and dissects the algorithms behind genAI. This book helps explain how AI works and why we need to understand how it arrives at its conclusions.

Fry, H. (2018). *Hello world: Being human in the age of algorithms*. W. W. Norton.

Fuchs, K. (2023, May). Exploring the opportunities and challenges of NLP models in higher education: Is Chat GPT a blessing or a curse? *Frontiers in Education*, *8*, 1166682. DOI: 10.3389/feduc.2023.1166682

Gao, H., Lindquist, M., & Serrano Vergel, R. (2024). *AI-Driven Avatars in Immersive 3D Environments for Education Workflow and Case Study of the Temple of Demeter*. Wichmann Verlag., DOI: 10.14627/537752059

García-Martínez, I., Fernández-Batanero, J. M., Fernández-Cerero, J., & León, S. P. (2023). Analysing the impact of artificial intelligence and computational sciences on student performance: Systematic review and meta-analysis. *Journal of New Approaches in Educational Research*, *12*(1), 171–197. DOI: 10.7821/naer.2023.1.1240

Gelana, F., & Campbell, A. (2024). The Possibilities of AI and Augmented Reality in Education. *2024 IEEE International Conference on Consumer Electronics (ICCE)*, 1–4. DOI: 10.1109/ICCE59016.2024.10444487

George, A. S., & George, A. S. H. (2023). A Review of ChatGPT AI's Impact on Several Business Sectors. *Partners Universal International Innovation Journal*, *1*(1), 1. Advance online publication. DOI: 10.5281/zenodo.7644359

Ghreir, H. (2023). The Impact of Using the Technology-Based Platform by The School Leadership on the Teachers' Evaluation. 3 Rd International Conference on Educational Technology and Online Learning – ICETOL 2023 Full Paper Proceedings, 131–136.

González-Calatayud, V.. (2021). AI-assisted student assessment in classroom instruction. *Educational Technology Research and Development*, *69*(5), 1017–1034.

Graesser, A. C.. (2017). Conversational agents in AI tutoring: An assessment. *Journal of Educational Psychology*, *109*(1), 20–34.

Graesser, A. C., Lu, S., Jackson, G. T., Mitchell, H. H., Ventura, M., Olney, A., & Louwerse, M. M. (2004). AutoTutor: A tutor with dialogue in natural language. *Behavior Research Methods, Instruments, & Computers*, *36*(2), 180–192. DOI: 10.3758/BF03195563 PMID: 15354683

Grájeda, A., Burgos, J., Córdova, P., & Sanjinés, A. (2024). Assessing student-perceived impact of using artificial intelligence tools: Construction of a synthetic index of application in higher education. *Cogent Education*, *11*(1), 2287917. DOI: 10.1080/2331186X.2023.2287917

Granić, A. and Marangunić, N. (2019). Technology acceptance model in educational context: A systematic literature review. British Journal of Educational Technology, 2572 - 2593.

Green, B. A. (2023). The flawed data underpinning AI fairness in education. *AI & Society*, *38*(1), 23–35.

Green, S., & Carter, B. (2022). Digital Literacy for AI: Preparing Educators and Students. *International Journal of Digital Education*, *27*(3), 45–60.

Green, T. D., & Donovan, C. B. (2024). "Educators' evolving roles in AI-enhanced learning ecosystems," Computers & Education. *Artificial Intelligence*, *5*(100098).

Gupta, D. G., & Jain, V. (2023). Use of artificial intelligence with ethics and privacy for personalized customer services. In *Artificial Intelligence in customer service: The next frontier for personalized engagement* (pp. 231–257). Springer International Publishing., DOI: 10.1007/978-3-031-33898-4_10

Habib, M., Faris, M., Qaddoura, R., Alomari, A., & Faris, H. (2021). A Predictive Text System for Medical Recommendations in Telemedicine: A Deep Learning Approach in the Arabic Context. *IEEE Access : Practical Innovations, Open Solutions*, *9*, 85690–85708. DOI: 10.1109/ACCESS.2021.3087593

Haleem, A., Javaid, M., & Singh, R. P. (2022). An era of ChatGPT as a significant futuristic support tool: A study on features, abilities, and challenges. *BenchCouncil Transactions on Benchmarks. Standards and Evaluations*, *2*(4), 100089. DOI: 10.1016/j.tbench.2023.100089

Hamash, M. A., Mohamed, H., & Tiernan, P. (2024). Developing a New Model for Achieving Flow State in STEAM Education: A Mixed-Method Investigation. *Sains Humanika*, *16*(3), 101–111. DOI: 10.11113/sh.v16n3.2163

Hamash, M., Ghreir, H., & Tiernan, P. (2024). Breaking through Barriers: A Systematic Review of Extended Reality in Education for the Visually Impaired. *Education Sciences*, *14*(4), 365. DOI: 10.3390/educsci14040365

Hamash, M., & Mohamed, H. (2023). Identifying the Level of Teacher's Maturity in the Impactful Technology Use (ITU) in Abu Dhabi Public Schools. *Innovative Teaching and Learning Journal*, *7*(2), 60–71. DOI: 10.11113/itlj.v7.135

Han, E., & Bailenson, J. N. (2024). Social Interaction in VR. In Han, E., & Bailenson, J. N. (Eds.), *Oxford Research Encyclopedia of Communication*. Oxford University Press., DOI: 10.1093/acrefore/9780190228613.013.1489

Hao, M., Wang, Y., & Peng, J. (2024). Empirical Research on AI Technology-Supported Precision Teaching in High School Science Subjects. *Applied Sciences (Basel, Switzerland)*, *14*(7544), 7544. Advance online publication. DOI: 10.3390/app14177544

Hard Fork AI is a podcast by the New York Times that focuses solely on the world of genAI. It is helpful because of its currency and relevance to the general population. https://www.nytimes.com/column/hard-fork

Harfoushi, O., & Hasan, D. (2018). Amazon Machine Learning vs. Microsoft Azure Machine Learning as platforms for sentiment analysis. *International Journal of Advanced Science and Technology*, *118*, 125–132. DOI: 10.14257/ijast.2018.118.12

Hassani, H., Silva, E. S., Unger, S., TajMazinani, M., & Mac Feely, S. (2020). Artificial intelligence (AI) or intelligence augmentation (IA): What is the future? *AI*, *1*(2), 8. DOI: 10.3390/ai1020008

Hernandez, P. (2023). Privacy Challenges in AI-Based Education Systems. *Computers & Security*, *130*, 103785.

Hidi, S., & Ainley, M. (2008). Situational interest personalization in AI tutoring. *Educational Psychologist*, *43*(3), 173–184.

Hmelo-Silver, C. (2004). Problem-Based Learning: What and How Do Students Learn? *Educational Psychology Review*, *16*(3), 235–266. DOI: 10.1023/B:EDPR.0000034022.16470.f3

Holmes, W., Bialik, M., & Fadel, C. (2019). Artificial intelligence in education: Promises and implications for teaching and learning. Center for Curriculum Redesign. Retrieved from https://curriculumredesign.org/wp-content/uploads/AI-in-Education-CCR-2019.pdf

Holmes, A., & Tuomi, A. (2023). AI literacy for educators: Building capacity for digital-age teaching. *British Journal of Educational Technology*, *54*(1), 45–61.

Holmes, J.. (2023). "Artificial Intelligence in Higher Education: Challenges and Opportunities," *AI & Society*, vol. 36, pp. 393–402, 2021C. Lee and P. Wang, "Predictive Analytics in Higher Education: AI for Student Success,". *Educ. Data Sci. Rev.*, *14*(2), 55–72.

Holmes, S., Bialik, K., & Fadel, C. (2019). *Artificial Intelligence in Education: Promises and Implications for Teaching and Learning*. Center for Curriculum Redesign.

Holmes, W., & Tuomi, I. (2022). State of the art and practice in AI in education. *European Journal of Education*, *57*(4), 542–570. DOI: 10.1111/ejed.12533

Hooshyar, D., Ahmad, R. B., Yousefi, M., Yusop, F. D., & Horng, S. J. (2015). A flowchart-based intelligent tutoring system for improving problem-solving skills of novice programmers. *Journal of Computer Assisted Learning*, *31*(4), 345–361. DOI: 10.1111/jcal.12099

Hooshyar, D., Azevedo, R., & Yang, Y. (2024). Augmenting Deep Neural Networks with Symbolic Educational Knowledge: Towards Trustworthy and Interpretable AI for Education. *Machine Learning & Knowledge Extraction*, *6*(1), 593–618. DOI: 10.3390/make6010028

Huang, C., Han, Z., Li, M., Wang, X., & Zhao, W. (2021). Sentiment evolution with interaction levels in blended learning environments: Using learning analytics and epistemic network analysis. *Australasian Journal of Educational Technology*, *37*(2), 37–53. DOI: 10.14742/ajet.6749

Huang, H.-M., Rauch, U., & Liaw, S.-S. (2010). Investigating learners' attitudes toward virtual reality learning environments: Based on a constructivist approach. *Computers & Education*, *55*(3), 1171–1182. DOI: 10.1016/j.compedu.2010.05.014

Huang, L. (2023). Ethics of artificial intelligence in education: Student privacy and data protection. *Science Insights Education Frontiers*, *16*(2), 2577–2587. DOI: 10.15354/sief.23.re202

Huang, X., & Qiao, C. (2024). Enhancing Computational Thinking Skills Through Artificial Intelligence Education at a STEAM High School. *Science & Education*, *33*(2), 383–403. DOI: 10.1007/s11191-022-00392-6

Hwang, G. J., & Tu, Y. F. (2021). Integrating learning management systems for adaptive feedback in AI-based tutoring. *British Journal of Educational Technology*, *52*(2), 649–662.

Hwang, G. J., & Tu, Y. F. (2021). Roles and research trends of artificial intelligence in mathematics education: A bibliometric mapping analysis and systematic review. *Mathematics*, *9*(6), 584. DOI: 10.3390/math9060584

Hwang, G.-J., Xie, H., Wah, B. W., & Gašević, D. (2020). Vision, challenges, roles and research issues of Artificial Intelligence in Education. *Computers and Education: Artificial Intelligence*, *1*, 100001. DOI: 10.1016/j.caeai.2020.100001

Hwang, G., Sung, H., Chang, S., & Huang, X. (2020). A fuzzy expert system-based adaptive learning approach to improving students' learning performances by considering affective and cognitive factors. *Computers and Education: Artificial Intelligence*, *1*(1), 100003. DOI: 10.1016/j.caeai.2020.100003

Idroes, G. M., Noviandy, T. R., Maulana, A., Irvanizam, I., Jalil, Z., Lensoni, L., Lala, A., Abas, A. H., Tallei, T. E., & Idroes, R. (2023). Student Perspectives on the Role of Artificial Intelligence in Education: A Survey-Based Analysis. *Journal of Educational Management and Learning*, *1*(1), 8–15. DOI: 10.60084/jeml.v1i1.58

Ilie, M. D., & Frăsineanu, E. S. (2019). Artificial intelligence applications in education: A review. Proceedings of the International Conference on Virtual Learning, 11, 105–110. Retrieved from https://www.icvl.eu/2019/abstracts/ICVL2019_Section_III_Paper01.pdf

Jackaria, P., Hajan, B., Mastul, A., & Sali, F. (2024). Generation AI in a Reimagined Classroom : Challenges, and Opportunities, pp. 174–176, .DOI: 10.4018/979-8-3693-3350-1.ch009

Jackaria, P. M., Hajan, B. H., & Mastul, A. R. H. (2024). A comparative analysis of the rating of college students' essays by ChatGPT versus human raters. International Journal of Learning. *Teaching and Educational Research*, *23*(2), 478–492. DOI: 10.26803/ijlter.23.2.23

Johnson, M., & Davis, L. (2023). Curriculum Development with AI: Innovations and Challenges. *International Journal of Educational Reform*, *31*(4), 220–235.

Johnson, P., & Brown, R. (2022). The Role of NLP in Academic Writing. *IEEE Transactions on Education*, *70*(2), 89–105.

Ka, C., Chan, Y., & Hu, W. (2023). Students' voices on generative AI: Perceptions, benefits, and challenges in higher education. *International Journal of Educational Technology in Higher Education*, *20*(1), 43. Advance online publication. DOI: 10.1186/s41239-023-00411-8

Kadiri, K., & Alabi, O. A. (2023). Revolutionizing Education with AI-Infused Smart Classrooms: A Case Study from Federal Polytechnic Offa. *ASUP Conference*. https://www.researchgate.net/publication/373897598_Revolutionizing_Education_with_AI-Infused_Smart_Classrooms_A_Case_Study_from_Federal_Polytechnic_Offa

Kamalov, F., Santandreu Calonge, D., & Gurrib, I. (2023). New Era of Artificial Intelligence in Education: Towards a Sustainable Multifaceted Revolution. *Sustainability (Basel)*, *15*(16), 12451. DOI: 10.3390/su151612451

Kaplan-Rakowski, R., & Wojdynski, T. (2018). Students' Attitudes Toward High-Immersion Virtual Reality Assisted Language Learning. SSRN Electronic Journal. DOI: 10.2139/ssrn.3255611

Kapoor, D. (2023). Ensuring Equity in AI-Powered Education: A Global Perspective. *International Journal of Educational Equity*, *12*(4), 210–225.

Kasneci, E., Sessler, K., Küchemann, S., Bannert, M., Dementieva, D., Fischer, F., Gasser, U., Groh, G., Günnemann, S., Hüllermeier, E., Krusche, S., Kutyniok, G., Michaeli, T., Nerdel, C., Pfeffer, J., Poquet, O., Sailer, M., Schmidt, A., Seidel, T., & Kasneci, G. (2023). ChatGPT for good? On opportunities and challenges of large language models for education. *Learning and Individual Differences*, *103*, 102274. DOI: 10.1016/j.lindif.2023.102274

Khandor, V., Rathod, N., Goda, Y., Shah, N., & Mangrulkar, R. (2023). *Textual Description to Facial Image Generation," in Generative Adversarial Networks and Deep Learning: Theory and Applications, Dwarkadas J. Sanghvi College of Engineering*. CRC Press., DOI: 10.1201/9781003203964-7

Khan, M. S., & Alghamdi, A. A. (2024). *Artificial Intelligence in Teaching and Teacher Professional Development*. ScienceDirect.

Khan, W. N. (2024). Ethical challenges of AI in education: Balancing innovation with data privacy. *Journal of AI Integration in Education*, *1*(1), 1–13. https://www.researchcorridor.org/index.php/jaiie/article/view/238

Khosravi, H., & Cooper, A. (2022). Personalized learning pathways using machine learning: Enhancing learner engagement and outcomes. *International Journal of Educational Technology in Higher Education*, *19*(1), 8–20.

Kim, S. W., Go, H., Hong, S. J., & Lee, Y. (2023). An Approach to the Utilization of Design Thinking in Artificial Intelligence Education. *International Journal on Advanced Science, Engineering and Information Technology*, *13*(6), 2198–2204. Advance online publication. DOI: 10.18517/ijaseit.13.6.19042

Kleebayoon, A., & Wiwanitkit, V. (2023). Artificial intelligence, chatbots, plagiarism and basic honesty [comment]. *Cellular and Molecular Bioengineering*, *16*(2), 173–174. DOI: 10.1007/s12195-023-00759-x PMID: 37096073

Koedinger, K. R.. (2013). Open Learner Models and self-regulated learning in AI tutoring. *International Journal of Artificial Intelligence in Education*, *23*(1-4), 138–157.

Kolomaznik, M., Petrik, V., Slama, M., & Jurik, V. (2024). The role of socio-emotional attributes in enhancing human-AI collaboration. *Frontiers in Psychology*, *15*, 1369957. Advance online publication. DOI: 10.3389/fpsyg.2024.1369957 PMID: 39474095

Kooli, C. (2023). Chatbots in education and research: A critical examination of ethical implications and solutions. *Sustainability (Basel)*, *15*(7), 5614. DOI: 10.3390/su15075614

Koos, S., & Wachsmann, S. (2023). Navigating the impact of ChatGPT/gpt4 on legal academic examinations: Challenges, opportunities and recommendations. *Media Juris*, *6*(2), 255–270. DOI: 10.20473/mi.v6i2.45270

Krathwohl, D. R. (2002). A Revision of Bloom's Taxonomy: An Overview. *Theory into Practice*, *41*(4), 212–218. DOI: 10.1207/s15430421tip4104_2

Kumar, A., & Singh, M. (2024). AI for Hypothesis Generation: A New Frontier. *AI & Data Science Review*, *15*(3), 201–217.

Kumar, R. (2023). AI-Powered Tutoring Systems: A New Era in Higher Education. *Journal of Educational Technology & Society*, *26*(1), 45–60.

Land, M. H. (2013). Full STEAM Ahead: The Benefits of Integrating the Arts Into STEM. *Procedia Computer Science*, *20*, 547–552. DOI: 10.1016/j.procs.2013.09.317

Lawrence, R.. (2022). Real-time monitoring in group-based learning through AI analytics. *Educational Technology Research and Development*, *70*(2), 401–420.

Lee, J., Wang, J., Brown, E., Chu, L., Rodriguez, S. S., & Froehlich, J. E. (2024). GazePointAR: A Context-Aware Multimodal Voice Assistant for Pronoun Disambiguation in Wearable Augmented Reality. *Proceedings of the CHI Conference on Human Factors in Computing Systems*, 1–20. DOI: 10.1145/3613904.3642230

Lee, T., Martinez, A., & Gupta, S. (2021). AI-Based Literature Summarization for Research Efficiency. *Computational Intelligence Journal*, *18*(1), 45–60.

Lester, J. C., Converse, S. A., Kahler, S. E., Barlow, S. T., Stone, B. A., & Bhogal, R. S. (1997). The persona effect: Affective impact of animated pedagogical agents. *Proceedings of the ACM SIGCHI Conference on Human Factors in Computing Systems*, 359–366. DOI: 10.1145/258549.258797

Liao, L., & Gu, F. (2022). 5G and artificial intelligence interactive technology applied in preschool education courses. *Wireless Communications and Mobile Computing*, *7629354*, 1–11. Advance online publication. DOI: 10.1155/2022/7629354

Lim, L. L. (2020). *The socioeconomic impacts of COVID-19 in Malaysia: Policy review and guidance for protecting the most vulnerable and supporting enterprises*. International Labour Organization.

Lin, H., & Chen, Q. (2024). Artificial intelligence (AI) -integrated educational applications and college students' creativity and academic emotions: Students and teachers' perceptions and attitudes. *BMC Psychology*, *12*(1), 487–487. DOI: 10.1186/s40359-024-01979-0 PMID: 39285268

Liu, J. (2024). Strategic AI Integration in Universities: Best Practices. *AI & Society, 38*(1), 150–170.

Liu, T.-Y., Jiang, Y.-H., Wei, Y., Wang, X., Huang, S., & Dai, L. (2024). Educational Practices and Algorithmic Framework for Promoting Sustainable Development in Education by Identifying Real-World Learning Paths. *Sustainability (Basel), 16*(6871), 6871. Advance online publication. DOI: 10.3390/su16166871

Llenada Santos, J. V. (2022). Comparative analysis of mobile applications for its integration in college mathematics subjects. EDUCATIO: Journal of Education, 6(4), 324-345. https://www.researchgate.net/profile/John-Vincent-Santos/publication/359516455_Comparative_Analysis_of_Mobile_Applications_for_its_Integration_in_College_Mathematics_Subjects/links/62425e7f5e2f8c7a03466d3a/Comparative-Analysis-of-Mobile-Applications-for-its-Integration-in-College-Mathematics-Subjects.pdf

Lopez, R. (2023). Evaluating AI's Impact in Higher Education. *Journal of AI Policy & Governance, 6*(3), 98–112.

Luckin, R., & Holmes, W. (2016). Intelligence Unleashed: An argument for AI in education. https://discovery.ucl.ac.uk/id/eprint/1475756

Luckin, R., ... (2023). "AI and education: Guidance for policy makers," OECD Education Working Papers, no. 253.

Luckin, R., Holmes, W., Griffiths, M., & Forcier, L. B. (2018). *Intelligence Unleashed: An Argument for AI in Education*. Pearson Education.

Lu, X.. (2021). Adaptive feedback in AI-based tutoring systems. *Educational Data Mining, 11*(2), 39–54.

MacIntyre, P. D., Schnare, B., & Ross, J. (2018). Self-determination theory and motivation for music. *Psychology of Music, 46*(5), 699–715. DOI: 10.1177/0305735617721637

Mahdaoui, A. (2022). Human-AI collaboration in educational AI tutoring. *Journal of Human-Computer Studies, 156*, 102758.

Makransky, G., & Petersen, G. B. (2021). The Cognitive Affective Model of Immersive Learning (CAMIL): A Theoretical Research-Based Model of Learning in Immersive Virtual Reality. *Educational Psychology Review, 33*(3), 937–958. DOI: 10.1007/s10648-020-09586-2

Mallillin, L. (2024). Artificial Intelligence (AI) Towards Students' Academic Performance. *Innovare Journal of Education*, 16 – 21. https://doi.org/.DOI: 10.22159/ijoe.2024v12i4.51665

Margot, K. C., & Kettler, T. (2019). Teachers' perception of STEM integration and education: A systematic literature review. *International Journal of STEM Education*, *6*(1), 2. DOI: 10.1186/s40594-018-0151-2

Marino, F., Chilà, P., Sfrazzetto, S. T., Carrozza, C., Crimi, I., Failla, C., Busà, M., Bernava, G., Tartarisco, G., Vagni, D., Ruta, L., & Pioggia, G. (2020). Outcomes of a robot-assisted social-emotional understanding intervention for young children with autism spectrum disorders. *Journal of Autism and Developmental Disorders*, *50*(6), 1973–1987. DOI: 10.1007/s10803-019-03953-x PMID: 30852783

Martin, C., DeStefano, K., Haran, H., Zink, S., Dai, J., Ahmed, D., Razzak, A., Lin, K., Kogler, A., Waller, J., Kazmi, K., & Umair, M. (2022). The ethical considerations including inclusion and biases, data protection, and proper implementation among AI in radiology and potential implications. *Intelligence-Based Medicine*, *6*, 100073. DOI: 10.1016/j.ibmed.2022.100073

Martinez-Maldonado, R.. (2015). Multi-surface classroom ecology for real-time interventions in AI tutoring. *Computers & Education*, *89*, 1–12.

Mavrikis, M.. (2019). Real-time analytics for classroom orchestration in AI-based tutoring. *Learning Analytics Review*, *24*, 201–219.

McLaren, B. M.. (2010). Supporting Collaborative Learning and E-Discussions Using Artificial Intelligence Techniques. *International Journal of Artificial Intelligence in Education*, *20*(1), 1–28.

McNamara, D. S. (2023). Academic integrity in the age of generative AI: Faculty roles and responsibilities. *AI and Ethics*, *4*, 125–134.

Melati, M. (2020). The Use of Zoom Cloud Meeting as an Innovative English Learning Media. E-Journal Karinosseff, 1(1).

Mhlanga, D. (2022). The role of artificial intelligence and machine learning amid the COVID-19 pandemic: What lessons are we learning on 4IR and the sustainable development goals? *International Journal of Environmental Research and Public Health*, *19*(3), 1879. DOI: 10.3390/ijerph19031879 PMID: 35162901

Milana, M., Brandi, U., Hodge, S., & Hoggan-Kloubert, T. (2024). Artificial intelligence (AI), conversational agents, and generative AI: Implications for adult education practice and research. *International Journal of Lifelong Education*, *43*(1), 1–7. DOI: 10.1080/02601370.2024.2310448

Milgram, P., & Kishino, F. (1994). A Taxonomy of Mixed Reality Visual Displays. *IEICE Transactions on Information and Systems*, *E77-D*(12), 1321–1329.

Min, S. A., Jeon, I. S., & Song, K. S. (2021). The effects of artificial intelligence convergence education using machine learning platform on STEAM literacy and learning flow. *Journal of the Korea Society of Computer and Information*, *26*(10), 199–208.

Mitchell, M. (2019). *Artificial intelligence: A guide for thinking humans*. Farrar, Strauss, & Giroux. An overarching guide to the development and understanding of artificial intelligence—the field and its history.

Mohammadkarimi, E. (2023). Teachers' reflections on academic dishonesty in EFL students' writings in the era of artificial intelligence. [DOI:]. *Journal of Applied Learning and Teaching*, *6*(2). Advance online publication.

Mohammed, A. S. (2023). Examining the Implementation of Artificial Intelligence in Early Childhood Education Settings in Ghana: Educators' Attitudes and Perceptions towards Its Long-Term Viability. *American Journal of Education and Technology*, *2*(4), 36–49. DOI: 10.54536/ajet.v2i4.2201

Möller, M., Nirmal, G., Fabietti, D., Stierstorfer, Q., Zakhvatkin, M., Sommerfeld, H., & Schütt, S. (2024). Revolutionising distance learning: A comparative study of learning progress with AI-driven tutoring. arXiv preprint arXiv:2403.14642.

Mollick, E. (2024). *Co-intelligence: Living and working with AI*. Penguin Random House. One of the best thinkers and writers in the area of genAI. Please visit Mollick's Substack called One Useful Thing.

Moore, E.. (2023). Infrastructure Readiness for AI in Higher Education. *IEEE Access : Practical Innovations, Open Solutions*, *10*, 45670–45685.

Moore, R. L., Jiang, S., & Abramowitz, B. (2023). What would the matrix do?: A systematic review of K-12 AI learning contexts and learner-interface interactions. *Journal of Research on Technology in Education*, *55*(1), 7–20. DOI: 10.1080/15391523.2022.2148785

Mousavinasab, E.. (2021). Bayesian networks in AI tutoring for predictive analytics. *Journal of Educational Data Science*, *7*(1), 89–105.

Nagaraj, B. K., Kalaivani, A., Begum, S., Akila, S., & Sachdev, H. K. (2023). The emerging role of artificial intelligence in stem higher education: A critical review. *International Research Journal of Multidisciplinary Technovation*, *5*(5), 1–19. DOI: 10.54392/irjmt2351

Naneva, S., Sarda Gou, M., Webb, T. L., & Prescott, T. J. (2020). A Systematic Review of Attitudes, Anxiety, Acceptance, and Trust Towards Social Robots. *International Journal of Social Robotics*, *12*(6), 1179–1201. DOI: 10.1007/s12369-020-00659-4

Nemorin, S., Vlachidis, A., Ayerakwa, H. M., & Andriotis, P. (2023). AI hyped? A horizon scan of discourse on artificial intelligence in education (AIED) and development. *Learning, Media and Technology*, *48*(1), 38–51. DOI: 10.1080/17439884.2022.2095568

Nguyen, A., Kremantzis, M., Essien, A., Petrounias, I., & Hosseini, S. (2024). Enhancing student engagement through artificial intelligence (AI): Understanding the basics, opportunities, and challenges. *Journal of University Teaching & Learning Practice*, *21*(06). Advance online publication. DOI: 10.53761/caraaq92

Nikolopoulou, K., Gialamas, V., & Lavidas, K. (2020). Acceptance of mobile phone by university students for their studies: An investigation applying UTAUT2 model. *Education and Information Technologies*, *25*(5), 4139–4155. DOI: 10.1007/s10639-020-10157-9

Nishiwaki, Y., Oshima, M., Hashimoto, K., & Tsuda, K. (2023). A study of sentiment analysis based on specific 6-emotion category for Thai language. *Information Engineering Express*, *9*(2), 80–89. DOI: 10.52731/iee.v9.i2.774

Nistor, E., & Stanciu, D. (2023). Rethinking the teacher's role in the age of AI. *Education Sciences*, *13*(2), 200–213.

Noble, S. (2018). *Algorithms of Oppression: How Search Engines Reinforce Racism*. NYU Press. DOI: 10.18574/nyu/9781479833641.001.0001

Nye, B. D. (2016). Socially engaging tools for AI tutoring in education. *Artificial Intelligence in Education*, *13*(1), 5–16.

O'Neil, C. (2016). *Weapons of Math Destruction: How Big Data Increases Inequality and Threatens Democracy*. Crown Publishing.

Obaigbena, A., Lottu, O. A., Ugwuanyi, E. D., Jacks, B. S., Sodiya, E. O., & Daraojimba, O. D. (2024). AI and human-robot interaction: A review of recent advances and challenges. *GSC Advanced Research and Reviews*, *18*(2), 321–330. DOI: 10.30574/gscarr.2024.18.2.0070

OECD. (2021). *Artificial Intelligence in Education: Challenges and Opportunities for Sustainable Development*. OECD Publishing.

Omirgaliyev, R., Kenzhe, D., & Mirambekov, S. (2024). Simulating Life: The Application of Generative Agents in Virtual Environments. 2024 IEEE AITU: Digital Generation, 181–187. DOI: 10.1109/IEEECONF61558.2024.10585387

Open, A. I. (2015, December 11). *Introducing OpenAI.* OpenAI. https://openai.com/blog/introducing-openai/

Ouédraogo, I. (2024). Mobile technology and artificial intelligence for improving health literacy among underserved communities (Doctoral dissertation, Université de Bordeaux; Université Nazi Boni (Bobo-Dioulasso, Burkina Faso). https://theses.hal.science/tel-04574957/

Owoc, M. L., Sawicka, A., & Weichbroth, P. (2019, August). Artificial intelligence technologies in education: benefits, challenges and strategies of implementation. In *IFIP International Workshop on Artificial Intelligence for Knowledge Management* (pp. 37-58). Cham: Springer International Publishing.

Palmer, L. E., Pagoto, S. L., Workman, D., Lewis, K. A., Rudin, L., De Luna, N., Herrera, V., Brown, N., Bibeau, J., Arcangel, K., & Waring, M. E. (2023). Health and education concerns about returning to campus and online learning during the COVID-19 pandemic among U.S. undergraduate STEM majors. *Journal of American College Health, 71*(8), 1956–1966. DOI: 10.1080/07448481.2021.1979009 PMID: 34666630

Pant, H. V., Lohani, M. C., & Pande, J. (2023). Thematic and sentiment analysis of learners' feedback in MOOCs. *Journal of Learning for Development, 10*(1), 34–47. https://jl4d.org/index.php/ejl4d/article/view/740. DOI: 10.56059/jl4d.v10i1.740

Park, J. S., O'Brien, J. C., Cai, C. J., Morris, M. R., Liang, P., & Bernstein, M. S. (2023). Generative Agents: Interactive Simulacra of Human Behavior (Version 2). arXiv. DOI: 10.1145/3586183.3606763

Pashevich, E. (2022). Can communication with social robots influence how children develop empathy? Best-evidence synthesis. *AI & Society, 37*(2), 579–589. DOI: 10.1007/s00146-021-01214-z

Patel, N. (2023). Ethical AI Implementation in Higher Education: A Review of Data Privacy Concerns. *AI and Ethics, 10*(1), 30–50.

Patel, R. (2022). Automated Feedback and Student Engagement: The Role of AI Tutors. *Computers & Education, 176*, 104391.

Pavlopoulos, A., Rachiotis, T., & Maglogiannis, I. (2024). An overview of tools and technologies for anxiety and depression management using AI. *Applied Sciences (Basel, Switzerland), 14*(19), 9068. DOI: 10.3390/app14199068

Pelau, C., Dabija, D. C., & Ene, I. (2021). What makes an AI device human-like? The role of interaction quality, empathy and perceived psychological anthropomorphic characteristics in the acceptance of artificial intelligence in the service industry. *Computers in Human Behavior*, *122*, 106–855. DOI: 10.1016/j.chb.2021.106855

Pellas, N., Kazanidis, I., & Palaigeorgiou, G. (2020). A systematic literature review of mixed reality environments in K-12 education. *Education and Information Technologies*, *25*(4), 2481–2520. DOI: 10.1007/s10639-019-10076-4

Peng, H., Ma, S., & Spector, J. M. (2019). Personalized adaptive learning: An emerging pedagogical approach enabled by a smart learning environment. *Smart Learning Environments*, *6*(1), 1–14. DOI: 10.1186/s40561-019-0089-y

Pesovski, I., Santos, R., Henriques, R., & Trajkovik, V. (2024). Generative AI for Customizable Learning Experiences. *Sustainability (Basel)*, *16*(3034), 3034. Advance online publication. DOI: 10.3390/su16073034

Picciano, A. G. (2012). The Evolution of Big Data and Learning Analytics in American Higher Education. *Online Learning : the Official Journal of the Online Learning Consortium*, *16*(3), 9–20. DOI: 10.24059/olj.v16i3.267

Pishtari, G., Sarmiento-Márquez, E. M., Rodríguez-Triana, M. J., Wagner, M., & Ley, T. (2023, August). Evaluating the impact and usability of an AI-driven feedback system for learning design. *European Conference on Technology Enhanced Learning* (pp. 324-338). Cham: Springer Nature Switzerland. DOI: 10.1007/978-3-031-42682-7_22

Piumsomboon, T., Clark, A., Billinghurst, M., & Cockburn, A. (2013). User-defined gestures for augmented reality. CHI '13 Extended Abstracts on Human Factors in Computing Systems, 955–960. DOI: 10.1145/2468356.2468527

Ployhart, R. E., & Vandenberg, R. J. (2010). Longitudinal Research: The Theory, Design, and Analysis of Change. *Journal of Management*, *36*(1), 94–120. DOI: 10.1177/0149206309352110

Poola, I., & Božid, V. (2023). Guiding AI with human intuition for solving mathematical problems in ChatGPT. *International Journal of Engineering and Scientific Research*, *11*(07). https://www.researchgate.net/profile/Indrasen-Poola/publication/373447147_Guiding_AI_with_human_intuition_for_solving_mathematical_problems_in_Chat_GPT/links/64ece15eee5ca306008c1f19/Guiding-AI-with-human-intuition-for-solving-mathematical-problems-in-Chat-GPT.pdf

Popenici, S. A., & Kerr, S. (2017). Exploring the impact of artificial intelligence on teaching and learning in higher education. *Research and Practice in Technology Enhanced Learning, 12*(1), 22. DOI: 10.1186/s41039-017-0062-8 PMID: 30595727

Puentedura, R. R. (2012). The SAMR model. [Image]. Available under CC BY-NC-SA 4.0 license.

Pu, L., Moyle, W., Jones, C., & Todorovic, M. (2019). The Effectiveness of Social Robots for Older Adults: A Systematic Review and Meta-Analysis of Randomized Controlled Studies. *The Gerontologist, 59*(1), e37–e51. DOI: 10.1093/geront/gny046 PMID: 29897445

Qi, X. (2023). ChatGPT: A Promising Tool to Combat Social Isolation and Loneliness in Older Adults with Mild Cognitive Impairment. *Neurology Live*, NA-NA. https://go.gale.com/ps/i.do?id=GALE%7CA776469898&sid=googleScholar&v=2.1&it=r&linkaccess=abs&issn=27674258&p=AONE&sw=w&userGroupName=anon%7E6320b905&aty=open-web-entry

Radianti, J., Majchrzak, T. A., Fromm, J., & Wohlgenannt, I. (2020). A systematic review of immersive virtual reality applications for higher education: Design elements, lessons learned, and research agenda. *Computers & Education, 147*, 103778. DOI: 10.1016/j.compedu.2019.103778

Raja, S., Jebadurai, D. J., Ivan, L., Mykola, R. V., Ruslan, K., & Nadiia, P. R. (2024). Impact of Artificial Intelligence in Students' Learning Life. In AI in Business: Opportunities and Limitations: Volume 2 (pp. 3-17). Cham: Springer Nature Switzerland.

Rakhimov, D., & Akbarov, F. (2021). Prospects for the introduction of artificial intelligence technologies in higher education. *Academicia: An International Multidisciplinary Research Journal, 11*(2), 929–934.

Rane, N. (2023). Enhancing mathematical capabilities through ChatGPT and similar generative artificial intelligence: Roles and challenges in solving mathematical problems.

Reeve, J. (2013). Self-determination theory and agentic engagement in personalized AI learning. *Educational Psychologist, 48*(4), 337–348.

Robinson, T., & Kim, D. (2023). AI Literacy Programs: Bridging the Gap Between Theory and Practice. *Journal of Educational AI, 14*(2), 78–93.

Roll, I., & Wylie, R. (2016). Evolution and revolution in artificial intelligence in education. *International Journal of Artificial Intelligence in Education, 26*(2), 582–599. DOI: 10.1007/s40593-016-0110-3

Russell, S. J., & Norvig, P. (with Chang, M., Devlin, J., Dragan, A., Forsyth, D., Goodfellow, I., Malik, J., Mansinghka, V., Pearl, J., & Wooldridge, M. J.). (2022). Artificial intelligence: A modern approach (Fourth edition, global edition). Pearson.

Sajja, R., Sermet, Y., Cikmaz, M., Cwiertny, D., & Demir, I. (2023). Artificial Intelligence-Enabled Intelligent Assistant for Personalized and Adaptive Learning in Higher Education (Version 1). arXiv. https://doi.org/DOI: 10.48550/ARXIV.2309.10892

Sajja, R., Sermet, Y., Cikmaz, M., Cwiertny, D., & Demir, I. (2024). Artificial Intelligence-Enabled Intelligent Assistant for Personalized and Adaptive Learning in Higher Education. *Information (Basel)*, *15*(596), 596. Advance online publication. DOI: 10.3390/info15100596

Saxena, D., Lamest, M., & Bansal, V. (2021). Responsible Machine Learning for Ethical Artificial Intelligence in Business and Industry. In Chkoniya, V. (Ed.), (pp. 639–653). Advances in Business Information Systems and Analytics. IGI Global., DOI: 10.4018/978-1-7998-6985-6.ch030

Sayed, G., Hassan, M. M., & Rizk, H. (2023). Quantitative methods in personalized learning: A meta-analysis of AI-driven educational tools. *Journal of Artificial Intelligence in Education*, *33*(4), 223–245. DOI: 10.1007/s40593-023-00211-8

Sayed, W. S., Noeman, A. M., Abdellatif, A., Abdelrazek, M., Badawy, M. G., Hamed, A., & El-Tantawy, S. (2022). AI-based adaptive personalized content presentation and exercises navigation for an effective and engaging E-learning platform. *Multimedia Tools and Applications*, *82*(3), 3303–3333. DOI: 10.1007/s11042-022-13076-8 PMID: 35789938

Scherer, R., Siddiq, F., & Tondeur, J. (2020). All the same or different? Revisiting measures of teachers' technology acceptance. *Computers & Education*, *143*, 103656. DOI: 10.1016/j.compedu.2019.103656

Schneider, S., Beege, M., Nebel, S., Schnaubert, L., & Rey, G. D. (2022). The Cognitive-Affective-Social Theory of Learning in digital Environments (CASTLE). *Educational Psychology Review*, *34*(1), 1–38. DOI: 10.1007/s10648-021-09626-5 PMID: 34226808

Schroeder, N. L., Adesope, O., & Gilbert, R. (2013). Virtual facilitators in AI tutoring systems. *Journal of Educational Psychology*, *105*(1), 50–63.

Selwyn, S. (2019). Should Robots Replace Teachers? AI and the Future of Education. *British Journal of Educational Technology*, *50*(6), 1285–1294.

Selwyn, S. (2023). *Should Robots Replace Teachers? AI and the Future of Education*. Polity Press.

Shane, J. (2019). *You look like a thing and I love you: How artificial intelligence works and why it's making the world a weirder place.* Voracious. Artificial intelligence responses can be funny. Shane shows how she trained small language models before the rise of ChatGPT and allows us a glimpse into how to work with genAI. Shane posts at ai-weirdness.ghost.io

Sharma, M. K. (2023). Ethical AI in Higher Education: Ensuring Fairness and Transparency. *IEEE Transactions on Ethics and AI*, *5*(1), 25–40.

Sherman, W. R., & Craig, A. B. (2003). Understanding Virtual Reality—Interface, Application, and Design. *Presence (Cambridge, Mass.)*, *12*(4), 441–442. DOI: 10.1162/105474603322391668

Shi, Y.. (2020). Social adaptive e-learning with Topolor in AI-based tutoring. *Journal of Educational Technology & Society*, *23*(4), 39–50.

Since starting this book chapter, a new GenAI startup has been launched. DeepSeek is a model that was trained at a significantly lower cost, but offers comparable performance to ChatGPT-4o and o1 (Gibney, 2025). It was also many orders of magnitude less expensive to build and subsequently operate (Cosgrove, 2025). This seems to foretell that there will be more disruptors of genAI in the near future (Whipple, 2025). A helpful guide can be found here, from the New York Times. As readers can see, the world of genAI continues to gain complexity.

Singh, P., & Rao, L. (2023). The Future of AI in Higher Education: Trends and Perspectives. *Journal of Emerging Educational Technologies*, *30*(4), 50–67.

Skjuve, M., Følstad, A., Fostervold, K. I., & Brandtzaeg, P. B. (2021). My Chatbot Companion - a Study of Human-Chatbot Relationships. *International Journal of Human-Computer Studies*, *149*, 1071–5819. DOI: 10.1016/j.ijhcs.2021.102601

Slater, M., & Wilbur, S. (1997). A Framework for Immersive Virtual Environments (FIVE): Speculations on the Role of Presence in Virtual Environments. *Presence (Cambridge, Mass.)*, *6*(6), 603–616. DOI: 10.1162/pres.1997.6.6.603

Smith, J. (2023). Artificial Intelligence in Academic Research. *Journal of AI Research*, *35*(4), 123–140.

Smith, J., & Brown, A. (2023). Artificial Intelligence in Education: Personalized Learning Approaches. *IEEE Transactions on Learning Technologies*, *15*(2), 102–115.

Spector, J. M., Ifenthaler, D., Sampson, D. G., & Isaias, P. (2021). Trends and research on artificial intelligence in education: A comprehensive review. *Computers in Human Behavior Reports*, *4*, 100125.

Sruthi, P., & Mukherjee, S. (2020). Byju's the learning app: An investigative study on the transformation from traditional learning to technology-based personalized learning. *International Journal of Scientific and Technology Research*, *9*(3), 5054–5059. https://www.academia.edu/download/62470661/Byjus-The-Learning-App20200325-12089-513ypi.pdf

Stevens, A., & Stetson, P. (2023). Theory of trust and acceptance of artificial intelligence technology (TrAAIT): An instrument to assess clinician trust and acceptance of artificial intelligence. *Journal of Biomedical Informatics*. Advance online publication.

Sugiarso, A., Nurjamin, A., Judijanto, L., Firdausiyah, L., & Hidayat, A. A. (2024). The Effect of Artificial Intelligence in Improving Student Learning Achievement in High School. *World Psychology*, *3*(1), 1–13. DOI: 10.55849/wp.v3i1.569

Sun, R. (2023). Comparative study of online learning and face-to-face learning. *SHS Web of Conferences, 180*, 04006. https://doi.org/DOI: 10.1051/shsconf/202318004006

Sundar, S. S. (2020). Rise of machine agency: A framework for studying the psychology of human-AI interaction (HAII). *Journal of Computer-Mediated Communication*, *25*(1), 74–88. DOI: 10.1093/jcmc/zmz026

Suntharalingam, H. (2024). Enhancing Digital Learning Outcomes Through the Application of Artificial Intelligence: A Comprehensive Review. *International Journal of Innovative Science and Research Technology*, *9*(4), 718–727. DOI: 10.38124/ijisrt/IJISRT24APR530

Suppes, P., & Jerman, M. (1970). Computer-Assisted Instruction. *The Bulletin of the National Association of Secondary School Principals*, *54*(343), 27–40. DOI: 10.1177/019263657005434305

Suzuki, T., Yamada, S., Nomura, T., & Kanda, T. (2019). Do People Prefer Robots Over Humans as Daily Communication Partners?: Relationship to Social Anxiety in Conjunction with the Appearance of the Robots. *Journal of Japan Society for Fuzzy Theory and Intelligent Informatics*, *31*(5), 789–796. DOI: 10.3156/jsoft.31.5_789

Tajik, A. (2025). Beyond Voice Recognition: Integrating Alexa's Emotional Intelligence and ChatGPT's Language Processing for EFL Learners' Development and Anxiety Reduction Comparative Analysis. DOI: 10.21203/rs.3.rs-5989702/v1

Talanquer, V. (2023). Interview with the Chatbot: How does it reason? *Journal of Chemical Education, 100*(8), 2821–2824. DOI: 10.1021/acs.jchemed.3c00472

Tanenbaum, C. (2016). Scalability of AI tutoring in global classrooms. *Global Education Review, 3*(4), 37–54.

Tang, P. M., Koopman, J., Mai, K. M., De Cremer, D., Zhang, J. H., Reynders, P., . . . Chen, I. (2023). No person is an island: Unpacking the work and after-work consequences of interacting with artificial intelligence. *Journal of Applied Psychology*. https://psycnet.apa.org/doi/10.1037/apl0001103

Terracina, A., & Mecella, M. (2014). Gaming@School: Combining Virtual Learning Environments and Intelligent Pedagogical Agents for a new Approach to Classroom Lessons. *European Conference on Games Based Learning*; Reading, 2, 843–847.

The Texas Computers in Education Association has many, many ideas for incorporating genAI into learning and teaching. https://blog.tcea.org/

These books, websites, and Substack sites will not only explain how generative artificial intelligence works, but also how to apply genAI in everyday life and guide colleagues and students in its implementation. Broussard, M. (2019). *Artificial Unintelligence: What computers misunderstand about the world.* MIT press. Broussard points out that AI systems, for all their usefulness, have still been created by humans.

Thompson, C., & Wright, H. (2023). AI in Classroom: A Teaching Assistant or a Replacement? *Educational AI Review, 9*(2), 80–95.

Thway, M., Recatala-Gomez, J., Lim, F. S., Hippalgaonkar, K., & Ng, L. W. (2024). Battling Botpoop using GenAI for higher education: A study of a retrieval augmented generation chatbots impact on learning. arXiv preprint arXiv:2406.07796.

Timms, M. J. (2016). Educational robots as social agents in AI tutoring. *Journal of Computer Assisted Learning, 32*(4), 336–348.

Tomar, S., & Verma, S. (2023). *Artificial Intelligence in Higher Education and Changing Roles of Educators*. ResearchGate.

Tribe, T. N., & Singha, S. (2023). Diversity and Inclusion in VR: A New Frontier in Learning. Open Science Framework. https://doi.org/DOI: 10.17605/OSF.IO/BY87D

Tricco, A. C., Lillie, E., Zarin, W., O'Brien, K. K., Colquhoun, H., Levac, D., Moher, D., Peters, M. D. J., Horsley, T., Weeks, L., Hempel, S., Akl, E. A., Chang, C., McGowan, J., Stewart, L., Hartling, L., Aldcroft, A., Wilson, M. G., Garritty, C., & Straus, S. E. (2018). PRISMA Extension for Scoping Reviews (PRISMA-ScR): Checklist and Explanation. *Annals of Internal Medicine*, *169*(7), 467–473. DOI: 10.7326/M18-0850 PMID: 30178033

Ullah, M., & Hafiz, M. (2022). Real-time analytics in AI tutoring through Bisis tools. *Educational Data Management Review*, *29*(3), 57–68.

UNESCO. (2021). *Recommendation on the Ethics of Artificial Intelligence*. United Nations Educational, Scientific and Cultural Organization.

Van Maris, A., Zook, N., Caleb-Solly, P., Studley, M., Winfield, A., & Dogramadzi, S. (2020). Designing ethical social robots—A longitudinal field study with older adults. *Frontiers in Robotics and AI*, *7*, 1. DOI: 10.3389/frobt.2020.00001 PMID: 33501170

VanLEHN, K. U. R. T.VanLEHN. (2011). The Relative Effectiveness of Human Tutoring, Intelligent Tutoring Systems, and Other Tutoring Systems. *Educational Psychologist*, *46*(4), 197–221. DOI: 10.1080/00461520.2011.611369

Vashishth, T. K., Sharma, V., Sharma, K. K., Kumar, B., Panwar, R., & Chaudhary, S. (2024). AI-driven learning analytics for personalized feedback and assessment in higher education. In *Using traditional design methods to enhance AI-driven decision making* (pp. 206–230). IGI Global., DOI: 10.4018/979-8-3693-0639-0.ch009

Vaze, A., Morris, A., & Clarke, I. (2024). CuriosityXR: Context-aware Education Experiences with Mixed Reality and Conversation AI. *2024 IEEE International Conference on Artificial Intelligence and eXtended and Virtual Reality (AIxVR)*, 41–49. DOI: 10.1109/AIxVR59861.2024.00013

Voskoglou, M. G., & Salem, A. B. M. (2020). Benefits and limitations of the artificial with respect to the traditional learning of mathematics. *Mathematics*, *8*(4), 611. DOI: 10.3390/math8040611

Wakelam, E., Jefferies, A., Davey, N., Sun, Y., Zawacki-Richter, O., Marín, V. I., & Wang, C. Y. (2020). Artificial intelligence innovation in education: A twenty-year data-driven historical analysis. *International Journal of Educational Technology in Higher Education*, *10*(1), 1–43.

Walkington, C., & Bernacki, M. (2014). Context personalization in math AI tutoring. *Mathematics Education Research Journal*, *26*(4), 795–813.

Wallen, T. (2023) Investigating the Emotional Impact of Social Robots. Department of computer and information science. Linköping University. https://liu.diva-portal.org/smash/get/diva2:1816944/FULLTEXT01.pdf

Wang, N., Johnson, W. L., Mayer, R. E., Rizzo, P., Shaw, E., & Collins, H. (2008). The politeness effect: Pedagogical agents and learning outcomes. *International Journal of Human-Computer Studies*, *66*(2), 98–112. DOI: 10.1016/j.ijhcs.2007.09.003

Webster, C., & Ivanov, S. (2020). Robotics, Artificial Intelligence, and the Evolving Nature of Work. In George, B., & Paul, J. (Eds.), *Digital Transformation in Business and Society*. Palgrave Macmillan., DOI: 10.1007/978-3-030-08277-2_8

White, A., & Singh, C. (2023). Hybrid Instructional Models: AI and Human-Centered Teaching. *AI in Education Journal*, *19*(1), 95–110.

Wienrich, C., & Latoschik, M. E. (2021). Extended artificial intelligence: New prospects of human-ai interaction research. *Frontiers in Virtual Reality*, *2*, 686–783. DOI: 10.3389/frvir.2021.686783

Williams, B. (2023). Intelligent Tutoring Systems in Higher Education. *IEEE Transactions on Learning Technologies*, *12*(4), 289–304.

Williamson, B., & Eynon, R. (2020). Algorithmic systems in education: Surveillance, autonomy, and equity in AI-driven learning platforms. *Learning, Media and Technology*, *45*(3), 254–267.

Wu, Y. (2023). Integrating Generative AI in Education: How ChatGPT Brings Challenges for Future Learning and Teaching. *Journal of Advanced Research in Education*.

Wu, R. (2021). Visualization of basic mathematics teaching based on artificial intelligence. *Journal of Physics: Conference Series*, *1992*(1), 042042. DOI: 10.1088/1742-6596/1992/4/042042

Wylie, R. (2023). Evaluating AI's role in professional education. *International Journal of Education and Research*, *115*, 102051.

Xie, Y., Wang, K., & Kong, Y. (2021). Prevalence of research misconduct and questionable research practices: A systematic review and meta-analysis. *Science and Engineering Ethics*, *27*(4), 41. DOI: 10.1007/s11948-021-00314-9 PMID: 34189653

Xu, W., Dainoff, M. J., Ge, L., & Gao, Z. (2023). Transitioning to human interaction with AI systems: New challenges and opportunities for HCI professionals to enable human-centred AI. *International Journal of Human-Computer Interaction*, *39*(3), 494–518. DOI: 10.1080/10447318.2022.2041900

Xu, Z. (2024). *AI in education: Enhancing learning experiences and student outcomes*. Applied and Computational Engineering.,

Yang, J., Chen, Y. L., Por, L. Y., & Ku, C. S. (2023). A systematic literature review of information security in chatbots. *Applied Sciences (Basel, Switzerland)*, *13*(11), 6355. DOI: 10.3390/app13116355

Yilmaz, F. G. K., Yilmaz, R., & Ceylan, M. (2024). Generative artificial intelligence acceptance scale: A validity and reliability study. *International Journal of Human-Computer Interaction*, *40*(24), 8703–8715. DOI: 10.1080/10447318.2023.2288730

Yim, I. H. Y., & Su, J. (2024). Artificial intelligence (AI) learning tools in K-12 education: A scoping review. *Journal of Computers in Education*, •••, 1–39. DOI: 10.1007/s40692-023-00304-9

Yu, H. and Guo, Y. (2022) Generative artificial intelligence empowers educational reform: current status, issues, and prospects, pp. 1–10, DOI: .DOI: 10.3389/feduc.2023.1183162

Yuen, S. C.-Y., Yaoyuneyong, G., & Johnson, E. (2011). Augmented Reality: An Overview and Five Directions for AR in Education. *Journal of Educational Technology Development and Exchange*, *4*(1). Advance online publication. DOI: 10.18785/jetde.0401.10

Yufeia, L., Salehb, S., Jiahuic, H., & Syed, S. M. (2020). Review of the application of artificial intelligence in education. *Integration (Amsterdam)*, *12*(8), 1–15.

Zacharaki, A., Kostavelis, I., Gasteratos, A., & Dokas, I. (2020). Safety bounds in human-robot interaction: A survey. *Safety Science*, *127*, 104–667. DOI: 10.1016/j.ssci.2020.104667

Zanetti, M., Iseppi, G., & Cassese, F. P. (2019). A "psychopathic" Artificial Intelligence: The possible risks of a deviating AI in Education. *Research on Education and Media*, *11*(1), 93–99. DOI: 10.2478/rem-2019-0013

Zawacki-Richter, O., Marín, V. I., Bond, M., & Gouverneur, F. (2019). Systematic review of research on artificial intelligence applications in higher education – where are the educators? *International Journal of Educational Technology in Higher Education*, *16*(1), 1–27. DOI: 10.1186/s41239-019-0171-0

Zhai, X. (2024). Transforming teachers' roles and agencies in the era of generative ai: Perceptions, acceptance, knowledge, and practices. *Journal of Science Education and Technology*, •••, 1–11.

Zhai, X., Chu, X., Chai, C. S., Jong, M. S. Y., Istenic, A., Spector, M., Liu, J.-B., Yuan, J., & Li, Y. (2021). A Review of Artificial Intelligence (AI) in Education from 2010 to 2020. *Complexity*, *2021*(1), 8812542. DOI: 10.1155/2021/8812542

Zhao, L., & Fernandez, D. (2023). Personalized Learning with AI: Challenges and Opportunities. *International Journal of Educational Technology*, *30*(1), 12–27.

Zhu, M., & Wang, Q. (2023). Exploring the impact of ChatGPT on education: Opportunities, challenges, and future directions. *Educational Technology Research and Development*, *71*(2), 235–250. DOI: 10.1007/s11423-023-10020-5

About the Contributors

Bosede Iyiade Edwards holds PhD in Educational Technology from Universiti Teknologi Malaysia (UTM) in addition to a Master of Education in Educational Technology from the same institution. She has a strong multidisciplinary academic background, with B.Sc. (Hons) Chemistry, Masters in Organic Chemistry and a PG Diploma in Education with over 25 years of experience in teaching, training, online learning, cognitive science, and instructional design. Dr. Edwards is currently a Senior Lecturer at the Center for Instructional Technology & Multimedia (CITM), Universiti Sains Malaysia (USM). Her research focuses on emerging technologies in education and future school. She explores themes including Artificial Intelligence (AI) and immersive media applications, adaptive learning, Human–Machine Interfaces, and the broad field of technology-aided instruction. She supervises graduate and doctoral research studies in these fields and others within the instructional technology and multimedia field. Dr. Edwards has authored several journal articles, conference papers and research books. She is passionate about interdisciplinary collaborations for student development, and leveraging technology to promote equity. She invests her free time in her hobbies, writing inspirational fictions for children and counseling books for adults, and giving free consultations on international education to school leavers and guidance to budding research scholars.

Hassan Abuhassna is an associate professor at Sunway University, Malaysia's Faculty of Education, specializing in educational technology. Prior to this role, he served as an assistant professor at Universiti Teknologi Malaysia (UTM), where he also completed a postdoctoral fellowship. Dr. Abuhassna earned his Ph.D. in Educational Technology from UTM and a Master's degree from Universiti Putra Malaysia (UPM). His research focuses on online education, MOOCs, and e-learning, with numerous publications indexed in prestigious databases such as Web of Science and Scopus. Dr. Abuhassna has successfully supervised seven Master's students and is currently supervising three Ph.D. candidates in their final semester. Throughout his academic career, he has demonstrated a strong commitment to advancing the integration of technology in education, contributing significantly to both research and pedagogy. His work continues to influence the field, positioning him as a respected figure in the academic community.

Damola Olugbade earned his PhD in Educational Technology from Obafemi Awolowo University, Nigeria, in 2018. He is a Principal Research Fellow at First Technical University, Ibadan, where he leads research on learning technologies and digital pedagogy. His work centers on integrating artificial intelligence (AI), learning cognition, and innovative educational technologies to enhance educational outcomes. Dr. Olugbade has made significant contributions through publications in prominent journals like Education and Information Technologies and the African Journal of Teacher Education. He frequently presents at international conferences on topics such as AI-driven education, technology-enhanced learning, and social media in education, advancing the practical applications of educational technologies in Nigeria and beyond.

Olayinka Anthony Ojo holds PhD in Educational Technology from Obafemi Awolowo University, Ile-Ife, and has a background in Computer Science. His work experience spans both the industry and academia, and he has been extensively involved with executive training in computer applications for top management staff of various organizations. He is well-versed in computer maintenance services, and development of computer solutions for top-rated companies. Dr. Ojo has taught various computer science and educational technology courses at the University of Ilesa, University of Ibadan, and Lagos State University. He is a professional examiner for the West African Examination Council (WAEC) and a lecturer and Postgraduate research supervisor at the National Open University of Nigeria (NOUN). Dr. Ojo served as a Senior Educational Technologist at the University of Medical Sciences, Ondo, Nigeria co-ordinating technology integration and training for the university academic staff. He is a dynamic researcher with published works in educational technologies and computer science. He is currently engaged with research in computing, network security and emerging technologies at the University of Bolton, United Kingdom. His research interests are in the application of computer and mobile technologies in teaching and learning.

Wan Ahmad Jaafar Wan Yahaya has been the Director at the Centre for Instructional Technology and Multimedia (PTPM), Universiti Sains Malaysia (USM), Penang, since 2016. He also serves as the President of the Malaysian Educational Technology Association (META). He is the Chairman of the Technical Committee on Audio, Video, Information Technology, and Communication

Equipment at the Department of Standard Malaysia, Ministry of International Trade and Industry Malaysia. He holds a PhD in Multimedia Education from the University of Leeds and a Master of Education (Computer in Education) from the University of Manchester, United Kingdom. In teaching, Prof. Dr. Wan Ahmad Jaafar Wan Yahaya has been focusing on Graphic 2D, 3D & Animation, Multimedia Project Management, Multimedia in Education, and 3D Visualizations and Animations. He has graduated over 30 PhD students. Some of his innovative creations and projects have won gold awards and special recognition in International Innovation, Invention, Design, and Technology competitions in Malaysia, Indonesia, Korea, and Geneva (Switzerland). He is the recipient of the Thailand Association International Honor Award for Outstanding Contributions to the field of Educational Communications and Technology for the year 2023.

***

Mohammed Abdul Wajeed is working as Professor in Computer Science and Engineering Dept. in Lords Institute of Engineering and Technology, Hyderabad. He completed PHD from Jawaharlal Nehru Technological University, Hyderabad.

Siti Nazleen Abdul Rabu is a senior lecturer at the Centre for Instructional Technology and Multimedia (CITM), Universiti Sains Malaysia (USM), Penang. Her research interests include instructional strategies in online learning, specifically looking into online learning discourse analysis, computer-supported collaborative learning (CSCL), including game-based learning and gamification.

Al-adzkhan N. Abdulbarie is currently taking his Bachelor of Secondary Education degree major in Mathematics at the Mindanao State University Tawi-Tawi College of Technology and Oceanography, Tawi-Tawi, Philippines.

Margaret Olusola Abimbola is a lecturer and Acting Head of the Department of Library and Information Science at the University of Ilesa. A widely published scholar, her research focuses on literacy development, bibliotherapy, and Ethics in Library and Information Science among others. With a strong commitment to academic excellence and innovation, Dr. Abimbola contributes meaningfully to the advancement of LIS education and research in Nigeria. Her work continues to influence teaching and scholarly discourse within the field.

Hana An Alvarado is a Pre-service Teacher taking Bachelor of Secondary Education major in Mathematics at the Mindanao State University- Tawi-Tawi College of Technology and Oceanography, Philippines. She is interested in Artificial Intelligence (AI) and its applications in mathematics education.

Taoufik Boulhrir is a professor of language and communication at Al Akhawayn University in Ifrane and an education expert in the UAE. Taoufik has a Master's in science of education, and PhD in Applied linguistics. His passion for education and research drives his contributions to teacher training, innovative pedagogy, reading literacy, and 21st century education. With over 15 years of education leadership and teaching experience, he has significantly impacted the education sector in the United States and the United Arab Emirates. Taoufik received the prestigious 2015 Abu Dhabi Reads award for his commitment to research-based practices in reading and literacy. As a strong advocate for educational technology, independent learning, and student-centered pedagogy, he is interested in exploring sustainability and the potential of Artificial Intelligence (AI) in Education.

Wati Sheena M. Bulkia is a staff at the College of Education, Mindanao State University- Tawi-Tawi College of Technology and Oceanography. She finished her Bachelors of Elementary Education Degree at the Mindanao State University-Tawi-Tawi College of Technology and Oceanography and is currently pursuing her Masters of Arts in Education major in Reading at the same university.

Olanrewaju Edwards is a strategy-minded and results-producing business professional with comprehensive executive experience in business and education development, management and operations. Background in Engineering and a Postgraduate Diploma in Education with over 20 years of experience in the international education and startup space. Currently exploring the role of Artificial Intelligence as a business tool for promoting efficiency and operations.

Hanan Ghreir is a dedicated researcher and experienced educator with over 10 years of teaching experience in biology, geology, and science. Her work spans the fields of educational technology, teacher development, and virtual reality (VR). With a strong foundation in teacher development coaching and digital learning implementation, Hanan has played a key role in supporting educators to enhance their instructional practices. Her research interests also include education leadership and data-driven leadership, where she explores innovative strategies to transform educational settings and create immersive learning experiences for both teachers and students.

Elizabeth A. Gross is Associate Professor of Library Science and Technology at Sam Houston State University and holds a PhD in Learning Design & Technology. Post-Doctoral work in engineering education uncovered the differences between graduate returner and direct pathway engineering students, and led to five journal articles and over a dozen proceedings papers and presentations. Her research interests include information needs of master's and early career school librarians, perceptions of school librarianship, social justice in the school library, and generative artificial intelligence as a tool for librarians and library users.

Mahmoud Hamash is a researcher and educator specialising in AI, immersive virtual reality (IVR), and digital learning in education. He is a funded SFI/d-real PhD researcher at Dublin City University, with a research collaboration at Tampere University. His work focuses on co-designing IVR environments for post-primary education, exploring their impact on student engagement, skill acquisition, and knowledge transfer. Mahmoud has a deep understanding of educational technology implementation.

Potchong M. Jackaria is an Associate Professor at the Department of Science and Mathematics Education, College of Education, Mindanao State University Tawi-Tawi College of Technology and Oceanography in Tawi-Tawi, Philippines. Before working at MSU-TCTO, he had extensive experience teaching in different public schools handling elementary-level mathematics. Assoc. Prof. Jackaria obtained his master's degree in Education in Administration and Supervision from MSU Tawi-Tawi College of Technology and Oceanography and a Master of Science Education Major in Mathematics from MSU-Iligan Institute of Technology. He was involved in teachers' training and is interested in research areas including mathematics teaching, education technology, professional development, and education policy.

Rahidin Moh. Jiripa is a mathematics teacher at the Mindanao State University-Tawi-Tawi College of Technology and Oceanography. He finished his BS mathematics and Masters of Science in Teaching Mathematics Degree at the same university.

Ng Man Yi was a Master in Instructional Multimedia (MIM) program at CITM and currently a PhD candidate at CITM, USM.

Al-sabrie Sahijuan obtained Master of Science in Teaching Mathematics at MSU-TCTO, and currently taking Doctor of Philosophy in Educational Management at MSU-TCTO. Serve as School Head at Pagasinan National High School of Ministry of Basic, Higher and Technical Education.

Al-adzran G. Sali is a BSED-MATHEMATICS major at MSU-TCTO specializing in Math Education related studies.

Aldammien A. Sukarno is currently taking Bachelor of Secondary Education degree major in Sciences at the Mindanao State University Tawi-Tawi College of Technology and Oceanography, Tawi-Tawi, Philippines.

Peter Tiernan is an Associate Professor of Digital Learning and Digital Literacy at the Institute of Education, Dublin City University. Peter is responsible for the design, delivery and evaluation of a broad range of modules at the Institute of Education, which enable teachers and other educators to harness the potential of technology in education while becoming critical evaluators of technology and the role it plays in teaching and learning, and society more broadly. Peter has led multiple nationally and internationally funded research projects, and has an extensive research publication record with multiple articles in top-tier international journals. His research covers the spectrum of digital learning, but he has a specialist interest in digital literacy and its development among students and wider society. Peter hosts a monthly education research podcast, 'Let's Talk Education Research', which focuses on disseminating new research and exploring new avenues for research collaboration. He is a member of the Educational Studies Association of Ireland (ESAI) executive, the Campus Entrepreneurship Educators Network (CEEN), and the Further Education and Training Research Centre (FETRC).

Daniel Vong is an AI and technology professional currently working with Wangi Lai PLT. With expertise in artificial intelligence, machine learning, and digital transformation, he focuses on developing innovative AI-driven solutions. Passionate about emerging technologies and education, Daniel actively contributes to promoting AI awareness through training and professional development programmes, bridging the gap between business needs and technological advancements. His experience spans AI research, product development, and strategic implementation in Malaysia's tech ecosystem.

Index

T

U

www.ingramcontent.com/pod-product-compliance
Ingram Content Group UK Ltd.
Pitfield, Milton Keynes, MK11 3LW, UK
UKHW050946290926
15470UKWH00005B/1672